"I'm thrilled to see this prac
who all have one thing in
with Mormons. An invaluable resource!"

**Lee Strobel**, Professor of Christian Thought at Houston Baptist University, bestselling author of *The Case for Christ*

"*Sharing the Good News with Mormons* is an elite book—not because it is hard to understand, but because it isn't. The authors have worked hard to make things very clear and practical. I know many of them and have deep respect for their fidelity to the historic Christian faith and the effort they have exerted to know why they believe and how to communicate that with others. The book is elite because it is rich in its content, broad in the topics covered, and first rate in every way. Happily, whoever reads this book will gain tools for communicating the gospel in all kinds of situations and to people outside of Mormonism as well. Get this book, study it, and share it with others."

**J.P. Moreland**, author and Distinguished Professor of Philosophy, Talbot School of Theology, Biola University

"The many creative and friendly approaches explored in this book eliminate the intimidation of sharing with Mormons. Each way is unique and is explained by contributors who have long practiced what they preach. Highly recommended!"

**Donna Morley, PhD**, author, adjunct professor at The Master's University, and cofounder of Faith and Reason Forum

"The book you hold in your hands represents an unprecedented treasury of practical wisdom and advice on how to share your faith in Jesus Christ with Latter-day Saints. Far from offering a one-size-fits-all approach to reaching Mormons for Christ, the contributors share a range of approaches they have developed over many years of effective, on-the-ground evangelistic interaction. It is a 'tactical toolbox' from which you may explore a range of approaches in search of the one (or more) that works best for you. During and after my time as a seminary professor in Utah I came to know and trust many of the contributors to this volume, and I can honestly say that a better and more credible collection of contributors can hardly be imagined."

**Ronald V. Huggins**, former Associate Professor of Historical and Theological Studies, Salt Lake Theological Seminary

"This jewel has enough facets to equip each of us for reaching Mormons, and those who leave the Mormon church, with commonsense twenty-first-century tools. Experts in their field have teamed up with general editors Eric Johnson and Sean McDowell to provide an informative work filled with practical training, riveting testimonies, and sound apologetics. Well done!"

**Judy Salisbury**, founder/president of Logos Presentations, author of *Reasons for Faith* and *Divine Appointments*

# SHARING THE GOOD NEWS WITH MORMONS

ERIC JOHNSON
SEAN McDOWELL
GENERAL EDITORS

HARVEST HOUSE PUBLISHERS
EUGENE, OREGON

Unless otherwise indicated, all Scripture quotations are from The ESV® Bible (The Holy Bible, English Standard Version®), copyright © 2001 by Crossway, a publishing ministry of Good News Publishers. Used by permission. All rights reserved.

Verses marked NIV are taken from the Holy Bible, New International Version®, NIV®. Copyright © 1973, 1978, 1984, 2011 by Biblica, Inc.® Used by permission. All rights reserved worldwide.

Verses marked KJV are taken from the King James Version of the Bible.

Cover by Jason Gabbert Design

Cover photos © Patrycja Zadros / Shutterstock

**Sharing the Good News with Mormons**

Published by Harvest House Publishers
Eugene, Oregon 97408
www.harvesthousepublishers.com

ISBN 978-0-7369-7406-6 (pbk.)
ISBN 978-0-7369-7407-3 (eBook)

Library of Congress Cataloging-in-Publication Data

Names: Johnson, Eric, 1962- editor.
Title: Sharing the good news with Mormons / Eric Johnson and Sean McDowell, co-editors.
Description: Eugene, Oregon : Harvest House Publishers, 2018. | Includes indexes.
Identifiers: LCCN 2018004242 (print) | LCCN 2018005444 (ebook) | ISBN 9780736974073 (ebook) | ISBN 9780736974066 (pbk.)
Subjects: LCSH: Missions to Mormons.
Classification: LCC BV2627 (ebook) | LCC BV2627 .S53 2018 (print) | DDC 289.3—dc23
LC record available at https://lccn.loc.gov/2018004242



**Printed in the United States of America**

18 19 20 21 22 23 24 25 26 / VP-JC / 10 9 8 7 6 5 4 3 2 1

# Contents

Section 3: Personal Approaches



Section 4: Invitational Approaches



Section 5: LDS Event Approaches

# Acknowledgments

This book would not be the same without the editing skills of Eric's oldest child, Carissa, and Mormonism Research Ministry associate Sharon Lindbloom. Both of you have made this book better and we are deeply indebted to you. Also, we want to thank those contributors who have provided a diversity of evangelistic methods described in this book and made this project possible. We believe your ideas will encourage many who will use these approaches in the upcoming years. May our Lord provide you with His richest blessing on your ministries. Finally, a book of evangelism aimed at a specific people group (Mormons) is a tough sell for most publishers, but our hats go off to Terry Glaspey and the team at Harvest House Publishers. You believed in this project from the very beginning and have been supportive each step of the way. Thank you for your ministry mindset and a sincere desire to see Mormons find their way to Jesus.

# Dedication

*Eric Johnson*

I dedicate this book to these mentors whose personal investment during my ministry formulation years through the 1980s helped direct my path:

Pastor Von (d. 2016)

Pastor Ray Hahn

Peter Barnes (d. 2012)

Jeff Howell

Dr. Gordon G. Johnson (d. 2011)

Bill McKeever

Finally, I dedicate this book to Jerald and Sandra Tanner, the mentors to all who have ever done ministry to the Mormon people. Your groundbreaking work, especially in the early years of countercult research, has been used mightily by God and set the foundation for what I do today. Your legacy is epic.

*Sean McDowell*

This book is dedicated to all the faithful people who share the good news with Mormons, whether they are mentioned in this book or not. I have the deepest respect and admiration for your faithfulness to share God's love and truth.

# Foreword by Josh McDowell

God loves Mormons. Let me say it again, and yet in a different way, to be sure it sinks in—*God loves the Mormon people*. God desires to be in a relationship with them, as He does with all people.

The stark reality, however, is that the gospel of The Church of Jesus Christ of Latter-day Saints is different than the gospel of the historic Christian faith. This should come as no surprise because Joseph Smith, the founder of Mormonism, claimed that God the Father and Jesus appeared to him as a 14-year-old boy to tell him that the entire Christian church had been corrupted in his day. This is also clear when comparing the teachings of the LDS Church—on the nature of grace, the person of Jesus, and requirements for the afterlife—with biblical Christianity.

Thus, it is critical that we have the courage, confidence, and training to share the good news with our LDS friends. And this is why I love the new book *Sharing the Good News with Mormons*, which is edited by Eric Johnson and my son, Sean McDowell. It is full of practical ideas to reach Mormons with the gospel of Jesus Christ. This is not a book of abstract ideas, and it is not merely a theological or apologetics book (although these kinds of books are vitally important). However, if we have knowledge without using the information in evangelism situations, what's the point? This book uniquely brings together a number of qualified Christian voices to offer a variety of practical approaches for lovingly reaching out to Mormons.

The variety of contributors in this book is one of its great strengths. After all, there is no "magic bullet" approach that works for everyone in evangelism. Even Jesus used a variety of different approaches when sharing truth with people. Sometimes He asked questions, other times He told stories, and He even engaged in heated debate (for example, see John 6–8).

This is certainly the case with evangelism to Mormons. There are a number of different ways that have proven effective in seeing Mormons come to Christ. The key is to find an approach (or approaches) that match your personality as well as your unique situation. And then when you find one, *go for it.* You don't need to have it all figured out before you begin. Just give it a try and learn along the way. God can (and will) use your efforts regardless of the results.

The chapters in this book were written by people from a range of backgrounds, including full-time missionaries to the LDS people as well as pastors, teachers, and scholars. Some chapters may resonate with you more than others. There are some you may want to read and apply right away. And there are some you may never want to read. That's okay. The whole point of this book is simply to equip *you* with some practical ways to lovingly reach out to Mormons.

Through my books, speeches, and personal conversations, I have had the privilege of leading many people to Christ, including some Mormons. Seeing people come to Christ is one of the greatest joys in the world. That's my hope for you. Take the strategies in this book and put them into practice and experience the joy of seeing the LDS people, whom God loves dearly, become transformed by the gospel. Go for it.

---

**Josh McDowell** is an internationally recognized speaker and the author or co-author of more than 150 books, including *Evidence that Demands a Verdict* and *More Than a Carpenter*.

Introduction:

# Should Christians Share the Good News with Mormons?

ERIC JOHNSON

It is not always easy for Christian believers to share their faith in this politically correct twenty-first century. Those who attempt to do so are criticized more than ever, even by some who identify as Christians.[1] Common questions raised by critics of evangelism include:

- Who are you to judge others?
- Isn't it bigoted to claim that your religion is the only way to truth?
- Why do you impose your values on others?

## Common Objections to Christian Evangelism to Mormons

Before we go any further, let's explain how we will refer to the Salt Lake City-based church—known officially as The Church of Jesus Christ of Latter-day Saints—and its membership throughout this book. According to LDS Church member Gary C. Lawrence:

> Our members are properly referred to as Mormons or as Latter-day Saints. Our church may be referred to by its full name or as the LDS Church. We prefer not to be called the Mormon Church.[2]

Thus, to be respectful and prevent any unnecessary arguments, we will refer to those who belong to this religion as "Latter-day Saints," "LDS," or "Mormons." While we will leave direct quotes using the term "Mormon Church" intact, we will not use this designation in our writing; instead, we will refer to the church using its full name or as "LDS Church."

With that said, let me make a guarantee. If you, as a Bible-believing Christian, try to discuss your faith with your LDS friends, family members, and neighbors, you will receive pushback. And, undoubtedly, you will be asked one of the following five questions:

- "Don't you believe Mormons are Christian?"
- "Hasn't the LDS Church changed its teachings to be more Christian?"
- "Aren't Christians (like you) hateful of Mormons?"
- "Don't you think I'm a good person?"
- "Can't we just work together for good?"

Allow me to provide a response to each question.

### *"Don't you believe Mormons are Christian?"*[3]

The Latter-day Saint who asks this question places the Christian in a catch-22 situation. Saying *yes* does nothing more than confuse the issue because Mormonism is a unique religion, with obvious essential doctrinal differences between the two faiths. Say *no* and it's off to what can too easily become a going-nowhere argument. ("We're Christian." "No, you're not." "Yes, we are!" etc.)

It becomes more confusing when Mormons adamantly contend that having the name of Jesus Christ in their church's title means they too are "Christian." They may even use terms such as *salvation by grace*, *atonement*, and *eternal life* that are commonly used in Christianity. This can make even the best-intentioned Christians want to go home, climb into bed, and pull the covers over their heads in frustration!

First and foremost, every Christian needs to know what he or she believes. Before hoping to engage a Mormon in a fruitful discussion, a solid foundation in understanding the basic teachings of the Bible is necessary. Learning about God's Word, including doctrine, should be a lifelong pursuit for *every* believer.

While the Mormon may think that he or she is a Christian, it helps to properly define terms. A good question to ask is, "What do you mean by [choose any doctrinal term]?" Listen carefully and you will hear a definition that probably doesn't sound the same as what your Sunday school teacher taught! But be ready to ask additional clarifying questions just to make sure you understand. To help the reader on this end, we have included 101 unique terms as defined by the average Mormon in Appendix 2. This tool will help the Christian reader comprehend what a Mormon means, especially for those terms also used in Christianity. We recommend using this feature while reading the book.

Only when these differences are evident is it possible to have a fruitful discussion with a member of another religion—or we end up talking past each other. Latter-day Saints who discover that you don't think Mormonism is synonymous with biblical Christianity may even declare that you are a Christian even though you don't think they are. While this might be their way to soften the tension, this response may come across as condescending. When this happens, I like to show how my position (i.e., not considering Mormonism to be the same as Christianity) is not intended to be personal. To make my point, I typically say,

> I haven't been baptized into the LDS Church—after all, I already was baptized at a Christian church—and I reject Joseph Smith as a prophet of God. I also don't believe the Book of Mormon is historical or scriptural. Would you say I am destined for exaltation in the celestial kingdom?

To better understand my question, we must define the words *exaltation* and *celestial kingdom* according to Mormonism. As defined in Appendix 2, *exaltation* means "becoming glorified as gods in the highest level of the celestial kingdom and living forever in the family unit." Meanwhile, *celestial kingdom* is "the only kingdom of glory where one may enjoy the presence of Heavenly Father and Jesus Christ as well as abide with one's family forever."

In other words, the faithful Mormon who is baptized into the LDS Church, gets married in the temple, and keeps all the church's commandments has the opportunity to become a god in the next life and live forever with his or her earthly family. Those who are *not* baptized in this religion and deny Mormonism's major teachings and practices—as I do—are *not* allowed to participate in Mormon temple rituals, which are essential ordinances necessary for those wanting to reach the celestial kingdom.

By asking if I am destined for exaltation (also known as "eternal life"), then, I am giving the Mormons a chance to make their own judgment call. Most likely they will respond, "I don't know." While they may say this, LDS leaders have made it very clear that the answer to the question is no, as they have regularly criticized Christian churches and their doctrines while maintaining the necessity of the "restored church" that was imperative since Christianity lost its authority during the "Great Apostasy."[4]

Another good response is this: "So if Mormon and Christian are synonymous terms, I must be a Mormon." This will cause some head scratching. Since those who reject the basic tenets of the LDS faith should not be considered Mormons, your point has been made. Words do have meaning and precision in any conversation with a Latter-day Saint is imperative for effective communication to take place.

### *"Hasn't the LDS Church changed its teachings to be more Christian?"*

Some will insist that the differences in beliefs are minimal. Others may claim that the LDS Church is moving closer to orthodoxy. While their current church leaders have tried to downplay their more controversial teachings, Mormons typically accept doctrines that are in juxtaposition to creedal Christianity, including:

- God the Father has a body of flesh and bones
- Jesus is not eternally God
- The addition of scripture beyond the Bible[5]

Don't assume your Mormon friend's belief, but ask if they believe the points above.[6] It is true that the rhetoric once prominent in the LDS hierarchy has softened in recent years while some (including Mormon apologists and professors at the church's universities) want to make Mormonism's doctrines sound almost synonymous with Christian teaching. Despite the change in approach, Mormonism continues to deny or distort every fundamental teaching of the historic Christian church when LDS beliefs are carefully considered.

### *"Aren't Christians (like you) hateful of Mormons?"*

Many Mormons can become defensive when evangelical Christians attempt to engage them in spiritual conversations. Any disagreement with Mormonism might be taken as direct criticism of the Mormon people. Christians must extend courtesy, respect, and patience to everyone despite our disagreements. After all, the apostle Paul says in Ephesians 4:15 that we should speak "the truth in love."

A term sometimes used to define well-meaning Christians who are attempting to share their faith with Latter-day Saints is *anti-Mormon*. The connotation is that someone who disagrees with Mormonism must be motivated by hatred for the Mormon people. This is far from accurate. One response to this unfair accusation is to ask, "Do Mormon missionaries knock on my door to share their faith with me because they 'hate' me?" Of course not! While they may disagree with those who are Christian, the missionaries generally will try their best to explain why Mormonism is true. Many faithful Mormon adults who are RMs ("returned missionaries") will resonate with this logic since they believe their service was dedicated to helping others, even when they disagreed with those on the other side of the door.

It comes down to this: If Mormonism and biblical Christianity are different in their view of biblical teachings, shouldn't Christian believers have concern for the spiritual welfare of those holding wrong beliefs? We believe the answer is yes, and this is the reason for this book.

### *"Don't you think I'm a good person?"*

While Latter-day Saints will generally plead that they are "good"—and I think we can agree that, generally, this is true—doing the right things is *not* enough to have one's sins forgiven. After all, isn't a Christian someone who knows he or she is forgiven of all sins? (See Matthew 1:21; 1 John 5:11-12.) It is impossible to keep God's perfect standard of holiness. Jesus Himself said in Matthew 7:21-23 that many will call out "Lord, Lord" at the judgment while pointing to their "good" works. Yet Jesus said they will be told, "I never knew you; depart from me, you workers of lawlessness."

People who consider themselves "good" enough to go to heaven do not understand the definitions of *holiness* or *sin*. As Jeremiah 17:9 puts it, "The heart is deceitful above all things, and desperately sick; who can understand it?"[7]

### *"Can't we just work together for good?"*

If Mormons belonged to a religious organization that agreed with the Bible on the essential issues of faith while rejecting heretical doctrines, it would be possible to unite and work together for good. Yet we would be fooling ourselves to think that we are on the same team when it comes to spiritual matters if we have contradictory beliefs. In Utah, some liberal Christian churches work together with Mormon congregations. For instance, I once attended a Christmas musical event at a Mormon chapel that included the members of a nearby Christian church along with the pastor. The choirs joined in a cantata while the bishop presented a spiritual talk to the mixed audience.

If Mormons are people who need to understand that forgiveness of sins is possible only by having a relationship with Jesus through faith alone as presented in the Bible—not through baptism, temple worship, or keeping commandments—we cannot pretend that these differences should be overlooked merely to get along or not rock the boat. Any need to evangelize is neutered through a desire to work together. It can be very confusing to both congregations. If Mormons who accept their church's heretical teachings are not forgiven of their sins, who will tell them the truth?

We will address a final question that Christians may be asked, though this one usually comes from fellow believers.

### *"Isn't 'lifestyle evangelism' the best way to share our faith?"*

According to this view, Christians should prioritize the living of a good life and let others observe their fruit without overtly evangelizing. Some have even cited a saying that has been falsely attributed to Saint Francis of Assisi: "Preach the gospel, use words if necessary."[8] There is no doubt that it is vital for a Christian to live a godly life, which only provides credibility to the Christian witness. However, this is not the *only* way to share one's faith. Good reasoning skills and purposeful evangelistic methods must also be utilized. Without intervention, some people are headed into an eternity of separation from God. As Romans 10:15 says:

> How are they to preach unless they are sent? As it is written, "How beautiful are the feet of those who preach the good news!"

The word *preach* translated here literally means "one who *is preaching*." Imagine a pastor who just stands up in the pulpit and stares back at the congregation. That would make no sense at all. Effective evangelism usually requires some type of oral or written communication—this was certainly true with the apostle Paul. A "silent witness" could be too quiet for Mormons to hear, as many Latter-day Saints might be living extremely moral lives that far outshine those of any Christians they know. In essence, Mormons may not see a Christian's "fruit" as much different from their own.

Now that we've dealt with some common objections to Christian evangelism to Mormons, let's take a closer look at this book's format.

## A Worm or a Fly?

Evangelism is like fishing. Some use fly rods, many like bait, and still others just put an empty hook at the end of their poles so they can take a nap! When it comes to sharing the Christian faith with others, there are a variety of ways to fish for people (Matthew 4:19). As you choose your approach, understand that this book is meant to deliver a potpourri of evangelistic strategies. Some ideas may resonate with you, while other concepts will not draw your interest at all.

When I walk through a restaurant's buffet line, I don't make a meal of everything offered. On my first go-round, I take samples of a variety of dishes before heading back once I've had a taste of each. Consider this book your evangelistic smorgasbord. Nibble on some of the ideas and see if an approach fits your taste. Learn how a method has worked for someone else. If you allow yourself freedom to explore, we think you will find some ideas here that will correlate with your own gifting. But as coeditor Sean McDowell says in the conclusion, don't get so bogged down by trying to partake in so many of the available dishes (the approaches offered in this book) that you end up becoming frustrated and not eating anything at all!

## A Tactical Toolbox

Often when I am speaking to a gung ho, tell-the-world-about-Jesus Christian who wants to share the faith with Mormons (and praise God for those who take evangelism seriously), I get asked, "What's the one way/question/strategy to get a Mormon to convert?" They're looking for what we call the "magic button." Imagine if the third-base coach on a baseball team merely had to flash the home-run sign before the batter could hit a home run. If a team hit home runs 100 percent of the time when the coach gave his cue, that would forever change the game!

Yet we all know no home-run signal is completely effective. In the same way, no evangelism strategy will work every time. If it did, we would have skipped the variety of methods in this book and just focused on the one that works for everyone on a consistent basis.

Terry Glaspey, the director of acquisitions for Harvest House Publishers, used a phrase that stood out to me as we discussed the idea for this book. He explained that the idea Sean and I proposed would be a "toolbox of tactics," something that could be offered to those who want to learn how to share the Christian faith with Mormons. After all, inside the average toolbox are many tools. Although I'm not much of a handyman, even my basic setup includes a hammer, several screwdrivers, a putty knife, an adjustable wrench, and duct tape. (Almost anything can be fixed with duct tape!) Depending on the assignment my wife Terri sends me on, I will use the appropriate tool to get the job done. Indeed, there are many ways to effectively share the gospel (which means "good news") with Mormons.

Sean and I are very excited to have 24 experienced Christians with a variety of backgrounds join us in this venture. Never before has such a diverse group of qualified believers been featured in one book focusing on Mormonism from an evangelical Christian perspective. These men and women bring plenty of experience to the table. Seven contributors hold professional doctoral degrees while several have little to no college experience. You'll also hear from several pastors and a number of qualified apologists, some of whom serve full time in Christian ministry while others are bivocational.

One thing they all have in common is this: Each contributor has a desire to equip you to effectively share the Christian faith by presenting a different approach to evangelize Latter-day Saints. In fact, they will each write as if their method is the best one anyone could ever use... while fully understanding that evangelism tactics are like ice cream flavors. What might be *their* favorite might not be *yours*, or mine for that matter. And that's okay. The passion with which they present is compelling.

With that said, feel free to take any idea presented here and go in a slightly different direction to make the strategy work for you. Indeed, creativity is encouraged! We won't pretend this book covers every successful evangelistic method. For instance, we decided not to include chapters talking about door-to-door evangelism, handing out Christian tracts in the streets, or utilizing service projects to gain relationships—all strategies I have used with great success over the years—because of space limitations. There might be other effective approaches, even some we don't know about.

I encourage you to be open-minded when considering options. I am reminded of the woman who told Dwight L. Moody, the great evangelist from the nineteenth century, that she didn't like the way he shared his faith. He asked, "Tell me, ma'am, how do you do evangelism?" "I don't," she said, to which Moody replied, "Well, I like my way of doing it better than your way of *not* doing it!" Be careful, then, when tempted to criticize a particular approach.

Not everyone will appreciate our desire to share biblical truth or jump for joy over the method(s) we use. Imagine if someone you knew had something green between her teeth and you decided to tell her. While your intention might have been good, perhaps your information shocked or embarrassed her. She might even have gotten upset and told you to mind your own business. This can happen. Speaking the truth comes with a risk. The alternative (not saying anything and letting her walk around looking like she was missing a front tooth) doesn't seem to be a good option. In the same way, every Christian who believes in the gospel message advocated in the Bible should be willing to take a chance by exposing others to the ultimate truth about the gospel, even with the possibility of offending someone.

Yet we need to be cautious because, like a sharp nail or screwdriver sticking up in a toolbox that can stab a person attempting to find a hammer, we don't want to go out of our way to intentionally offend people. Being a jerk when sharing Christian beliefs will only detract from the presentation. Appropriate tactics do matter. However, remaining silent and keeping the gospel hidden is not the loving thing to do.

## Are You Ready?

While you are looking through your tactical toolbox, you'll see that these chapters are arranged in six particular themes. Please understand that they don't have to be utilized in chronological order since they don't build on each other. A short summary at the beginning of each chapter will help you determine what that strategy is about. Knowing a little more about it will prepare you to adequately consider the material.

We include two additional tools that I want to mention here. The first is the six "Spotlight" interviews featuring full-time Christian missionaries. This allows a showcase of other ministry strategies that have been successfully used all over the United States. In addition, our book has a website (www.SharingWithMormons.com) that contains additional information not found in the book, including bonus chapters. Be sure to check this out. Even if you have little background with Mormonism, this book and the information available on the website will be an asset for anyone who wants to learn practical strategies on how to effectively and lovingly share the Christian faith with Mormons.

Finally, you may like some more information on Mormonism or other apologetic topics. Here are some excellent Internet resources from some of the contributors to this book (in alphabetical order):

- BeggarsBread.org: General apologetics, including Mormonism (Fred Anson)
- Carm.org: General apologetics, including Mormonism (Matt Slick)
- ColdCaseChristianity.com: General apologetics (J. Warner Wallace)
- EvidenceMinistries.org: Mormonism and Jehovah's Witnesses (Keith and Becky Walker)
- Irr.org: General apologetics, including Mormonism (Joel Groat, Robert Bowman)
- MormonInfo.org: Mormonism (Rob Sivulka)
- Mrm.org: Mormonism (Bill McKeever, Eric Johnson, Sharon Lindbloom, Randy Sweet)
- NGIM.org: General apologetics (David Geisler and Brian Henson)
- RatioChristi.org: General apologetics (Corey Miller)
- SeanMcDowell.org: General apologetics (Sean McDowell)
- StrivingforEternity.org: General apologetics (Andrew Rappaport)
- Theopedia.com: Encyclopedia of Christianity (Aaron Shafovaloff)
- UnveilingMormonism.com: Mormonism (Lynn Wilder)
- Utlm.org: Mormonism (Sandra Tanner)

I'm so glad you picked up *Sharing the Good News with Mormons.* Regardless of which approach(es) you take, may the Lord bless and guide you in your endeavors!

## SECTION 1

# Basic Training Approaches

In the military, it is referred to as basic training. In college, they may give a 101 designation to a course that introduces a subject, such as English or history. And football coaches call the first week of practice "hell week." The first section of this book is meant to be an introduction to material that will be important when having conversations with Latter-day Saints whose ideas may be different from what is taught in their church.

Most Mormons who leave their religion end up heading toward agnosticism or atheism. They feel burned by organized religion. In fact, a common saying among many Mormons is, "If the church isn't true, nothing else is." This type of thinking is akin to throwing the baby out with the bathwater. Just because Mormonism isn't true doesn't mean that Christianity is false. Thus, Christians need to be equipped by understanding foundational issues related to their faith, especially when Mormons come to them with their doubts about their beliefs.

We'll begin with a chapter by Mark Mittelberg, who takes a closer look at understanding different worldview perspectives. Comprehending the thinking process of the person you're speaking with will help you know how to better approach the conversation. In chapter 2, I (Sean) explore a few arguments for the existence of God, which can be used to help guide the former Mormon (or possibly soon-to-be former

Mormon) to the realization that God does exist, even if the religion of Mormonism is not true.

Many who are dissatisfied with Mormonism may come to the conclusion that the Bible is outdated and cannot be considered a reliable source of authority. Why should anyone in the twenty-first century accept the authority of the Bible? In chapter 3, Matt Slick presents a case to show that the Bible is a trustworthy historical document that contains God's communication for humanity today. Finally, while Mormons make a case for a belief in Jesus, those who are leaving their faith often put Jesus on a shelf and want nothing to do with Him. Dr. Rob Bowman presents evidence in chapter 4 for a historical Jesus, including the use of the resurrection, that can help draw the Latter-day Saint back to a reasonable belief in the Savior as revealed in the Bible.

Remember, it is important to be ready with an answer to why Christianity is true (1 Peter 3:15). That's our goal in this section. But it is equally important to treat Mormons with dignity and respect as image-bearers of Christ. These chapters are tools to help lovingly guide Mormons (or former Mormons) to the only truth that can set them free.

1

# Helping Our Friends Evaluate Truth Claims
## The Straight-Thinking Approach

MARK MITTELBERG


### Summary

All people, whether they recognize it or not, adhere to a worldview by which they make sense of the world they live in. This is also true in the arena of faith. Most people employ at least one of six different approaches as they determine what to believe and why. Recognizing and understanding each of these approaches is the first step toward confident and effective evangelism.


### Introduction

Everyone has faith in *something*. Buddhists believe in the eightfold path. Muslims follow the five pillars of Islam. Atheists assume there is no creator. Mormons hold that "living together forever" in a family unit is possible. And Christians trust that Jesus is the Son of God who died for their sins.

To be effective in reaching people for Christ, it is important to understand *why* others believe the way they do. According to 1 Corinthians 9:20-23, Paul modeled the importance of knowing our audience. To Jewish people he deliberately communicated as a Jew "in order to win Jews. To those under the law I became as one under the law…to those outside the law I became as one outside the law" and "to the weak I became weak, that I might win the weak." In fact, the apostle said, "I have become all things to all people, that by all means I might save some. I do it all for the sake of the gospel, that I may share with them in its blessings."

This chapter will explore six ways people decide what to believe through what I call the *six faith paths*.[1] As we'll see, some are more reliable than others. Most of them can be found within the Latter-day Saint community. Once we can identify which ones our friends are using, we'll be better prepared to point them toward a biblical faith.

## The Six Faith Paths

### *1. Relativistic Faith Path: "Truth is what you make it."*

The first of the six approaches people take to choosing their faith is the *relativistic faith path*. People with this view choose what to believe by deciding what they *want* to believe—and then thinking that reality conforms to those beliefs. People who take this approach often say things like, "I've got my truth; you've got yours—let's just get along."

Christians need to be strong advocates of tolerance by supporting people's right to choose their own beliefs. That doesn't mean everybody is right. Tolerance and truth are entirely different. I'll support the rights of groups to say, for example, that Jesus was actually an exalted mushroom (there are some who do teach that), but that doesn't mean I have to agree with them. An important aspect of tolerance is the freedom to disagree and debate about spiritual ideas—and not pretend that everyone's beliefs are equally valid.

Those who attempt to provide evidence for Christianity to relativists will be dismissed as presenting nothing more than "your truth." But relativism will not work in any other area of life, so why should it be trusted in the spiritual realm? Suggest that they go to Hollywood and try driving on Highway 101 in a relativistic manner by deciding that the sign by the road saying "101" is, for them, the speed limit. If they happen to meet a highway patrolman, they can simply explain, "My truth is that my speed limit is 101, so just let me be."

How do you think *that* will work out? Probably not so well. With incredulity, the officer will reply, "Look, when you're out here on the highway there's just *real truth*. And the truth is that the speed limit is 65, so you're going to pay a hefty fine!"

Relativistic highway driving doesn't work—nor does relativistic dieting, relativistic investing, or relativistic anything. The truth is that in real life *the real truth* must be discovered and dealt with. It's not what we want things to be or think they ought to be. Truth is *what really is*. Imagining or wishing things were different has no effect on how things really are. That's the case in the physical world, but also in the spiritual world.

In recent years, many Latter-day Saints have sidled up to this approach more than they might realize. Perhaps this is one reason why many Mormons don't try very hard to convert their evangelical Christian friends to their faith—because, after all, they think these "other Christians" are "good" and are merely on their own truth path. Those holding this perspective may leave evangelism to the short-term missionaries who may or may not knock on the Christian's door.

The real question is this: *What reasons are there to believe or not believe in any religion, including Mormonism or historic Christianity?* Relativism can't answer that question; it can only lead one to choose a belief and to act as if it is really true. That's a roll of the dice that I don't want to take with my life—and one we should try to convince our friends they don't want to take with their lives either. Instead, we need to urge them to find a more reliable faith path, one that will lead them to a trustworthy faith based on real facts.

### *2. Traditional Faith Path: "Truth is what you've always been taught."*

The second approach is the *traditional faith path*. This approach accepts beliefs as hand-me-downs. Your friends on this path might not even think about what they believe or why—they simply accept what they were taught growing up. This person says, "My parents, grandparents, and great-grandparents were all Mormons, so I'm a Mormon, and I'll always be one."

What can we say to someone with this mindset? We can ask how they know their parents were right, because they could have been wrong—mine could have been and yours could have been. So how do we find out whose parents, and whose belief systems, are correct? We cannot discover the truth by blindly clinging to traditions.

You might encourage your friends to think of the last holiday they had with their extended family. Urge them to consider the people around the dinner table and ask themselves: "Which of these relatives do I respect enough to entrust my eternity to?" That's what they're doing when they unthinkingly perpetuate hand-me-down beliefs and traditions. I love my relatives and enjoy being around them, but I won't let a single one of them do my thinking for me or decide on behalf of me and my children what we're going to believe.

Instead of supporting a blind journey down the traditional faith path, the Bible commands believers to "test everything; hold fast what is good. Abstain from every form of evil" (1 Thessalonians 5:21-22 ESV). And Jesus cautioned His listeners about the dangers of letting tradition stand in the way of obeying what God has said (Mark 7:5-13).

The traditional path is a natural way to begin as children. At some point, however, we need to grow up spiritually and think for ourselves, examine the reasons behind the traditions we've been taught, and seek truth with God's help until we're confident we are on the right path. This journey can be relationally tumultuous—leading us to explore biblical teachings that other family members might not be open to considering. Jesus promised that if we will ask, seek, and knock, we will find not just truth but the surpassing rewards that come with knowing the God of truth Himself (Luke 11:9-13).

### *3. Authoritarian Faith Path: "Truth is what you've been told to believe."*

Similar to the last approach, the *authoritarian faith path* is also passive, but this one can come with much more force. The authoritarian teacher exclaims, "You *will* believe this!"

I saw this once when I took a church group on a trip to an Islamic mosque. The imam (someone who leads prayer at the mosque) had everyone sit down so he could give an overview of the tenets of Islam. While he was at it, he decided to teach a few things about Christianity as well. He adamantly declared that "God is not divided; he does not have a son." I knew Muslims also deny that Jesus died on the cross and reject claims about His resurrection, so I raised my hand and said,

> I'm curious about something. Jesus's followers walked and talked with Him for several years. They also reported that He repeatedly claimed to be the Son of God, that they watched Him die on the cross, and that three days later they saw and talked and ate with Him after He was resurrected. They wrote down detailed accounts of what they heard and saw. These have been preserved in thousands of manuscript documents. Now, correct me if I'm wrong, but what Islam teaches us about Jesus seems to be based on the words of one man, Muhammad, who six hundred years after the time of Christ was sitting in a cave when, he claimed, an angel spoke to him and told him these things weren't so. What I'm curious about is whether you have any historical or logical reasons for why we should accept that viewpoint over and against the actual historical record?

The imam glared at me and declared, *"I choose to believe the prophet!"* With this statement, the discussion was over. For him, the authority of his religion was all he needed. If he had deeper reasons backing up his faith, he chose not to share them.

In Mormonism, "official church doctrine" is expounded upon numerous times in biannual General Conference sessions, church manuals, and teachings at local Sunday services. Leaders demand adherence from their followers. Mormonism's founder Joseph Smith set the pace when he said, "God made Aaron to be the mouth piece for the children of Israel, and He will make me be god to you in His stead, and the Elders to be mouth for me; and if you don't like it, you must lump it."[2] Although they wouldn't say it exactly as Smith did, many LDS parents, bishops, and stake presidents come across with the same attitude.

How should we respond? First, make it clear that we're not

anti-authority—we all will be influenced and led by authorities in our lives. But, second, we need to submit to the *right* authorities by measuring them against biblical standards (Acts 17:11). "Watch out for false prophets," Jesus warned. How? "By their fruit you will recognize them," He explained (Matthew 7:15-16 NIV).

### *4. Intuitive Faith Path: "Truth is what you feel in your heart."*

The fourth approach is the *intuitive faith path*, exhibited in the person who says, "Why do I need evidence when my spirit tells me what's true?"

In the Star Wars movie *A New Hope*, Obi-Wan Kenobi teaches Luke Skywalker to use his lightsaber. "Don't trust your eyes," he said. "Your eyes will deceive you." Instead, he puts a hood over Luke's face so he can't see anything and says, "Just feel the Force." This *sounds* so spiritual. When you talk to your friends who think this way, ask them if they've ever tried making financial investments simply by following their hearts or trusting their feelings. They'd quickly go broke.

Or ask them if they've attempted to drive to some side-street address in the heart of a major city based on instinct alone, without GPS. Sure, they might have gotten lucky and found their way on occasion, but usually they'll become frustrated and realize that their senses—and GPS!—were created for a reason.

God will sometimes give us an intuitive sense about things. Yet we need to be careful. The heart, according to the Bible, is deceitfully wicked (Jeremiah 17:9). Solomon, the wisest man who ever lived, warned in Proverbs 14:12, "There is a way that seems right to a man, but its end is the way to death."

Intuition is like a flashing yellow light in a dark intersection: it signals to pay attention, but it doesn't tell you everything you need to know. You still need to look both ways, figure out what the real situation is, and act accordingly. Spiritual intuition is similar to that. It might give some clues, but you still need to search for solid truth and reliable evidence to be confident you're on the right track.

### *5. Mystical Faith Path: "Truth is what you think God told you."*

Those who take the *mystical faith path* choose what they believe based on experiences they consider supernatural. They are therefore supremely confident in what they believe. "Why should I listen to your academic arguments," they wonder, "when I already know what God has shown me?" I most commonly see this approach in Mormons who testify that they prayed to God, asking Him to show them if the Book of Mormon was true. When they felt a strong sense that it was, it became "case closed"—and they can't understand why you're so hesitant to become a Latter-day Saint as well.

What should we say to our friends who are on the mystical faith path? First, we shouldn't deny that God can and does speak today. He didn't lose His voice two thousand years ago. Jesus said in John 10:27, "My sheep hear my voice, and I know them, and they follow me."

But caution is in order, however, as the Bible warns in 1 John 4:1, "Dear friends, do not believe every spirit, but test the spirits to see whether they are from God, for many false prophets have gone out into the world" (NIV). And 1 Thessalonians 5:21 cautions that we should "test everything; hold fast what is good." The message of Scripture is, first, to be open to hearing God's voice, but, second, to be careful about what you accept as being from God.

How can we test such things? By applying the pattern in the Bible, which is to test alleged new revelations against what we already know to be from God. For example, Paul warned in Galatians 1:8, "Even if we or an angel from heaven should preach a gospel other than the one we preached to you, let them be under God's curse!" (NIV). In other words, don't automatically put stock in a message received through a mystical experience unless it passes the test and brings a message consistent with what has already been shown to be true from the Bible.

Mormonism's message that there are many gods contradicts the clear and consistent monotheistic teachings of both the Old and New Testaments (Isaiah 45:5; John 17:3). If your Mormon friends say God told them it's true, show them how the Bible says that they need to "test all things" and not to believe every spirit—even if it's an angel standing right in front of them—when it contradicts what God has already revealed.

### *6. Evidential Faith Path: "Truth is what logic and evidence point to."*

The sixth approach, the *evidential faith path*, is the most consistently trustworthy method for determining truth, as it relies primarily on reason and evidence to lead one toward faith.[3] We can't think, evaluate ideas, or make decisions without logic. Some may claim that they don't trust logic while trying to make their point logically. Or sometimes they'll say that logic is "Western" and is not accepted by the other half of the world living in the East. As Indian-born apologist Ravi Zacharias says, "Even in India we look both ways before we cross the street. It is either the bus or me, not both of us!'"[4] And need we argue for the importance of evidence that is experienced through the five senses? All scientific research relies on it; it's the foundational tool of the justice system and is what we use every day to figure out what is true.

Logic and evidence are inescapable, so let's employ them well. More than that, the Bible—which is itself supported by reason and evidence—tells us to test truth claims. Jesus often pointed to evidence to verify His claims, including fulfilled prophecies, miracles, His divine knowledge and insights, His sinless life, and ultimately His resurrection from the dead. He also warned us, as we saw earlier, to examine the words and fruit of those who claim to be prophets to see whether the evidence substantiates their claims.

Looking back over the other faith paths, we see that this mix of logic and evidence helps us evaluate the *relativistic faith path*, determining it to be faulty because truth needs to square with what is real. It provides the tools to test our *traditions* to determine which ones are worth holding on to, and to assess the credentials and messages of the *authorities* in our lives. It also helps us size up our *intuitive* instincts and confirm or disconfirm our *mystical* encounters.

More than that, it provides an ensemble of reasons for accepting the biblical Christian message.[5] Studying these reasons will strengthen your own faith while giving you the confidence to effectively communicate that faith to your Mormon friends as we "become all things to all people...for the sake of the gospel."

---

*Mark Mittelberg (Denver, Colorado) is the Executive Director of the Center for Strategic Evangelism, in partnership with Houston Baptist University. His books include* The Case for Christ Devotional: Your Daily Moment of Truth *(with Lee Strobel),* The Questions Christians Hope No One Will Ask (With Answers), Confident Faith, *and* The Reason Why Faith Makes Sense. *He is also the primary author of the* Becoming a Contagious Christian *training course, which has been translated into more than 20 languages.*

2

# Sharing the Reasons for God
## The Evidence Approach

DR. SEAN MCDOWELL


## Summary

Those who are disillusioned with Mormonism are often enamored with agnosticism and atheism. Their conclusion is that, since the LDS Church isn't true, nothing else must be either. Unfortunately, many who come to this conclusion have never considered the evidence readily available to show that God does exist.


## Introduction

A few years ago, I had a conversation with a lady who was in the process of leaving the LDS Church. The further her husband ascended in the leadership of Mormonism, the more they both became disheartened with the practices and teachings of the faith. Given how deeply their lives were intertwined with their church, the decision to leave was costly, painful, and disillusioning. And of course, they were trying to figure out what was next. The last I heard, she left Mormonism and began to dabble in New Age beliefs. Her story is not unusual.

Several websites and podcasts are committed to chronicling the stories of people who leave Mormonism.[1] Many former church members feel disillusioned after learning about some of the falsehoods at the root of their faith[2] and decide to abandon organized religion entirely. Rather than separate the fabrications in Mormonism from creedal Christianity, many embrace the mind-sets of atheism, agnosticism, and New Ageism. The writings of popular atheists such as Richard Dawkins, Sam Harris, and Michael Shermer are especially popular among ex-Mormons. Since many questioning Mormons have been taught, "If the church isn't true, nothing is," they abandon religion entirely when their LDS faith crumbles.

Why would someone abandon belief in God after discovering problems with Mormonism in particular? One answer is that the power of psychological matters such as anger and distrust cannot be underestimated.

## Why Abandon All Theistic Beliefs?

First, Mormons are taught to base their beliefs on experience and blind faith apart from evidence. For instance, Alma 32:17-18 in the Book of Mormon says, "Yea, there are many who do say: If thou wilt show unto us a sign from heaven, then we shall know of a surety; then we shall believe. Now I ask, is this faith? Behold, I say unto you, Nay; for if a man knoweth a thing he hath no cause to believe, for he knoweth it." In other words, faith involves believing something *we do not know*. If we knew it, through some miracle or sign, there would be no need for faith. In this view, faith and knowledge are opposites.

The Bible proposes a different relationship between faith and reason. Rather than opposites, the Bible models faith *built* upon evidence. For instance, Exodus 14:31 says, "Israel saw the great power that the LORD used against the Egyptians, so the people feared the LORD, and they believed in the LORD and in his servant Moses." God performed a miracle first, and *then* the people were called to believe in Him and His spokesman Moses. Jesus also gave signs so people could have a confident faith supported by evidence (Mark 2:10-11; John 20:30-31).

I suspect the reason that the Book of Mormon teaches this view of faith and knowledge is the lack of substantive evidence for Mormonism. When there is no convincing external evidence corroborating a belief, it must be based upon experience, feeling, and blind faith. No wonder so many Mormons abandon faith when they encounter evidence against their beliefs—they haven't been taught to think evidentially about faith.

Second, many Mormons are simply unaware of the evidence for God in general and Christianity in particular. Few have heard of the scientific, philosophical, and historical evidence for Christian theism. The reality is not that Mormons have investigated the evidence and found it wanting. Rather, many simply have not encountered the evidence at all.

I believe the evidence approach can be useful for ministering to practicing Mormons and ex-Mormons.

## The Evidence Approach and Practicing Mormons

The evidence approach has two goals. First, it can help practicing Mormons think more biblically (and consistently) about the relationship between evidence and faith, so if they end up doubting the LDS Church at some point in the future, they may pause and consider the evidence before entirely abandoning Christian theism. Second, it can establish the Christian as a thoughtful person who cares about them, so if they ever become open to considering non-Mormon religious options, they might turn to you for direction. People from a variety of religious backgrounds have come to me for spiritual direction *years* after our first conversations. Part of the evidence approach is to reveal that you are both thoughtful and caring; if a Mormon experiences a faith crisis, you may be the first person who comes to his or her mind.

There are many ways to start an evidence-based conversation with a Mormon. Personally, I have found a couple questions helpful. First I like to ask, "If you were not a Mormon, would you still believe in God? Why or why not?" This can be helpful because it encourages people to think about their beliefs as objectively as possible and to consider them from a different angle.

Depending on their response, I sometimes follow up by asking, "Have you ever considered the philosophical and scientific evidence for the existence of God? If so, what do you think about it?" In my experience, most Mormons are unfamiliar with the evidence but will be curious about what you mean. And they will feel unthreatened by this question since they already believe in God. Many will inquire about the specific evidence you are referring to, and if you are ready, the conversation is off and running!

Another question I like to ask is, "If you were not a Mormon, would you still believe in the resurrection of Jesus? Why or why not?" As with the question above, this one is meant to encourage them to probe deeper into the *reasons* for their beliefs. While the conversation may go a variety of directions, you might be surprised by how many people will ask you about your own beliefs. If they do, you have the opportunity to explain how Christianity would be false without the resurrection of Jesus (1 Corinthians 15:14, 17), and also provide the *positive* evidences for its historicity.

## The Evidence Approach and Ex-Mormons

For ex-Mormons, the evidence approach has a different goal: to help them separate false ideas about faith that they adopted from the LDS Church and to reconsider positive evidences for Christianity. This is (of course) easier said than done. And these kinds of conversations can take *years* and may require an immense amount of commitment and patience.

The reality is that many ex-Mormons have unwittingly adopted a certain epistemological approach to religion that is different than that of classical Christianity. Until they can learn to separate from bad thinking about faith (such as the idea that faith is blind), they will not likely be open to considering the evidence for Christianity. For ex-Mormons who are open to discussing faith, here is a simple question I have found helpful: "Even though you feel burned by the LDS Church, have you ever considered the positive evidence for creedal Christianity?" Chances are they have not heard the evidence and may inquire about what you mean. If so, go for it!

You may also ask a follow-up question to help them think through how they may have adopted some faulty assumptions about religion from the LDS Church: "How has your experience in the LDS Church shaped the way you think about religious faith as a whole? You disagree with Mormon doctrine, but do you disagree with *how* you learned to even approach religious issues?" The idea is to help surface some of the unconscious assumptions they may have inadvertently adopted from Mormonism. And the goal, quite naturally, is to begin discussing and analyzing those assumptions.

Remember, the evidence approach is not meant to downplay the importance of emotional issues ex-Mormons experience as a result of leaving their faith. These issues are often raw, real, and deep. The last thing we want to do is ignore or dismiss those real emotions. In fact, before we even get to the evidence, it is often helpful to spend considerable time simply listening to their story and being a good friend. These kinds of conversations can take a long time, but the goal is to help direct them to the Christian faith through positively engaging the evidence for faith.

## Three Principles for the Evidence Approach

If you choose to adopt the evidence approach, please keep three things in mind. First, keep the focus on the positive evidence for Christianity and try to avoid criticizing Mormon doctrine and history. Few people like to have their beliefs challenged. In the minds of many Mormons, if you criticize their faith, you are criticizing them *personally*. Not long ago I used the evidential approach with a couple of college-aged Mormons who recently returned from their missions. After our 90-minute conversation (which we all enjoyed immensely, by the way), I sent them a copy of *More Than a Carpenter*, a book I co-authored with my father Josh McDowell, which provides evidence for the New Testament account of Jesus but says nothing critical about Mormonism. There is certainly a time and place for criticizing Joseph Smith and Mormonism, yet it should be done in a judicious and careful manner.

Second, ask questions. Jesus asked dozens of questions, even when He knew the answers. He often responded to a question with another question. Why? One reason is that He wanted people to think so they might personally wrestle with truth and hopefully come to faith. If asked generously and strategically, questions can be a nonthreatening way of getting Mormons (and really *anyone*) to consider the positive evidence for Christianity.

Third, be kind and generous. The purpose of the evidence approach is not to trap someone and to try to argue him or her into the kingdom. The goal is simply to lovingly guide someone to consider the positive evidence for creedal Christianity. Many Mormons (as well as Muslims, atheists, and others) have asked me what I believe because I *first* listened to their beliefs and treated them with generosity and kindness.

## A Primer on the Evidence for God

In this final section, I want to lay out some powerful evidence for faith that can play a central role in the evidence approach. Christian apologists have done a remarkable amount of work to make the case for Christian theism. Many of these evidences go beyond the scope of this chapter, such as the argument from reason,[3] consciousness,[4] the Cambrian explosion,[5] fine-tuning,[6] fulfilled prophecy,[7] the reliability of the Bible,[8] and ontology.[9] I have found the following arguments particularly helpful in conversations with Mormons.

### *The Cosmological Argument*

This argument begins with the observation that the universe had a beginning, which is demonstrable by science and philosophy. Given that something can't begin to exist without a cause, it seems eminently reasonable to believe that a transcendent cause (outside of the universe) is responsible for its existence. Since matter, time, and energy simultaneously came into existence at a finite point in the past, the cause is plausibly timeless, immaterial, intelligent, powerful, and personal. Simply put, the beginning of the universe points to a Beginner.[10]

This argument can be particularly powerful in conversations with Mormons for two reasons. First, it raises questions about the plausibility of the Mormon belief in the eternal succession of gods. And further, it points toward the existence of one eternal, timeless, powerful God who is worthy of worship.[11]

### *The Design Argument from DNA*

While the cosmological argument makes the case for God as the cause of the entire universe, the DNA argument points to design *within* the universe. It begins with the reality that cellular organization and the development of living creatures are orchestrated by genetic information. Human DNA, for instance, contains the information equivalent of roughly 8,000 books (to be conservative). Natural forces such as chance and necessity have overwhelmingly failed to explain the origin of biological information. Yet we know minds can produce information. Simply put, the vast amount of information contained in living organisms points to an Author of Life.

This argument often finds warm reception from Mormons since they already believe in an intelligent designer. Its value is helping them realize that, despite Mormon teachings, faith is not the opposite of knowledge. There are good reasons for faith in God. And if DNA points to God, what else does?

### *The Moral Argument*

This argument draws a connection from the reality of objective moral values to the existence of God. If God does not exist, moral values and duties are ultimately subjective and nonbinding. Yet we know objective moral values and duties are real. We don't need to be persuaded that, for instance, torturing babies for fun is wrong. All reasonable people know this. Therefore, since moral values and duties do exist, God must as well. Simply put, the existence of moral values points to a universal Moral Lawgiver.

This argument can be particularly influential to Mormons for a couple reasons: (1) it is rooted in Scripture (Romans 2:14-15), and (2) Mormons tend to care deeply about the moral behavior of both individuals and the society, and thus resonate with the philosophical case for an objective moral law.

### *The Argument for the Resurrection of Jesus*

This can be made in a variety of ways, but typically it involves establishing a few well-documented historical facts, such as the death of Jesus, the discovery of the empty tomb, the multiple appearances of Jesus, and the transformation of the disciples. Presenting these facts together indicates how the historical resurrection is the best explanation for them. Unlike the previous three arguments, this argument points specifically to the Christian God.

This argument is particularly powerful because it can be based upon how historians normally approach their task.[12] It also *indirectly* raises some troubling questions for the Mormon historical record. Consider two examples. First, there is significant external historical evidence from archaeology and extrabiblical written sources for the life and death of Jesus.[13] On the other hand, external evidence for the reliability of the Book of Mormon is lacking.

And second, the case for the resurrection largely depends upon the reliability of the witnesses—the disciples of Jesus. In chapter 5, cold-case detective (and former atheist) J. Warner Wallace explains that there are three broad motives at the heart of misbehavior: financial greed, sexual or relational desire, and pursuit of power. There is no evidence the apostles were motivated by *any* of these. They sacrificed material gain and willingly suffered for their faith. Yet the same cannot be said for Joseph Smith.[14]

Again, there are many other evidences for the faith. The person who employs the evidence approach should feel freedom to be flexible in what evidences he or she utilizes. Just as readers may choose different tactics in this book depending on the person and circumstance, the wise person will use evidence that fits the individual person.

## Conclusion

The goal of the evidence approach is actually quite modest: to encourage practicing Mormons to examine the evidential roots of their faith, and to discourage ex-Mormons from entirely abandoning theism while considering the positive case for creedal Christianity. The goal is to plant seeds in the minds of current and former members of the LDS Church that may later come to fruition. If you are willing to lovingly engage people with the evidences for faith, through question-asking and with kindness, you might be amazed at how God can use you to minister to others. Go for it!

---

*Sean McDowell, PhD (San Juan Capistrano, CA) is an associate professor of apologetics at Talbot Theological Seminary, an international speaker, and the author of more than 18 books, including the updated* Evidence that Demands a Verdict: Life-Changing Truth for a Skeptical World *(with Josh McDowell) (Nashville, TN: Thomas Nelson, 2017). He also teaches high school part-time and is the Resident Scholar for Summit, California. You can follow him on Twitter at @Sean_McDowell and his blog at www.seanmcdowell.org.*

3

# Did God Really Say So?
## The Reliability-of-the-Bible Approach

MATT SLICK


### Summary

Although the King James Version of the Bible is the official translation for the LDS Church, many Mormons put little trust into these 66 books as God's Word for today. In fact, Article 8 of Mormonism's Articles of Faith states that the Bible is "true as far as it is translated correctly." Yet the evidence shows that the Bible is reliable and can be trusted.


### Introduction

One of the most important questions non-Christians ask as they consider Christianity is whether or not the Bible is trustworthy. In fact, if meddling translators and monks changed what was originally written (called the "autographs"), the words and deeds that the Bible attributes to Jesus should not be trusted. However, if the Bible is accurate and can be trusted, its words have authority for people today. Every Christian should be ready to deal with criticism about the Bible's truthfulness, accuracy, and authority, especially in conversations with Mormons who are leaving (or have even left the "Church") and are critical of "religion."

## The Reliability of the Biblical Manuscripts

The Bible's autographs are inspired by God, as 2 Timothy 3:16 indicates: "All Scripture is breathed out by God and profitable for teaching, for reproof, for correction, and for training in righteousness." The words *breathed out* literally mean that the Bible originates with God. Jesus said in Luke 24:44-45, "'These are my words which I spoke to you while I was still with you, that everything written about me in the Law of Moses and the Prophets and the Psalms must be fulfilled.' Then he opened their minds to understand the Scriptures." The scriptures referred to here are the entire Old Testament.

One thing that Mormons or skeptics may point out is that no autographs of the Bible have been preserved. But this cuts both ways since the original Book of Mormon manuscripts (the gold plates) are not available either. According to LDS leaders, the angel Moroni took the plates back from Joseph Smith. Therefore, they are not available for scholars to examine. The Book of Mormon was supposedly translated by the "power of God," yet there have been almost 4,000 changes to it since it was first produced. Some of those changes are mere spelling corrections, but others are significant. If Smith translated the Book of Mormon accurately through the guidance by God, why were any changes ever needed?[1]

Although many Christians have wanted to debate this point, the Bible's autographs have been lost and are no longer available. When God inspired the Bible, it was perfect. Nevertheless, through the copying method over the years, various textual problems have crept in. Do these textual problems undermine the reliable transmission of the Bible, rendering it untrustworthy? Not at all. We don't need to have the original documents to demonstrate their accuracy any more than a prosecutor needs a body to prove that a crime has been committed. Inferences are drawn from the evidence at hand, and a reasonable conclusion can be drawn from the extant biblical manuscripts.

We must understand that before the autographs were lost, they were copied very carefully. Experts consider the copying method to be exceptionally precise. The Old Testament was written in Hebrew while the New Testament was written in Greek. In both languages the letters are also used as numbers. In English there are both letters and numbers. So, whenever a word is written in either of those languages, they are writing numbers. This means that every word has a mathematical value.

When the professional copyists were doing their sacred work on the Old Testament documents, they would copy one letter/number at a time. When they were finished with any particular page, they added the numbers of the copy and compared it to the numbers on the original. If there was any discrepancy at all, the copy was discarded (or sometimes relegated to use as a second-rate teaching document). This method of copying is remarkably accurate because the copyists considered their work to be transmitting the very words of God.

In many cases, the earliest New Testament manuscripts weren't copied by professionals who adhered to this strenuous criterion,[2] but they still took great care in handling the Word of God because they understood the serious nature of their work and felt the weight of that responsibility on them.[3] For this reason, and many more, we have good reason to believe that the copies of the Old and New Testament documents have been well preserved from the time of the original writings until today.

As far as the New Testament, Mormon scholars acknowledge the accuracy of the writings that go back 2,000 years. Some Mormons will be surprised with Brigham Young University professor Lloyd Anderson, who, in a paper delivered in 1963, explained why he felt that 99 percent of all verses of the New Testament were correct:

> One can disagree with the textual assumptions behind some of the modern translations of the New Testament and still not be overly concerned with differences that are immaterial. For a book to undergo progressive uncovering of its manuscript history and come out with so little debatable in its text is a great tribute to its essential authenticity. First, no new manuscript discovery has produced serious differences in the essential story. This survey has disclosed the leading textual controversies, and together they would be well within one percent of the text. Stated differently, all manuscripts agree on the essential correctness of

> 99 percent of all the verses in the New Testament. The second great fact that such a survey demonstrates is the progress that has placed the world in possession of manuscripts very near to the time of their writing. One would have to be a student of ancient history to appreciate how much superior the New Testament is to any other any book in its manuscript tradition.[4]

While the copies of the original documents are not perfect, they are very close to it. Critics often mistakenly assume that even the copies are supposed to be perfect. If your Mormon or atheist friend makes this assumption, point out that God never said the copies would be perfect. They then may ask how the Bible can be trusted at all. The answer is that the copies have been preserved with precise care.

Let me give you some examples that you can use in your witnessing encounters. Of the 5,800-plus Koine Greek manuscript copies of the New Testament along with the additional 24,000-plus copies in other languages, there is little variation, as Anderson accurately pointed out above. Of this very slight number, the majority of the variants are easily corrected by comparing them to other copies that don't have the "typos" or by simply reading the context. Copying mistakes occur in such ways as word repetition, spelling, or a single word omission due to the copyist missing something when moving his eyes from one line to another. The variants are very minor. None of them affect core doctrinal truths, and the words and deeds of Christ are reliably transmitted.

The Bible is so remarkably accurate in its transmission from the originals to the present copies that, when compared to any other ancient writings, it is light-years ahead regarding the number of manuscripts and their dating. If the Bible were to be discredited as unreliable, for the sake of consistency, it would also be necessary to discredit the ancient writings of Homer, Plato, and Aristotle along with other authors because none of them are as well preserved as the Bible. Homer's *Iliad*, Plato's *Tetralogies*, Aristotle's works, and Herodotus's history are far less well preserved than the books of the New Testament. Critics should be consistent in how they apply their criticism across all ancient writings and not hold the Bible to a double standard.

Still, some say that since there are copyist errors, the entire Bible must not be reliable. But this reasoning is weak. Should a science textbook be considered unreliable because there is a misspelled word or two in it? Should the whole document be disregarded for a few spelling errors? Of course not!

The logical fallacy known as the fallacy of composition states that what is true of the part is true of the whole. For example, "The engine is blue. Therefore, the car is blue." People employing this logical fallacy when criticizing the Bible say that what is true of one copyist's error is true of the whole Bible. Again, this is not sound reasoning.

As far as the Old Testament is concerned, the best evidence for its accuracy in transmission is in the Dead Sea Scrolls found in caves of Qumran in 1947. These documents were mainly written in Hebrew and Aramaic by a Jewish sect known as the Essenes between the third century BC to first century AD. About 250 Old Testament manuscripts were discovered in 11 caves along the northwest shore of the Dead Sea in Israel. The entire book of Isaiah, dated about 125 BC, was found intact. This is particularly important since it predated the oldest existing copy of Isaiah at that time by roughly a thousand years. When this was compared to the known versions from AD 900 called the Masoretic Text, the scroll demonstrated the remarkable accuracy of the copying method used with biblical documents.

There is also very little doubt about the existence of many of the Old and New Testament cities mentioned in the Bible. Many "biblical" archaeologists working in the Holy Land are secular and are neither Jewish nor Christian, yet they continue to utilize the Bible in their work because it is accurate and provides historical information useful in understanding the sites. Places such as Arad, Bethel, Capernaum, Chorazin, Hazor, Jericho, and Shechem have all been verified as authentic places, just as the Bible reported.[5]

Unfortunately, many laypeople shedding doubt on this issue have not studied the reliability of the biblical documents. Instead, they often parrot what biblical critics say. Some even cite popular atheist writers such as Richard Dawkins and the late Christopher Hitchens who are ill informed about evidence for biblical reliability. Many Mormons may not know that these same men also mock Mormonism. A deeper study of these biblical documents would benefit those who minimize God's Word.

## More Questions about the Bible

Mormons and skeptics frequently bring up other common issues to degrade the Bible's authority. Let's deal with some of the questions they ask about the Bible's reliability and provide some answers.

### *"Hasn't the Bible been rewritten so many times it can't be trusted?"*

Some people think the Bible was written in one language, translated to another language, then translated into yet another and so on until it was finally translated into English. They infer that, since it was translated so many times into different languages throughout history, it must have become corrupted. The telephone game analogy is often used as an illustration. In this game one person tells another person a sentence, who then tells it to another person, who tells yet another, and so on until the last person hears a sentence that has little or nothing to do with the original one. The only problem with this analogy is that it doesn't fit the facts of biblical transmission at all.

When critics bring up the telephone game, ask, "Can you tell me how you think the Bible has come to us?" Far too often, critics have never seriously thought about this. They just assume the worst. Maybe they believe that throughout history, translators have put their own spin on things so much that the original meaning has long been lost. This is wrong because that isn't how translations are done. For example, they are not made by translating from Greek into German into Latin and then into English. On the contrary, a good modern translation of the Bible is made by utilizing the copies of the original languages and writing straight into the target language like German, Spanish, and French.

### *"What about the other books?"*

The Bible mentions other books, including the Book of Wars (Numbers 21:14), the Book of Jasher (Joshua 10:13), the Book of the Kings of Israel and Judah (2 Chronicles 27:7; 35:27; 36:8), and two other letters to the Corinthians. Critics erringly conclude that because the Bible sometimes refers to other books, this must mean that they are lost scripture. Just because biblical writers reference other books does not mean they believe these book were inspired. The exception, of course, is when the Bible references other inspired books within itself. Nevertheless, these books are not *lost* books of the Bible. They were just never considered inspired to begin with.

The Deuterocanonical books (Apocrypha) contain those books that were included in the Greek Septuagint (LXX) but were not part of the Hebrew Bible. The word *apocrypha* comes from the Greek *apokryphos,* which means "hidden." It is used in a general sense to describe a list of books written by Jews between 300 and 100 BC. More specifically, it refers to the seven additional books that were added to the Roman Catholic canon in 1546 in its reaction to the Protestant Reformation.

The Pseudepigraphal books are "false writings." They are a collection of early Jewish and "Christian" writings composed between 200 BC and AD 200, such as 3 and 4 Maccabees and the Psalms of Solomon. However, they too were known during the days of the early church and were never considered Scripture because they were not authoritative, inspired, or genuinely written by either prophets or apostles. Since these books were not lost and were never part of the Bible to begin with, they have no bearing on the validity of the Bible.

### *"What about the many Bible 'contradictions'?"*

Bible difficulties, or *apparent* Bible contradictions, exist. When someone brings up the standard objection that "the Bible is full of contradictions," I encourage you to ask, "Do you know of any? Could you give me an example?" Almost always there is no answer. If, however, someone produces a supposed contradiction, point out that a contradiction occurs when one statement makes another statement impossible. In other words, a contradiction is when someone both affirms and denies the same proposition in the same way and at the same time. Differences in descriptions of accounts are not contradictions.

One common example of an apparent contradiction involves comparing Acts 9:7 with Acts 22:9. In the first passage, it says that the men who were with Saul heard "a voice, but seeing no man." In the second, it says that "they heard not the voice of him" (KJV). The Greek word *akouo* is translated "hear" in the KJV in both verses. However, other versions, such as the New American Standard Bible, translate the word "understand" in Acts 22:9, "And those who were with me saw the light, to be sure, but did not understand the voice of the One who was speaking to me." The word *akouo* does not carry the narrow meaning assigned to the English word "hear." In many cases, such as Acts 2:22 and 7:2, this word means "listen" or "take heed." Furthermore, even the KJV translates the same word as "understand" in 1 Corinthians 14:2. The men with Paul heard the sound, but they did not understand what they were hearing nor did they take heed to it. Therefore, there is no contradiction in the above two passages.[6]

## Doubt God's Word; Change God's Word; Contradict God's Word

Since God is infinite, omniscient, and omnipotent, He is perfectly capable of preserving His Word. After all, it represents Him. For the Enemy to accomplish his work of deceiving people, three things must occur as revealed in Genesis chapter 3:

1. *Doubt God's Word.* Verse 1 cites the serpent asking, "Did God actually say, 'You shall not eat of any tree in the garden'?"
2. *Change God's Word.* God is quoted in verse 3 as saying, "You shall not eat of the fruit of the tree that is in the midst of the garden, neither shall you touch it, lest you die."
3. *Contradict God's Word.* The serpent says in verse 4, "You will not surely die."

Don't let anyone cause you to doubt God's Word. Otherwise, you will end up contradicting God Himself and believing lies.

## Conclusion

Christians should believe the Bible because it is the Word of God. It is authoritative, true, and inspired. However, convincing people that the Bible is the Word of God is another task. After all, people have their preconceptions, which are often difficult to overcome. Nevertheless, you can rest assured that God's Word has stood the test of time and is the trustworthy message from God that guides humanity into truth.

---

*Matt Slick (Nampa, Idaho) is the founder and president of the Christian Apologetics and Research Ministry (CARM), which he began in 1995. The website carm.org is one of the most popular Christian apologetic websites on the Internet. Matt earned his bachelor's degree from Concordia University (Irvine, California) in 1988 and his master's of divinity degree from Westminster Theological Seminary in Escondido, California, in 1991.*

4

# Who Is the Real Jesus?
## The Christ-Centered Approach

DR. ROBERT M. BOWMAN JR.


### Summary

While Mormons are adamant about their belief in Jesus, those who leave Mormonism often lose this faith. In fact, many ex-Mormons move toward atheism or agnosticism and abandon any trust in Jesus. This is a shame because it was men—LDS leaders—and not Jesus who let them down. The overwhelming evidence for a historical Jesus who is the risen Savior can be offered as a message of hope.


### Introduction

The Church of Jesus Christ of Latter-day Saints claims to be centered on Jesus Christ. Mormons are fond of pointing out that His name is in the name of their church. They also refer to the Book of Mormon as a scripture about Christ that presents a Christ-centered faith: "And we talk of Christ, we rejoice in Christ, we preach of Christ, we prophesy of Christ" (2 Nephi 25:26). From a faithful LDS perspective, Mormonism offers a more robust knowledge of Jesus Christ than can be found in traditional Christianity or than can be gleaned from the Bible alone.

On the other hand, many Mormons eventually recognize that the Latter-day "prophets" and additional scriptures of their religion are not reliable or trustworthy sources of Christian belief. When this happens, these now-former Mormons typically become unsure of *everything* they have believed about Jesus Christ. They often wonder if they can continue to have faith in Christ at all.

Those who are transitioning out of Mormonism, or who have already left it, need to know the truth about Jesus Christ. They need to find reliable information about Him that will not crumble upon examination like LDS stories about Jesus visiting the Nephites or appearing to Joseph Smith. The Christ-centered approach is simply a way to talk to former and transitioning Mormons about who Jesus Christ really is.

### "Who Do You Say That I Am?"

Just as Jesus asked His disciples who they believed He was (Matthew 16:15), we should ask others what they believe about Jesus. It's always a good idea to ask questions first to get an accurate gauge on their beliefs. Don't assume you know what they think or be in a rush to tell them what you believe. Rather, listen and hear their point of view (Proverbs 18:13; James 1:19).

If they express ideas about Jesus that are erroneous, be gentle and conversational rather than harsh and condemning (Proverbs 15:1; 2 Timothy 2:25; James 1:19-20; 1 Peter 3:15). False prophets and teachers must be identified and exposed as such (Matthew 7:15-23; 2 Peter 2:1; 1 John 4:1-6), but those who have been following those false teachers are best persuaded by truth spoken in love (Ephesians 4:15).

An alarming number of former Mormons are becoming skeptical about Jesus. They may be unsure what is true about Christ. Perhaps they still think He died on the cross and rose from the dead, but beyond those basic truths, they don't know what to believe. All too often they have doubts about Jesus's death and resurrection. They may think of Jesus as, at best, a great teacher and example. At worst, they may have accepted the fringe atheist propaganda that Jesus never existed, which is a popular view also among many who have abandoned traditional Christianity for atheism. If a former Mormon confidently advocates this "Jesus mythicist" position, frankly, it will be very difficult to persuade him or her to rethink that view. Nevertheless, Christians should be prepared to counter this extreme position to help prevent those who are on the fence from falling off it.

## "If Christ Has Not Been Raised"

The central fact about Jesus Christ is the resurrection. The apostle Paul wrote, "If Christ has not been raised, then our preaching is in vain and your faith is in vain" (1 Corinthians 15:14). To put the matter in the simplest terms: If Christ did not rise from the dead, Christianity is false; if Christ did rise from the dead, Christianity is true and ought to be embraced. From a practical point of view, then, find out early in the conversation whether your friend believes that Jesus rose from the dead. If the answer is no, try to find out why they don't; if they do, build on that all-important common ground when turning to other questions about Jesus.

People who express uncertainty or skepticism about Jesus's resurrection offer various reasons for questioning its truth. Most of the objections challenge the *sources*, the *facts*, or the *possibility* of the resurrection.

### *Doubts About the Sources*

Once Mormons have lost faith in some of the sources of teaching about Jesus that they have accepted within the LDS religion, they commonly lose faith or, at the very least, doubt all sources, including the Bible. Evangelical Christians often want to respond to these doubts by asserting the absolute trustworthiness of the Bible as the written Word of God. That is the right way to view Scripture because it is the way Jesus viewed Scripture (Matthew 5:17-18; Mark 7:13; 12:24; John 10:35).[1]

Mormons, though, have been taught to view the Bible with some suspicion, and that suspicion becomes greatly magnified once they begin doubting Mormonism. If we base our use of the Bible on its being inspired, those with doubts will be distracted from the issue of the person of Christ by the myriad of criticisms made against the Bible.

To avoid getting sidetracked, reframe the issue. Invite them to view the New Testament—especially the Gospels—as historical documents. Now the issue is not whether the Gospels are totally without error but whether they are good historical sources about Jesus. The case for accepting them as such can be summed up in two simple points:

1. The Gospels are *biographies*. A biography is a book intended to tell the story of a real person's life. Luke's preface (Luke 1:1-4) states explicitly that the Gospel of Luke is meant to tell the truth about Jesus based on eyewitness testimonies. Recent scholarship has demonstrated that the Gospels are biographies in the style of ancient Greco-Roman writings.[2] Like those writings, the Gospels are narratives about one individual, focusing on the most important events of His life. Thus, even if there are questions about *details*, the Gospels are not myths or fables.
2. The Gospels are *the earliest biographical sources*. All biblical scholars, even those who are liberal and secular, agree that the New Testament Gospels were written in the first century, roughly 25 to 75 years after Jesus's death.[3] No alternative sources date that early.

In short, the Gospels are simply the best sources of historical information available about Jesus. Nothing else even comes close. We can explain confidently to former Mormons that, while the Book of Mormon has no historical support, the Gospels are just what they claim to be: ancient biographies about Jesus written by authors living close enough to the time of Jesus to have had access to eyewitness accounts of His life, teachings, death, and resurrection.

### *Doubts About the Facts*

Many people haven't thought seriously about what *did* happen if they deny that Jesus rose from the dead. They may simply dismiss the resurrection as a later legend without wrestling with the question of how this legend supposedly originated. We can help people understand the issue better by asking them to think about how the Christian movement itself got started. What led a group of Jews in the first century to begin proclaiming that a man named Jesus of Nazareth had risen from the dead? Let's consider how skeptics typically respond to this question.

1. *Did the story of Jesus's resurrection originate later?* Skeptics often claim that the resurrection was a later fiction, legend, or myth devised by Christians many years after Jesus's death. However, the earliest references to Jesus's resurrection come not in the Gospels but in Paul's letters, including 1 Thessalonians, which scholars date to AD 50-51. That's less than 20 years after Jesus died (probably in AD 33). That's too short a time for Jesus to be a wholly mythical figure.

2. *Did Jesus not really die on the cross?* Some non-Christians claim that Jesus didn't actually die on the cross at all. The many variations on this claim all say that *someone* made up the story of Jesus dying on the cross. The main problem with this claim is that crucifixion was such a shameful, humiliating form of death that no one would have chosen to invent the story of their religious founder dying in that way. As Paul admitted: "We preach Christ crucified, a stumbling block to Jews and folly to Gentiles" (1 Corinthians 1:23).

3. *Was Jesus not a real person?* As mentioned earlier, some skeptics have gone so far as to claim that Jesus never existed but was a later fiction invented on the basis of earlier myths. Frankly, the majority of historians—religious or nonreligious—do not take this claim seriously. Whereas only Mormons consider Lehi, Nephi, and the other Book of Mormon characters to be historical personages, the only people who deny the historical existence of Jesus are a few atheists. The four Gospels, Acts, and 1 Timothy all refer to Jesus's execution by the order

of Pontius Pilate, a historical figure who ruled Judea as its governor from AD 26 to 36 (Matthew 27; Mark 15; Luke 3:1; 23; John 18–19; Acts 3:13; 4:27; 13:28; 1 Timothy 6:13). The Roman historian Tacitus confirmed that Christ "suffered the extreme penalty during the reign of Tiberius at the hands of one of our procurators, Pontius Pilatus" (*Annals* 15.44).[4] Were this evidence about anyone other than Jesus, even the most hardened skeptic would agree that it was proof enough.

### *Doubts About the Possibility*

Most skeptics disbelieve in Jesus's resurrection simply because, if it happened, it would be a miracle. In the Western world today, skepticism about the miraculous or supernatural continues to grow. It is rather understandable that former Mormons, upon realizing that Joseph Smith's fantastic claims to supernatural visitations and gifts were fraudulent, would become cynical about such claims in general, even the resurrection. We can make the following four points in response to such skepticism.

1. *One case of fraud does not prove that all other claims are fraudulent.* For example, the fact that some insurance claims are fraudulent does not mean that all of them are. The fact that Joseph Smith lied about seeing the risen Jesus in 1820 does not mean that Paul and the other apostles lied about seeing the risen Jesus in the first century.

2. *Miracle claims should be evaluated by the evidence.* We should assume neither that all miracle stories are true nor that they are all false, but should instead evaluate these stories based on the evidence.

3. *General skepticism about miracles is a modern, Western, culturally narrow way of thinking.* Most people in most societies throughout history have believed in some kind of supernatural dimension to the world. It is only in the

past three centuries or so, and only in nations of Western cultural origins, that disbelief in the miraculous has been an issue at all. This fact doesn't prove that the supernatural exists, but it suggests that one should be cautious in dogmatically assuming that miracles are impossible.

4. *If God exists, miracles like the resurrection are possible.* Of course, many skeptics, including many former Mormons, also doubt the existence of God. Here's one way of addressing this problem: Ask if they would agree to say, at least for now, that God's existence is possible but not certain. If so, there should be a willingness to take an objective look at the evidence for the resurrection.

Note that the goal in making any of these four points is to encourage skeptics to consider the evidence. Once they agree to do so, it is possible to move ahead on the assumption that God's existence, and therefore the miraculous, is at least possible.

## "My Lord and My God"

If your former- or transitioning-Mormon friend believes that Jesus Christ rose from the dead, this point of agreement is common ground for discussing what else we should believe about Christ. If the individual no longer trusts the LDS Church's prophets and extrabiblical scriptures, where will they look for the truth about Jesus, and what will they find there?

We have already pointed out that the New Testament writings, most notably the Gospels and the epistles of Paul, are our earliest and best sources of information about Jesus. Once a person comes to the realization that the Mormon sources are not reliable while also recognizing that Jesus did rise from the dead, the natural place to look for further understanding of Jesus is the New Testament. After all, the New Testament writers were Christians because they were convinced that what Jesus said was true. Therefore, we should be able to find in the New Testament writings at least some fairly reliable information about who Jesus was and what He taught.

If the skeptic believes that Jesus rose from the dead and is ready to hear what else the New Testament says, we can begin addressing more directly the question of who Jesus is and how He is related to God. A helpful approach is to begin with the words of Jesus as recorded in the Gospels, and from there move out to the rest of the New Testament to show what it consistently teaches about Jesus.

The Gospel of Mark reports what Jesus said when He was asked what the greatest commandment was:

> Jesus answered, "The most important is, 'Hear, O Israel: The Lord our God, the Lord is one. And you shall love the Lord your God with all your heart and with all your soul and with all your mind and with all your strength.' The second is this: 'You shall love your neighbor as yourself.' There is no other commandment greater than these" (Mark 12:29-31).

Jesus's answer here is quite consistent with the fact that He was a Jewish teacher. The commandment He identified as the most important (Deuteronomy 6:4-5) is known in Judaism as the *Shema* (the Hebrew word translated "hear"). It was at the time (and still is today) the central confession or "creed" of the Jewish faith. The commandment epitomizes their belief that the Lord, who created the world and everything in it, is uniquely God. While ancient Judaism recognized the existence of many supernatural beings (and occasionally even called them "gods"), they recognized only one God as the Creator and Ruler of all things. This belief in one God is the consistent position of the New Testament writings (1 Corinthians 8:4; 1 Timothy 2:5; James 2:19).

What was surprising, even jarring, is what Jesus said about Himself. Without explicitly saying "I am God"—a statement that would no doubt have been misunderstood as claiming to be the Father—Jesus made numerous statements that placed Him on God's level. He forgave people's sins (Matthew 9:1-8; Mark 2:1-12) and claimed that He would be the Judge on the Day of Judgment (Matthew 25:31; Mark 12:36). He claimed that He would be present with His disciples wherever they went in all the nations (Matthew 18:20; 28:20). He invited His apostles to pray to Him about anything (John 14:14). After His resurrection, Jesus accepted worship from the disciples (Matthew 28:17) and accepted Thomas's affirmation that Jesus was "my Lord and my God" (John 20:28).

Several of the New Testament writings likewise affirm that Jesus Christ was God in ways that clearly indicated Jesus had the same divine status as the Father (Romans 9:5; Titus 2:13; Hebrews 1:8-12; 2 Peter 1:1). John tells us that Christ, before He became a human being, had *always* been God: "In the beginning was the Word, and the Word was with God, and the Word was God" (John 1:1). The apostles taught that the preexistent Christ, the divine Son, was the One through whom all created things came into existence (John 1:3; Colossians 1:16; Hebrews 1:2). Thus, creation itself, which the Old Testament credited solely to God, is now understood to have been the work of both the Father and the Son.

Paul interpreted the confession of the *Shema* to include both the Father and Jesus Christ in the one divine Creator of Jewish monotheism: "For us there is one God, the Father, from whom are all things and for whom we exist, and one Lord, Jesus Christ, through whom are all things and through whom we exist" (1 Corinthians 8:6).

In other places Paul expanded the monotheistic confession to include explicitly the Spirit (1 Corinthians 12:4-6; Ephesians 4:4-6). Jesus had revealed the existence of this third person, the Holy Spirit (John 14:26; 16:13-14). The very act of Christian baptism as instituted by Christ is a profession of faith in the three divine persons of the Father, Son, and Holy Spirit (Matthew 28:19), without denying the monotheistic faith that Jesus affirmed.

## Conclusion

As Mormons read and study the New Testament freed from Mormon presuppositions and doctrinal baggage, seeking in its pages the truth about Jesus, they will have a better appreciation of its teachings. They will grow in the grace and knowledge of the true Jesus and glorify Him (2 Peter 3:14-18).

---

*Dr. Robert M. Bowman Jr. (Rockford, Michigan) is the executive director of the Institute for Religious Research (IRR.org) in Cedar Springs, Michigan. He holds MA and PhD degrees in biblical studies and has lectured frequently at universities and seminaries throughout the United States. Rob is the author of a dozen books, including the co-author of* Putting Jesus in His Place: The Case for the Deity of Christ *(with J. Ed Komoszewski; Grand Rapids, MI: Kregel, 2007).*

# Spotlight

## BRETT KUNKLE

*Brett Kunkle served for many years at Stand to Reason (www.str.org) and in 2017 started a ministry called MAVEN aimed at training Christian young people (www.maventruth.com). Instead of just teaching students about Mormonism in a classroom setting, Brett has taken almost a thousand students and leaders on mission trips to Utah since 2000. Because more than half of those living in Utah are Mormon, Brett specifically instructs the students on the essential doctrines of Mormonism so they can learn how to share their faith effectively in a different religious culture.*

**Eric and Sean: Why did you begin taking students to Utah?**

Brett: I took my first trip to Utah as a Biola University student in the spring of 1995 and it had a profound impact on my life. I was a part-time youth pastor at the time and realized that mission trips to Utah could be a powerful tool in teaching theology to students and giving them a passion for the Great Commission without boring them.

**Eric and Sean: What are some of the specific types of outreach you like to focus on while you are in Utah?**

Brett: I have two goals for the trip: (1) to help Christian students know what and why they believe; and, (2) to help Christian students cultivate a love for lost people. I structure my trips to get students into conversations with as many Mormons as possible because such discussions help accomplish both purposes. I typically start by having them spend a full day in downtown Salt Lake City, touring Temple Square and teaching them to ask lots of questions. We encourage students to engage in friendly and respectful conversation with the Temple Square missionaries and other LDS representatives while not shying away from serious questions about LDS beliefs. I also love to take students to Utah college campuses where they can buy lunch in the cafeteria and sit down with Mormon students.

**Eric and Sean: If someone were to ask you, "Why would you take students to Utah instead of a foreign country for a mission trip?" how would you respond?**

Brett: For me, it's not *either* foreign missions *or* a Utah mission trip, it's a *both/and.* Take the students on foreign mission trips because there are many things God will teach them through that experience. But also take them to Utah. First, they'll interact with people who live in the same American cultural context, so the students get incredible training and experience sharing the gospel with people in Utah who are similar to their family, friends, and coworkers at home. Second, the trip is unique in that there is a focus on studying and knowing theology and Scripture. The trip challenges them to really understand what they believe about God, salvation, and other theological topics while getting them to know their Bibles much better.

**Eric and Sean: A parent might be concerned that their child could become interested in converting to Mormonism by learning too much about this religion. Is this a valid concern?**

Brett: I have never had a single person on one of my trips become interested in converting to Mormonism. In fact, the overwhelming response is just the opposite. When students discover for themselves that there is tremendous biblical, historical, and philosophical evidence for their Christian faith, *and* they begin to uncover the powerful arguments against Mormonism, it only strengthens their faith.

**Eric and Sean: How have these trips affected your students after they got back home?**

Brett: There are many stories of students who come home and immediately begin sharing Christ with their Mormon friends. Other students bring a new passion for God's Word home with them. A couple of weeks after one trip, a mom shared how her daughter had been studying the Bible every day since the experience. Stories like this are typical.

**Eric and Sean: If you were to give advice to a youth pastor who was thinking about organizing a mission trip to Utah, what factors should be taken into consideration?**

Brett: First, train the students *before* the trip by giving them good theological and biblical training. My philosophy is truth first before exposing them to error. Second, the activities on the Utah trip should be engineered to help get students into fruitful conversations with Mormons. The feedback I get is that the individual conversations they have are their favorite aspect of the trip.

# SECTION 2

# Reasoning Approaches

It's raining cats and dogs," Tweedledee screamed as he ran into the house. To which his friend Tweedledum replied, "If that's the case, I wonder if they will all need to be walked."

What's the problem with this response? Obviously a misunderstanding has stifled effective communication. After all, literal cats and dogs did not come from the sky, just a heavy rain.

Good logic and thinking skills are vital. God has given human beings minds with which to think. And He expects us to use them (Mark 12:30). When we cross the street, we look both ways—or, at least, we should! When we put our taxes together, we read the instructions. When Christians want to determine if someone is telling us the truth about spiritual issues, we should use our Bibles and check out the claims to see if they stand the test (1 Thessalonians 5:21). Otherwise, we are too likely to embrace heretical teachings that contradict the Word of God.

In chapter 5, J. Warner Wallace uses his skills as a cold-case detective to consider the evidence exposing the foundational elements of Mormonism. If the observer carefully uses deductive skills and objectively considers the evidence against Joseph Smith and the LDS religion, too many problems that do not correspond to historical truth become evident. In chapter 6, Dr. Corey Miller explains why a testimony should not supersede the evidence against Mormonism. Then in chapter 7, Bill McKeever discusses how two historical events—Joseph Smith's First Vision as well as the Book of Mormon—are integral to Mormonism's claim on truth. If there are major problems with both events, what are ways to bring these up to a Latter-day Saint who is willing to listen? Finally, Chip Thompson shows in chapter 8 how to utilize surveys to guide a conversation, providing a systematic approach to encourage Mormons to think through a variety of important topics.

While reason alone cannot bring a person to God, it certainly can be useful in getting the Mormon to think through issues that had never before been considered. These approaches might be exactly what is needed to help set the Mormon free.

5

# Investigating Mormonism
## The Case-Making Approach

J. WARNER WALLACE

### Summary

Police detectives are trained to collect evidence and present what they find. If the case is sufficiently compelling, the district attorney will file the case and eventually present it to a jury. What does the evidence suggest about Mormonism? And is there sufficient evidence, for or against the claims of Mormonism, to make the case to a jury?

### Introduction

I was an atheist and a police detective when I first examined the Christian and Mormon scriptures. It was my investigative skills that helped me verify the truth claims of Christianity, even as they falsified the truth claims of Mormonism. In the many years since I became a Christian, I've had conversations with Mormon believers to share what I discovered as a trained detective. I begin by describing the nature of criminal investigations, and then I show how the simple principles of good detective work can help determine if Mormonism is true.

### Investigating Joseph Smith

Criminal investigations focus on five key aspects of criminal activity:

1. The *motives* of the suspect in question
2. The *planning* executed prior to the commission of a crime
3. The *opportunity* a suspect has to commit the crime
4. The *overt acts* performed by a suspect in the commission of the crime
5. The *subsequent evidence of a crime* discovered following the suspect's overt acts

As I explain what I discovered about Joseph Smith and his claims related to the Book of Mormon in evangelistic conversations, I describe these five aspects of criminal activity:

### *The Motives of Joseph Smith*

All crimes, from simple thefts to gruesome homicides, are motivated by one of three desires: sexual lust, financial greed, and the pursuit of power. Each was present in the life of Joseph Smith.

#### Sexual Lust

Mormon leaders admit that Smith took between 30 to 40 wives for himself, claiming that God revealed polygamy to be a holy practice.[1] Emma, his first wife, never fully accepted this practice and remained skeptical about Joseph's divine revelations related to polygamy.[2]

#### Financial Greed

Smith relied largely on the financial support of his followers. Hundreds of members contributed to projects he initiated, and Smith's writings included divine commandments for the prophet to be sustained by his people. At one early point in Mormon history, Smith claimed to have received a revelation from God to establish a bank in Kirtland, Ohio. He told his followers that God promised him the bank would never fail, which proved to be a false prophecy and led to the bankrupting of many church members.[3]

#### The Pursuit of Power

Smith enjoyed a power base possessed by few others of his generation.

He was the general of his own militia, the Nauvoo Legion. He also served as the chief justice of the court and was the Nauvoo city mayor. In 1843, he announced his candidacy for president of the United States.[4]

### *Joseph Smith's Planning*

Evidence surrounding Smith's early history reveals the manner in which he prepared to write the Book of Mormon.

#### Smith Learned How to Be a Local Treasure Digger

He first learned about treasure digging from a traveling magician and diviner who visited Palmyra prior to 1825. At 20 years of age (approximately six years after he claimed that he saw God the Father and Jesus), charges were filed against Smith for his fraudulent efforts as a treasure digger.[5] He was charged as "a disorderly person and an impostor" in Bainbridge, New York in March 1826.[6]

#### Smith Learned How to Use a "Seer Stone"

He imitated the diviner he met in his youth and utilized "seer stones" that he believed were supernatural.

#### Joseph Smith's Opportunity to Commit the Act

Joseph did not create the Book of Mormon in a historical vacuum, and he wasn't alone in his efforts to seize the opportunity to start a new religion.

#### The Second Great Awakening

The Second Great Awakening took place during the first half of the nineteenth century, which resulted in tremendous religious excitement throughout New England, including in Joseph Smith's hometown. The local churches were not established enough to help teach and mentor those who were interested in learning biblical truth. As a result, many religious groups (all claiming to be true) emerged in the area.

#### Cultural Fascination with Native Americans

Several authors during this time speculated about the origin of the Native Americans. In 1823, Ethan Smith (no relation to Joseph Smith) wrote *View of the Hebrews,* which described Native Americans as descendants of the Hebrews who had migrated to the North American continent. A second edition of the book was published in 1825, five years prior to the publication of the Book of Mormon.

#### Local Interest in Treasure Digging

The practice of treasure digging was a well-accepted activity for many people in lower economic status at the time, particularly in the Palmyra area where Joseph Smith was raised.

### *Evidence of Joseph Smith's Overt Acts*

The chief instrument by which Smith convinced others to follow him was the Book of Mormon, allegedly written from gold plates that he said he found buried in the ground near Palmyra, New York. His prior interests and activities contributed to the story of their discovery and subsequent translation.

#### Elements from *View of the Hebrews*

There are many significant parallels between the Book of Mormon and *View of the Hebrews*. Even B.H. Roberts, a well-known Mormon apologist and historian, described parallels between the two books, including the claim that American Indians descended from Israelites and the description of a buried "lost book" with "yellow leaves."

#### Use of the King James Version (kjv)

Smith claimed that God provided him with the translation of the gold plates so the people of America could read the history and "scripture" in the 1830s. But he also used Elizabethan English in his text so it would match the spiritual-sounding language his potential followers would have understood.

#### Entire Chapters from the kjv

Whole chapters from the kjv, practically word for word, were incorporated into the Book of Mormon. For instance, nearly 20 complete chapters of Isaiah and Malachi were copied without alteration.

### Uncorrected KJV Translation Errors

Scholars now know the KJV translation Smith used contains many translation errors when compared to the latest and most recent manuscript discoveries. The Book of Mormon, however, cites the inaccurate passages without correcting these errors.

### Specious KJV Passages

Several passages in the KJV translation are now known to be late additions to the text, based on the latest discoveries of early biblical manuscripts. Joseph transferred some of these specious passages into the Book of Mormon when he copied it from the KJV.[7]

### Anachronisms

Perhaps the biggest evidence of an overt act related to the Book of Mormon is the presence of anachronisms. In many places in the Book of Mormon, Smith writes about things the allegedly ancient characters would not have known (because an event had not yet occurred in history, or an object had not yet been invented or introduced).

### Paraphrases from Long Before the Earthly Life of Jesus

Smith quotes or paraphrases Jesus in the Book of Mormon, placing these quotes within the Mormon chronology long before Jesus ever lived to make the original statements.[8]

### New Testament Paraphrases... Before the New Testament Was Written

When quoting an Old Testament passage, Smith often cites a New Testament paraphrase of the passage rather than returning to the Old Testament verse, even though the Book of Mormon was allegedly written *before* the New Testament was penned.[9]

### Describing the "Gospel" Long Before It Was Revealed

The biblical authors said the "good news" about salvation through Christ was made known to the Jew and Gentile alike, but it was a mystery prior to the appearance of Jesus and its full revelation after the

Resurrection (Ephesians 3:3-7; Colossians 1:26; 1 Peter 1:1-12; Romans 16:25-26). Smith reveals the Gospel message out of sequence approximately 570 years prior to its revelation in the New Testament (2 Nephi 25:19, 23; 2 Nephi 26:12; 2 Nephi 30:2; 2 Nephi 31:17).

### Describing the Church Long Before It Was Founded

Jesus repeatedly described the church as something yet to come (Matthew 16:18 and Acts 2:47). The Book of Mormon, however, claims the church was already formed as early as 147 BC, nearly two hundred years before it actually happened (Mosiah 18:17).

### Defining "Christians" Long Before They Were Named

The followers of Jesus were first called "Christians" in the first century in the city of Antioch (see Acts 11:26), but the Book of Mormon describes people being called "Christians" as early as 73 BC (Alma 46:15).

### The Gift of the Holy Ghost Long Before Pentecost

The Holy Spirit was promised by Jesus, and then bestowed upon the believers for the first time on the day of Pentecost (Luke 24:49 and Acts 2:1-4). Smith, however, describes people receiving the gift of the Holy Spirit as early as 545 BC (2 Nephi 31:12-13).

### Words Used in the "Ancient" Text Long Before They Existed

The Book of Mormon uses words not available at the time it supposedly happened. For example, the word *Bible* is attributed to authors who are supposedly writing between 559 BC and 545 BC (see 2 Nephi 29:3-4, 6, 10), even though the Greek word *biblia* was not used until the fifth century AD. Smith also repeatedly used the word *Christ* in places dated hundreds of years before the coming of Christ and hundreds of years before the invention of the Greek word from which the English word *Christ* is transliterated.

### Events Written in the Past Tense Long Before They Occurred

Smith writes about events as if they had already occurred, even though they would not have yet occurred in the Book of Mormon chronology. In 2 Nephi 31:6, 8, for example, the baptism of Jesus ("Lamb of God") is described as though it had already occurred almost six centuries before Jesus came.

### Animals in the Americas Long Before They Arrived There

The Book of Mormon references several animals on the continent, even though these species didn't arrive in North America until centuries later. For example, it mentions horses (Alma 18:9; Alma 18:12; Alma 20:6; 3 Nephi 3:22), elephants (Ether 9:19), cows and goats (1 Nephi 18:25; Enos 1:21; Ether 9:18), and pigs (Ether 9:8; Ether 9:17-18).

### Crops in the Americas Long Before They Existed

Smith also errantly describes grains not yet present on the American continent during the time period described by the Book of Mormon, including barley (Mosiah 7:22; 9:9; Alma 11:7, 15) and wheat (Mosiah 9:9; 3 Nephi 18:18).

### Weapons Used by Native Americans Long Before They Were Invented

Smith repeatedly describes weapons of war supposedly used by people in the Book of Mormon. No archeological evidence supports the existence of these weapons or articles of war, including chariots (Alma 18:9-10,12; Alma 20:6; 3 Nephi 3:22) and metal swords (2 Nephi 5:14; Mosiah 8:11).

### Modern Innovations

Smith inaccurately includes inventions and innovations unavailable during the period described in the Book of Mormon, including a metal-based monetary system (Alma 11:5-19), silk fabric (1 Nephi 13:7,8; Alma 1:29; Alma 4:6; Ether 9:17; Ether 10:24), compasses (1 Nephi 16:10; 1 Nephi 18:12; 1 Nephi 18:27; Alma 37:38), and glass windows (Ether 2:22-23).

Like the Bible, the Book of Mormon claims to be the true history of a vast population that lived, built cities, engaged in commerce, waged war, and developed a complex culture. If true, archaeological evidence of this vast civilization should be abundant. There is not, however, a single archaeological discovery confirming any detail from the Book of Mormon, even though the Bible has plenty of archaeological support.

### *Subsequent Evidence Related to Joseph Smith*

Several events occurred following the alleged translation of the Book of Mormon that indicate Smith committed a fraudulent act.

#### The Original Plates Became Unavailable

Smith guaranteed that subsequent investigators of his claims would be unable to examine the gold plates; he claimed these plates were returned to the angel Moroni.

#### "Eyewitnesses" Changed Their Claims

Smith claimed three witnesses observed the plates, but these witnesses (Martin Harris, Oliver Cowdery, and David Whitmer) only said they observed the plates after repeated and persuasive efforts on his part to convince them of their observations. Cowdery later became a Methodist and confessed his regret for having any connection with Mormonism. Meanwhile, Harris also eventually left Mormonism and admitted that he only saw the plates in a "visionary or entranced state."

#### Smith Disguised and Protected His Translation Efforts

Most modern accounts of Smith's translation process depict him reading and translating the plates word for word with a scribe by his side, usually sitting at the same table. The real "translation" process was very different, according to those who were present. The plates remained hidden throughout the translation process; in some instances, Smith sat behind a curtain as he recited the text to his helpers.

#### Smith Was Unable to Duplicate the Lost 116 Pages

Martin Harris's wife, Lucy, became suspicious of Smith's translation activity; she suspected he was trying to defraud her husband. After

Smith and Harris (working as his scribe) penned approximately 116 pages of the Book of Mormon, Harris began to have serious doubts about the authenticity of the work. He told Smith about Lucy's concerns, and Smith ultimately allowed Martin to take the transcript home. While there, the transcript allegedly disappeared. Smith was unable to retranslate the lost pages, even though he reportedly still had access to the gold plates from which the translation first resulted. Instead, he said God redirected him to replace the lost material with information found on yet another set of metal plates he claimed to possess. Lucy Harris remained unconvinced.

#### An Even More Obvious Act of Fraud

Although the original gold Book of Mormon plates are unavailable to examine, this is not the case with the Book of Abraham. Smith allegedly translated this ancient Egyptian papyrus he acquired in 1835. When he first saw the papyri, he claimed they contained the writing of Abraham. Smith "translated" the document, now called the Book of Abraham in the Pearl of Great Price. The original papyrus scroll was lost for a number of years but was rediscovered in 1967. When translated by experts both in and outside the LDS Church, the document contains *nothing* remotely similar to what Smith claimed in his translation.[10]

### Conclusion

The evidence implicating Joseph Smith is cumulative and convincing when considered as a criminal investigation:

1. Joseph Smith possessed a *motive* to defraud his followers. He had much to gain financially, sexually, and from a perspective of power.

2. Smith's life prior to writing the Book of Mormon provided him with experiences from which he could *plan* his forgery. His time as a treasure digger, his involvement with seer stones, and his experience with the criminal justice system prepared him to deceive others.

3. Smith had the perfect *opportunity* to make his false claims given the religiously charged environment of New York State in the nineteenth century, preexisting ideas about Native Americans, and the cultural interest in treasure digging.
4. Smith's *overt acts* of fraud are evidenced in the text of the Book of Mormon. He borrowed from the *View of the Hebrews* outline and used archaic King James Version language to construct his narrative. He inserted errors and questionable passages while including a number of anachronistic passages as well.
5. The behavior of Smith (and his accomplices) following the translation of the Book of Mormon provide *subsequent evidence* of his fraudulent activity. Smith made sure the gold plates were unavailable for inspection, the "eyewitnesses" made questionable statements following their original testimony, Smith could not repeat his efforts to translate the book, and he committed an obvious act of fraud in his translation of the Book of Abraham.

Whenever I engage people who want to know the truth about Mormonism, I use this outline, incorporating as much of the evidence as I have time to explain and showing how Smith's actions were consistent with someone who fraudulently attempted to deceive his followers.

---

*J. Warner Wallace is a senior fellow at the Colson Center for Christian Worldview and adjunct professor of apologetics at Biola University. He wrote* Cold-Case Christianity *(Colorado Springs, CO: David C. Cook, 2013),* God's Crime Scene *(Colorado Springs, CO: David C. Cook, 2015), and* Forensic Faith *(Colorado Springs, CO: David C. Cook, 2017). He has a master's degree in theological studies from Golden Gate Baptist Theological Seminary and has appeared in faith-based productions such as* God's Not Dead 2, Jesus Revealed, *and* Mining for God.

6

# Undermining Confidence in a Mormon's Personal "Testimony"
## The Police-Lineup Approach

DR. COREY MILLER


### Summary

Many Christians fail to realize the central role that a testimony plays in the Mormon psyche, preventing heartier and seemingly more important discussions on essential matters such as God and salvation. To have a truly fruitful conversation, it is vital for the Christian to wean the Mormon's reliance on it early in the discussion by casting doubt about which testimony is most reliable.


### The Authority of Testimony

In their conversations with Mormons, too many Christians are left dumbfounded and deflated upon realizing that the Latter-day Saint testimony takes preeminence over facts and logical arguments. There is a place for discussing essential doctrines, but eliminating this communication barrier is necessary to fruitfully address those issues.[1] Mormons must first begin to doubt before they can believe what the Christian shares.

Anyone who engages with Mormons frequently will encounter "the testimony." In fact, personal testimonies are the featured event on the first Sunday of every month at LDS meetinghouses all over the world. A testimony goes something like this: "I bear you my testimony. I know Joseph Smith is a prophet of God. I know the Book of Mormon is the word of God. And I know that The Church of Jesus Christ of Latter-day Saints is the one true church!" Mormonism is founded upon "priestly" authority as well as the teachings of prophets, apostles, and the Standard Works. Nonetheless, it is often the testimony that proves to be most influential for a Mormon.

"Testimony," Apostle Boyd K. Packer once said, "is to be *found* in the *bearing* of it. Somewhere in your quest for spiritual knowledge, there is that 'leap of faith,' as the philosophers call it."[2] Somehow, "bearing" the testimony helps discover it. Elsewhere, Packer revealed the nature of testimony: "Bear testimony of the things that you hope are true, as an act of faith."[3] It bears similarity to the sort of wish fulfillment ridiculed by atheists like Karl Marx and Sigmund Freud.

Dallin Oaks, a member of the First Presidency, described the testimony as a "'burning in the bosom' (see D&C 9:8-9)...which signifies a feeling of comfort and serenity."[4] Seventy Gene Cook encouraged its deployment in evangelism: "Sincere feelings conveyed from heart to heart by means of testimony convert people to the truth where weak, wishy-washy, argumentative statements will not."[5]

An official LDS church manual proclaims, "In order to know that the Book of Mormon is true, a person must read, ponder, and pray about it. The honest seeker of truth will soon come to feel that the Book of Mormon is the word of God."[6] President Spencer W. Kimball even warned that failure to bear one's testimony frequently could result in a loss of merit points toward the heavenly goal.[7] It seems the church leaders teach that the more expressively one's testimony is told and repeated, the truer and more deeply rooted it becomes. It is often delivered with such tenacity that one might be tempted to conflate it with veracity.

## Turning a Problem into Opportunity

Religious testimony *can* be a legitimate form of knowledge, as there is strong philosophical grounding and biblical precedent as well as rhetorical power in sharing a testimony. The problem is not that a testimony is subjective, but that it is sometimes *too* subjective, as in the LDS case. Only testimonial reports that contradict truth or fail to be adequately supported (or supportable) by evidence are problematic.

We can build a bridge in the conversation by learning "Mormonese," what I call the natural language of Latter-day Saints.[8] Building some common ground with Mormons by affirming the practice of the testimony in general helps cultivate a receptive rather than a defensive posture. To undermine their confidence in the subjective testimony, the Socratic dialogue (i.e., asking questions) is more effective than direct frontal assault. Good questions foster reflection rather than deflection. Given the high number of LDS adults who have served in church missions, most Mormons are conditioned to see themselves as teachers who have a repository of religious truth.

To undermine confidence in the LDS testimony, I find it helpful to use what I call the police-lineup approach. A police lineup is a process by which a witness's alleged identification of a suspect is confirmed on some level that can be admissible as evidence in a court trial. Along with several foils—people of similar height, build, and complexion—the suspect is placed against a wall next to them as they face in the direction of the witness, who stands behind a one-way mirror to allow for anonymity. The goal is to identify the real culprit in contrast to lookalikes who are eliminated in the process of consideration. The person behind the glass must determine which of these people, if any, is responsible for the crime.

Mormonism claims to be the true representation of God. But which Mormonism? There are numerous competing Mormon sects, yet not all of them can be true.[9] In discussing the various versions of Mormonism, all retell the story of the "First Vision" that is believed to have taken place in 1820 when Smith was only 14. During that time, many different Protestant churches sought converts through revivals. Smith claimed that he went into the forest and prayerfully sought an answer to his question about which church to join. Although there were several varying versions, the official account is that God the Father and Jesus Christ appeared to Smith in the First Vision and told him that he should join none of them since all were apostate; they also said that the Christian pastors did not have the necessary authority to represent God. Smith was then called to restore what was lost.

The legitimacy of Mormonism hinges on this story and its teachings of the "Apostasy" and the "Restoration." Mormon missionaries recount this story to people in their first missionary discussion, noting that the multiplicity of churches today removes any hope of confidence in religious knowledge without modern revelation and a living prophet available to guide humanity.

A steep burden of proof here is often left unchallenged. These assertions require one to believe that for nearly two millennia following the death of the last of Jesus's apostles, the priestly authority was lost, leaving millions of Christian thinkers and devotees misinformed, misled, or otherwise severely lacking until Smith emerged to restore the faith. Before introducing the police-lineup approach concerning the Restoration, I start by suggesting the problem of the Apostasy by appealing to their imagination. Consider my initial response to the First Vision:

> I appreciate what you've shared, but let me present you with a similar scenario. Suppose we were out in the wilderness together and I briefly journeyed off on my own. When I return, I inform you that I just encountered God. I saw Him! He spoke with me! Moreover, he told me that all religions, including Mormonism, were apostate and in need of restoration. Would you believe me if I claimed to have seen God and then asked for you to leave your religion, begin donating money to my movement, and follow me as your spiritual leader?

It is important to insist upon a response, even though they probably will be suspicious and can anticipate your direction. I would follow with this:

> What is more probable on the face of it: one man's claim to literally see God, who informed him that millions of

> brilliant and godly Christians were lost with respect to the nature of God and salvation, or that this one man was lost? If my encounter in the forest sounds incredible, and you would not believe me, how is this different from committing yourself to the words of Smith now and asking me to do the same?

The Mormon will come to feel just what this experience reveals: the steep burden of proof to establish the Great Apostasy required to make sense of a Restoration whereby one is called to place all one's trust in one man over and against history. The burden becomes increasingly steep considering Jesus's statements denying any such total apostasy (Matthew 16:17-19; 28:18-20), even if small-scale apostasy is mentioned elsewhere in the New Testament (1 Timothy 4:1).

Mormons may bear their testimony in response, creating an opportunity for the police-lineup illustration. Invoke the illustration even if they do not bear testimony at that time. Remember, the goal is to undermine their confidence in subjective testimony such that every time they bear it, regardless of your presence, they will be unable to feel confident given the residue of doubt. They will be more open to consider other truths once this obstacle has been successfully undermined, subverted, or demolished.

## Problems with the Personal Testimony

If it is not already apparent, the LDS testimony is significantly problematic. One shortcoming is that a subjective testimony is taken as the primary criterion for truth, which leads to a sort of subjectivism. The police-lineup approach considers the fact that there are dozens of Mormon splinter groups. However, as previously mentioned, the LDS Church is not alone—dozens of other churches each claim Joseph Smith as their founder; each group says it has a direct link to a restored priesthood authority. Furthermore, members from each group cite the same Book of Mormon passage (Moroni 10:4-5) to support their personal testimonies.

To illustrate the problem, suppose you inquire about which Mormon sect you should join. You need only name a few.[10] Ask them to imagine gathering one representative from each competing sect in a room to bear their testimonies. Each would undoubtedly bear a sincere and similar testimony with equal tenacity. Yet they will all contradict each other at serious points—not to mention that each thinks the other to be apostate. This demonstrates that tenacity cannot be confused with veracity. Ask:

> How might an investigator conclude which of all these Mormon sects is true? Which of these is really the "one true" church? Logically, since they are all contradictory to one another, at best only one can be true and all others false. At worst, they are all false.

Invoking imagination again with an illustration, continue:

> Suppose I were standing before a lineup of representatives of various Mormon sects, each with its own set of prophets and apostles, bearing testimonies. How would I determine which one is true? How do you know your church is true and not another? As I see it, you have a few options. Either you can judge their hearts and call them liars or insincere. Or you can claim that, though sincere, they were somehow deceived by a lying spirit. If your testimony is true, are the others insincerely lying or sincerely deceived?

Get a commitment. Because of the current cultural aversion to making judgment calls about others, they will likely choose the latter and conclude that these others are either self-deceived or deceived by a lying spirit. Continue penetrating the issue, asking:

> Since you believe that people can be sincerely deceived after praying about the Book of Mormon, how do you *know* that you are not sincerely deceived in your testimony?

Point out the apostle Paul's warning when speaking of the possibility of people being deceived even by an angel of light (Galatians 1:6-9; 2 Corinthians 11:14). Then reiterate,

> How do you know you are not the one who is deceived when competing Mormon sects testify of an equally emotive feeling of peace and serenity? It seems to me that a subjective testimony cannot be relied upon as the sole criterion of truth. Furthermore, if Mormonism teaches a foreign god or means of salvation contradicting the Bible, biblical Christians should no more pray about this than pray over whether it is right to murder. After all, if God has already spoken on something, there is no need to ask Him to change His mind. It is not wise to rely on a merely subjective testimony as the primary criterion of truth—especially if eternity hangs in the balance. Would you agree?

## Clinching the Conversation

Having undermined their testimony, I culminate by passionately deploying my testimony and sharing the most explicit statement in Scripture that tests the legitimacy of a subjective testimony.[11] Speaking with tenacity, I will testify in Jesus Christ alone and my belief that provides me with eternal life and a relationship with God forever.[12] Read 1 John 5:9-13 as translated in the New International Version, emphasizing what I have italicized:

> We accept human *testimony*, but God's *testimony* is greater because it is the *testimony* of God, which he has given about his Son. Whoever believes in the Son of God accepts this *testimony*. Whoever does not believe God has made him out to be a *liar*, because they have not believed the *testimony* God has given about his Son. *And this is the testimony*: God has *given* us eternal life, and this life is in his Son. Whoever has the Son has life; whoever does not have

> the Son of God does not have life. I write these things to you who believe in the name of the Son of God so that you may *know* that you have eternal life.

Then ask the clinching questions:

> Do you have this testimony? If you died today, do you know that you would experience eternal life with Heavenly Father merely by having the Son? If not, is God a liar?

Based upon biblical testimony, I do, in fact, *know* that I have eternal life because I trust in Christ's work alone, doing good works in grateful response to the salvation I presently possess solely on the merits of Christ. If it were based on anything I could do, I could not know this. But I know this both by the Spirit (Romans 8:16) and the testimony of Scripture. Mormonism does not offer the confidence that my testimony has in harmony with God's testimony, namely, whoever "has the Son" can *know* that eternal life with Heavenly Father is assured.[13]

---

*Dr. Corey Miller was a sixth-generation Mormon raised in Utah who converted to Christianity and then earned four graduate degrees. He serves as the president/CEO of Ratio Christi: Campus Apologetics Alliance (www.ratiochristi.org) and is an adjunct professor in philosophy and comparative religions at Indiana University-Kokomo. He co-edited* Is Faith in God Reasonable? Debates in Philosophy, Science, and Rhetoric *(Routledge, 2014) and co-authored* Leaving Mormonism: Why Four Scholars Changed their Minds *(Kregel, 2017).*

7

# Joseph Smith's First Vision and the Book of Mormon
## The Historical Approach

BILL MCKEEVER


### Summary

When theological problems within Mormonism do not seem to shake a Mormon's testimony, historical problems sometimes will. Mormon leaders have pointed to certain events that are necessary for Mormonism to be true, and Christians can use these events to have a productive conversation.


### Introduction

The bodily resurrection of Jesus Christ is a historical event that must be true or the claims of Christianity fall apart. As the apostle Paul affirmed, if Christ did not rise from the grave, the Christian's faith is useless and believers remain in their sins (1 Corinthians 15:16). In the same way, Mormonism has two "do-or-die" historical events. One is the First Vision when Joseph Smith claimed he was visited by both God the Father and Jesus Christ in the spring of 1820. The second is the angel Moroni leading Smith to an ancient set of gold plates known as the Book of Mormon. Showing the problems with these events can be useful in evangelistic conversations with a Mormon.

## The First Vision

According to Gordon B. Hinckley, Mormonism's fifteenth president,

> Every claim that we make concerning divine authority, every truth that we offer concerning the validity of this work, all finds its roots in the First Vision of the boy prophet...If the First Vision did not occur, then we are involved in a great sham. It is just that simple. [1]

It is rare to find a Mormon who is not familiar with Smith's First Vision testimony. Most are familiar with the version in the 1838 account, which can be found in the Pearl of Great Price. Smith recounted that when he was 14 years old and living with his family in the area of Palmyra, New York, there arose "an unusual excitement on the subject of religion." Smith was concerned by the fact that "some were contending for the Methodist faith, some for the Presbyterian, and some for the Baptist."

Deeply troubled, he took James 1:5 as his guide and proceeded to go into the nearby woods to ask God which of all the churches were true. During that encounter according to the first chapter of Joseph Smith—History found in the Pearl of Great Price, he claimed that he "saw two Personages, whose brightness and glory defy all description, standing above me in the air. One of them spake unto me, calling me by name and said, pointing to the other—This is My Beloved Son. Hear Him!"[2] When he asked these personages "which of all the sects was right," he reported,

> I was answered that I must join none of them, for they were all wrong; and the Personage who addressed me said that all their creeds were an abomination in his sight; that those professors were all corrupt; that: "they draw near to me with their lips, but their hearts are far from me, they teach for doctrines the commandments of men, having a form of godliness, but they deny the power thereof."[3]

Joseph Smith claimed that this experience led to him being persecuted:

> I soon found, however, that my telling the story had excited a great deal of prejudice against me among professors of religion, and was the cause of great persecution, which continued to increase; and though I was an obscure boy, only between fourteen and fifteen years of age, and my circumstances in life such as to make a boy of no consequence in the world, yet men of high standing would take notice sufficient to excite the public mind against me, and create a bitter persecution; and this was common among all the sects—all united to persecute me.[4]

No evidence supports this claim. While Smith did, on very rare occasions, speak of a first heavenly visitation, the details are not always consistent. For example, in his 1832 diary, Smith testified that he was concerned about his personal forgiveness of sins, not which church is true. When he prayed in his "sixteenth year," he said he was visited only by "the Lord." In this version, Smith said he already knew the churches were corrupt and teaching false doctrine.[5]

An unpublished account dated November 9, 1835 stated that Smith was "about 14 years old." No revival is mentioned, but Smith does introduce two unidentified personages and many angels. He says nothing about corrupt churches.[6]

In a November 14, 1835 account, Smith does not mention a revival or that he was told that the churches were wrong. He does say that he was visited by "angels," but nothing was said about the Father or the Son. In the first published version of the First Vision (September 1840), Smith failed to mention the revival but said he was visited by two unidentified "glorious personages." He learned from these personages that the churches were teaching "incorrect doctrines."[7]

It was not until 1842 that the church published what is known as Smith's 1838 account. This version has become the church's official version.[8] Today Mormon missionaries use the First Vision to invite investigators to join the "only true and living church" that possesses the "restored Gospel." Missionaries are instructed to explain how "a universal apostasy occurred following the death of Jesus Christ and His Apostles. If there had been no apostasy, there would be no need of a Restoration."[9]

Meanwhile, Smith's account in the Pearl of Great Price gives enough details about this "religious excitement" that it is possible to accurately pinpoint the exact revival he described. The historical event described by Smith took place in 1824, not 1820. "Great multitudes" were not added to the churches in 1820, but statistical records show considerable growth in 1824.[10]

This date creates another problem. If this 1824 revival led Smith to pray about which church was true, then the appearance of the angel Moroni in 1823 (described below) becomes his actual "first vision." Mormon historians must be aware of this incongruity since the church tenaciously sticks to the erroneous 1820 date. The contradictions surrounding this truly fantastic event have caused many to conclude that Smith fabricated the story and embellished it as the years went by.[11]

## The Book of Mormon

Besides the First Vision, Mormonism is dependent upon the story of the origin of the Book of Mormon. Apostle Jeffrey R. Holland insisted that

> everything of saving significance in the Church stands or falls on the truthfulness of the Book of Mormon and, by implication, the Prophet Joseph Smith's account of how it came forth is as sobering as it is true. It is a "sudden death" proposition. Either the Book of Mormon is what the Prophet Joseph said it is, or this Church and its founder are false, a deception from the first instance onward.[12]

Seventy Tad R. Callister explained that, if the Book of Mormon "is true, then Joseph Smith was a prophet and this is the restored Church of Jesus Christ, regardless of any historical or other arguments to the contrary."[13]

According to Joseph Smith—History 1:34, the angel Moroni appeared to Smith on September 21, 1823, to tell him that "there was a book deposited, written upon gold plates, giving an account of the former inhabitants of this continent, and source from which they sprang."

Born as a mortal man about 14 centuries earlier, Moroni had buried the plates in a stone box near the Smith home. Smith was not allowed to retrieve the plates for another four years. Several LDS historians and official church manuals have used the story given by Lucy Mack Smith, the mother of the Mormon prophet, to explain when and how Smith took the plates from their earthly hiding place.[14] She reported that her son took the plates and, "wrapping them in his linen frock, placed them under his arm and started for home." After "traveling some distance," he

> came to a large windfall, and as he was jumping over a log, a man sprang up from behind it and gave him a heavy blow with a gun. Joseph turned around and knocked him down, then ran at the top of his speed.[15]

She said her son was attacked at least two more times as he traveled the three miles between the place where the plates were hidden and his home. There is no record of Smith rendering his assailants unconscious or incapacitated. It must be assumed, then, that he was able to outrun them, even though he would have been hindered by a slight limp caused by a childhood surgery.

## The Weight of the Gold Plates

In hundreds of conversations I've had with members of the LDS Church, I have found that virtually everyone is familiar with the basic story of the gold plates; however, very few have ever stopped to seriously consider the details of the story. Contemporaries of Smith gave varying dimensions for the plates as well as a wide range of estimated weights.

Smith claimed that the record he received from the angel was "six inches wide and eight inches long, and not quite so thick as common tin." He also said the "volume was something near six inches in thickness, a part of which was sealed."[16] Given these dimensions, the plates were one-sixth of a cubic foot. Since gold weighs 1,204 pounds per cubic foot, this would equal about two hundred pounds. We can agree with Apostle John Widtsoe who said, "If the gold were pure, [the plates] would weigh two hundred pounds, which would be a heavy weight for a man to carry, even though he were of the athletic type of Joseph Smith."[17]

In an effort to reconcile the weight of gold plates, Mormons have offered several clever explanations, including "Joseph was a buff farm boy." Though I'm sure Smith probably was a strong young man, it is highly unlikely that he could "carry and run with" plates weighing more than his own body weight. When Mormons realize the silliness of such an argument, they often move on to what I call "the miracle theory"; after all, couldn't God give Smith supernatural strength to carry such a load?

While I certainly do believe that God could have given Smith divine strength, this theory is refuted by Mormon leaders and apologists who work hard to concoct theories that get the weight of the plates down to a manageable level. If God truly intervened by bestowing Smith and others with superhuman abilities, this effort would be unnecessary. Rather than insist in a miracle, Widtsoe offered the following theory:

> For the purpose of record keeping, plates made of gold mixed with a certain amount of copper would be better, for such plates would be firmer, more durable and generally more suitable for the work in hand. If the plates were made of eight karat gold, which is gold frequently used in present-day jewelry, and allowing a 10 percent space between the leaves, the total weight of the plates would not be above one hundred and seventeen pounds—a weight easily carried by a man as strong as was Joseph Smith.[18]

It seems obvious that Widtsoe didn't see the need for a miracle if the plates were only a mere 117 pounds, a weight he claims is "easily carried." But is this even plausible? I decided to create a visual experiment by producing a set of plates made out of sheet metal. These plates are the same dimension (8 by 6 by 6 inches) as Smith's gold plates but are "only" eighty pounds in weight. For many years I have used these plates on a public street outside an annual Mormon pageant in central Utah to invite passersby to "lift the plates." I ask if the Mormon volunteer believes that Smith's plates were created out of the *metal* gold. Rarely does anyone deny this; after all, Joseph Smith—History 1:34 cites Moroni telling Smith that there was "a book deposited, written upon *gold* plates."

My 80-pound plates are not impossible to lift, but those who take me up on my challenge normally conclude that plates this size are extremely heavy. At this point, I explain how these replica plates are just 40 percent of the weight of Smith's plates. If they were made of gold, the 80-pound weight would have to be doubled (add 80 pounds) with a half stack (add 40 pounds) on top of that! It seems obvious that it would be impossible to carry such a weight for any considerable distance (with a limp), much less the three miles mentioned by Smith's mother.

Replica plates are not absolutely necessary to make this challenge effective. When illustrating this point, suggest that your Mormon acquaintances lift and carry two bags of Portland cement (a bag weighs about 92 pounds) the next time they visit a hardware store. While there, they might try carrying six 16-by-8-by-8-inch concrete blocks (a block weighs 34 pounds). Or challenge them to lift five boxes of printer paper (a box containing 10 reams weighs about 40 pounds) at an office supply store. Or ask them to go to the gym and lift two 100-pound grip plates…at the same time. You get the idea. Be creative to show the impossibility of such a feat.

Though LDS leaders often continue to use the phrases "gold plates" or "plates of gold," some Mormons interpret this to be a reference to the color of the plates rather than the content of the metal. If so, ask them to explain what kind of metal was used that could withstand being buried in the ground for centuries. The selections are very limited, but one alloy has become the most common answer from Latter-day Saints. Dr. John Sorenson, a former professor from Brigham Young University who is a strong defender of the Book of Mormon, wrote,

> R. H. Putnam has argued persuasively that the Book of Mormon plates that were in Joseph Smith's hands were of *tumbaga*. (Had they been unalloyed gold, they would have been too heavy for a single person to carry.)[19]

Tumbaga is an alloy composed mostly of gold and copper, the percentage or carat weight of each metal varying dramatically. Like Sorenson, Putnam did not believe that Smith needed supernatural strength to carry the plates:

> The plates were not so heavy that a man could not carry them. Joseph Smith was a man of youth and vigor, yet Mormon was 74 years of age when he turned them over to his son. (See Morm. 6:6) We are not led to believe that the weight of the plates was a great hindrance. The witnesses testified that they had "hefted" them, indicating the weight seemed tolerable.[20]

Putnam stated that the tumbaga plates could not have been made of an "extremely low-gold alloy because of the danger of electrolysis and brittleness." At the same time, he surmised that they "were probably not of an extremely high-gold-alloy either, since the weight would thereby be increased."[21]

Given these factors, Putnam surmised that plates made of 8-carat gold with "3-percent native impurity would weigh 106.88 pounds." Assuming that the plates were not perfectly flat, he then arbitrarily added an amazing 50 percent air gap, not just a 10 percent air gap as John Widtsoe did. This, he believed, would bring the plates' weight down to around 53 pounds.

By doing this, Putnam created another problem. Smith claimed to have translated only the top two inches of the plates since the bottom four inches were sealed. A 50 percent air gap drops that to a mere one inch, which is hardly enough space for a book as extensive as the Book of Mormon.

## Conclusion

Understanding the problems with the First Vision and Book of Mormon accounts has shaken the faith of many Latter-day Saints, especially in recent years. When doctrinal discrepancies don't seem to faze a Mormon, the history may. It could be the jolt necessary for a Latter-day Saint to realize how problematic Mormonism's history really is, opening the door to sharing gospel truth.[22]

---

*Bill McKeever is the founder and director of Mormonism Research Ministry, based in the Salt Lake City, Utah, area. He hosts the daily radio program* Viewpoint on Mormonism *(mrm.org/podcast). He also has authored* In Their Own Words *(Morris, 2016) while coauthoring (with Eric Johnson)* Answering Mormons' Questions *(Kregel, 2013) and* Mormonism 101 *(Baker, 2015).*

8

# Using Surveys to Reveal Truth to Mormons
## The Polling Approach

CHIP THOMPSON


### Summary

Starting a conversation with a stranger is difficult. Starting a conversation on spiritual issues is even harder. But what if there were a tool that could be used to guide such a conversation and get to the heart of the issue? Surveys can be effective in breaking the ice with a Latter-day Saint and creating a meaningful conversation.


### Introduction

Using surveys is a nonconfrontational evangelistic approach that can initiate dialogue with Mormon people in virtually *any* public setting. Based in Ephraim, Utah, Tri-Grace Ministries (TGM) has been hosting Christian mission teams for the past quarter of a century. Because this tactic works so well with those who have no practical experience sharing their faith with Mormons, it has become one of our primary strategies.

One of the advantages of the polling approach is that the initial conversation is completely scripted, which allows for an inexperienced Christian believer to confidently approach Latter-day Saints of all ages and engage them one-on-one. Once the ice is broken and the Mormon is engaged, it becomes much easier for the Christian to lead the conversation toward sharing the gospel. TGM has created several public surveys on a variety of topics that can be used with Latter-day Saints, even though *none* of them mention Mormonism by name. (*Note:* Each survey can be accessed online as a free PDF and printed by going to trigrace.org/resources/surveys.html.) This chapter will be best understood if you can read it alongside the surveys.

In this chapter, we will discuss three TGM surveys: The Jesus Survey, the Bible Survey, and the Social Questionnaire on Relative Truth. These will serve as examples of how the polling approach can be a powerful witnessing tool.

## The Jesus Survey

Although LDS Church leaders claim to *believe in* Jesus, they really don't *believe* Jesus. What do I mean by that? In Mormonism, Jesus is like the church mascot, making this religion appear Christian, though in reality He is not very important in the day-to-day life of the average Mormon. Before proceeding further in this chapter, it would be a good idea for you to take this survey for yourself. It consists of six straightforward true/false and multiple choice questions and will only take three to four minutes.

Evangelical Christians usually get at least four of the six questions correct, but Mormons will usually miss at least four. Before continuing with this chapter, go to the second page of the survey and review the correct answers as taught by Jesus. This survey exposes how Mormons follow the teachings of Joseph Smith rather than Jesus Christ. Many Mormons truly believe that the doctrines of their church were taught by Jesus. Because their church discredits the Bible and discourages them from reading it, most Mormons are shocked when they discover how their heartfelt religious beliefs don't line up with Jesus Christ's teachings in the Bible. Let's consider each topic in the Jesus Survey.

### *Question #1: Topic—the Forgiveness of Sins*

**Mormonism**—Mormon scripture is clear about what is required for forgiveness. Doctrine and Covenants (D&C) 1:32 says, "Nevertheless, he that repents and does the commandments of the Lord shall be forgiven." D&C 76:52 says, "That by keeping the commandments they might be washed and cleansed from all their sins." For those who repent and return to their sins, D&C 82:7 warns, "And now, verily I say unto you, I, the Lord, will not lay any sin to your charge; go your ways and sin no more; but unto that soul who sinneth shall the former sins return, saith the Lord your God."

Compare how Jesus forgave sinners in His real-life interactions with people by reviewing the answers given on the second page of the survey. Mormon theology directly conflicts with the immediate and unconditional forgiveness offered by Jesus.

### *Question #2: Topic—the Pre-Mortal Existence or Preexistence*

**Mormonism**—According to an LDS Church manual:

> God is not only our Ruler and Creator; He is also our Heavenly Father. All men and women are literally the sons and daughters of God. "Man, as a Spirit, was begotten and born of heavenly parents, and reared to maturity in the eternal mansions of the Father, prior to coming upon the earth in a temporal [physical] body" (*Teachings of Presidents of the Church: Joseph F. Smith* [1998], 335). Every person who was ever born on earth is our spirit brother or sister.[1]

The Mormon doctrine of the pre-mortal existence of all human beings has many theological problems. In this survey, the focus is on the places in the Bible where Jesus claims He was the only person who had preexisted with the Father in heaven. It is important for Christians to understand what Jesus taught on this topic because preexistence is one of the primary doctrines of Mormonism's worldview. Jesus denied the idea of the preexistence in John chapters 5 through 8 as well as 17, which can be seen on the second page of the survey. In total conflict with LDS theology, Jesus states that only He preexisted with the Father in heaven.

### *Question #3: Topic—Temple Marriage or Eternal Celestial Marriage*

**Mormonism**—According to Seventy F. Burton Howard:

> The prophets have uniformly taught that the consummate and culminating element of God's great plan for the blessings of his children is eternal marriage... President Howard W. Hunter described celestial marriage as "The Crowning Gospel Ordinance."[2]

Eternal marriage is one of the foundational teachings of Mormonism and, again, Jesus totally contradicts this idea in Matthew 22:23-33. An interesting twist is that the Book of Mormon—claimed by Joseph Smith to be "the most correct book of any book on earth"[3]—never once mentions temple marriage!

### *Question #4: Topic—LDS Priesthood Authority*

**Mormonism**—The church manual *Gospel Principles* states,

> The priesthood is the eternal power and authority of God. Through the priesthood He created and governs the heavens and the earth. By this power the universe is kept in perfect order. Through this power He accomplishes His work and glory, which is "to bring to pass the immortality and eternal life of man" (Moses 1:39). Our Heavenly Father delegates His priesthood power to worthy male members of the Church. The priesthood enables them to act in God's name for the salvation of the human family. Through it they can be authorized to preach the gospel, administer the ordinances of salvation, and govern God's kingdom on earth.[4]

The beliefs about the Aaronic and Melchizedek priesthoods are, by far, the most emphasized gospel doctrines in the LDS Church. Jesus, however, must not have considered the topic of priesthood authority to be important because He never discussed either the Aaronic or Melchizedek priesthoods with His disciples.

### *Question #5: Topic—the Great and Total Apostasy of the Christian Church*

**Mormonism**—Latter-day Saints are taught that Joseph Smith met with God the Father and Jesus Christ when he was 14 years old. According to Joseph Smith—History 1:19 in the LDS scripture Pearl of Great Price, when Smith asked which of all the Christian churches were right and which he should join, he was told to "join none of them, for they were all wrong; and...all their creeds were an abomination in his sight; that those professors were all corrupt; that: 'they draw near to me with their lips, but their hearts are far from me.'"

In light of Jesus's prophecies concerning His church (see these biblical passages on page 2 of the Jesus survey), the Mormon doctrine of the "Great and Total Apostasy" of the failed Christian church would mean that Jesus was a false prophet.

### *Question #6: Topic—Hell and Eternal Punishment*

**Mormonism**—Most Mormons despise the Christian view of hell with a passion. They don't like to picture a place of fiery judgment where any of God's sons and daughters are destined for eternal torment. In LDS theology, everyone except the "sons of perdition" will have the opportunity after death to repent and eventually be saved. (This is why temple work for those who are already dead plays such an important role in Mormon temples around the world.) Except for a select few apostate Mormons who become "sons of perdition," Mormonism teaches that all humans are destined to one of three kingdoms of eternal glory.

However, Jesus spoke more about eternal punishment in hell than glory in heaven. It is ironic that Mormonism minimizes the doctrine of hell because the Book of Mormon warns how the Devil will deceive people into believing that there is no such thing as an eternal hell. Second Nephi 28:21-22 says,

> Others will he [the devil] pacify, and lull them away into carnal security, that they will say: All is well in Zion; yea, Zion prospereth, all is well—and thus the devil cheateth their souls, and leadeth them away carefully down to hell. And behold, others he flattereth away, and telleth them there is no hell; and he saith unto them: I am no devil, for

> there is none—and thus he whispereth in their ears, until he grasps them with his awful chains, from whence there is no deliverance.

Even though the Jesus Survey never mentions Mormonism and only discusses the actual teachings of Jesus, this concept of hell is a huge challenge to Mormons because their heartfelt beliefs clearly conflict with what Jesus taught. Many may be shocked by the number of questions they miss, so it's important to offer the survey and its answers so the person is able to study the issues at a later time. If possible, exchange contact information for future interaction.

## The Bible Survey

One of the greatest hurdles in evangelizing Latter-day Saints is dealing with their internal distrust of the Bible. This religion has planted seeds of doubt in subtle ways that cause Mormons to question the trustworthiness of God's written Word. The eighth Article of Faith found in the Pearl of Great Price states, "We believe the Bible to be the word of God so far as it is translated correctly." First Nephi 13:24-27 in the Book of Mormon describes a "great and abominable church" that corrupted the Bible and removed many "plain and most precious" truths of the gospel. If Satan can convince people that the Bible is not trustworthy, where will they ever find truth?

Like the Jesus Survey, the Bible Survey is easy to use because it is nonconfrontational; it is simply a tool to provide historical information that gives reasons to trust the Bible. As Mormons take the survey, they might even say, "You are going to give me the answers at the end of the survey, aren't you? I have no idea what the correct answers are."

Print the survey and take it for yourself before proceeding any further. After taking it, review the correct answers. As others take the survey, allow opportunities for discussion or to ask any questions they might have.

At some point, you can say, "I not only believe the Bible has never been changed, but I can prove it to you." Often Mormons will respond, "How can you prove something like that?" A TGM witnessing tool called

"The Plain and Precious Truths Visual" provides a simple explanation to show how the Bible has never been changed in any significant way. It may seem simplistic at first, but by explaining two historical facts about the Bible, it is possible to show how the Bible is a reliable and trustworthy guide.[5] This chart, as well as a video tutorial to show how to use the visual with Mormons, can be found under the Resources tab on our website.

All of this will be new information for most Mormons, so it is important to give them both the printed questions and answers to take home so they can study on their own. This may give them a reason to read the Bible and think about what Jesus Christ taught. Conclude your discussion with a challenge to read the Gospel of John with a fresh set of eyes because what is recorded in the Bible has never been changed. Again, if it's possible to exchange contact information, the conversation can continue later.

## The Questionnaire on Relative Truth

This questionnaire is a tool to initiate conversation with Mormons and even atheists so the ice can be broken and deeper religious dialogue can occur. The approach is used to draw people into conversation. It works well with Mormons because twenty-first-century Mormons have been inundated with morally relativistic ideas. Mormons will often insist, "We are Christians just like you!" They may also say, "We believe the exact same things as all other Christians. After all, the name of Jesus Christ is in the name of our church." If your LDS friends have responded this way, you have experienced Mormon relativism.

This phenomenon does not align with the foundational First Vision account of Joseph Smith. As mentioned earlier, Smith claimed that the Christian denominations "were all wrong" and "all their creeds were an abomination" in God's sight; in addition, God said that the Christian pastors "were all corrupt." In light of this inconsistency, this questionnaire does not directly challenge Mormon theology; instead, it opens a door for the Christian to discuss the subject of relativism. The Christian will need to be prepared to provide follow-up questions. Following are a few examples of answers given by Mormons and how these can be used as a springboard for deeper dialogue.

**Question #3. Are personal feelings a good way to determine what truth is?**

Yes No

Why?

One LDS person wrote, "Because I believe that you can feel if something is right."

Possible questions in response:

- Can you explain the difference between a right feeling and a wrong feeling?
- If you feel like something is right, do you think that always makes it true?
- What if we feel differently about the same topic? Do you think both of our feelings would be true?
- If we disagree but we both feel strongly about our feelings, how do you think we might discover which of us is right?

**Question #6. How do your personal feelings affect what you believe about truth?**

One Mormon answered, "Intuition—if I feel that it is true, I believe it to be the truth."

Possible questions in response:

- What do you mean by intuition?
- Do you believe your intuition is always dependable?
- Have your feelings ever let you down?
- Was there ever a time when you thought something was true and later found out it wasn't? (I only ask because I know I have had that kind of experience in my life.)
- If you discovered that your intuition was wrong, how might you find the truth?

**Question #7. How does truth affect your life?**

A Mormon answered, "Truth is a guide for what you feel is right or wrong."

Possible questions in response:

- Would you say that a truth claim is only true if you feel like it is right?
- Could something be true even if you don't feel good about it?
- If we had a disagreement about what is right and what is wrong, how might we find the truth?

**Question #8. In your opinion, what is the truth about the afterlife?**

Another Mormon replied, "We will have a chance to decide how close to God we want to be."

Possible questions to ask:

- What do you think God would do if a really bad person wanted to live in heaven right next door to Him?
- What do you think a person needs to do to make it to the highest kingdom where God dwells? (That's where I want to go.)

## Conclusion

We have had great success using the polling approach to enter into nonconfrontational dialogue with LDS people. It helps break the ice by requiring Mormons to think about things they don't normally consider. We suggest you try it for yourself and see if this might be something that works for you!

---

*Daniel (Chip) Thompson (Ephraim, Utah) and his wife Jamie moved their family from Phoenix, Arizona, to Ephraim, Utah, in 1991 to start the Ephraim Church of the Bible. They later founded Tri-Grace Ministries and began a Christian club at Snow College as well as the coffeehouse the Solid Rock Café. Chip authored* Witness to Mormons in Love: The Mormon Scrapbook *(Ephraim, UT: Gospel4U Publications, 2014).*

## Spotlight

### MICAH WILDER

*One day during his two-year Mormon mission, Micah Wilder—who cofounded the Adam's Road Ministry* (www.AdamsRoadMinistry.com)*—met a Christian pastor in Florida who gave him advice that forever changed his life. Micah's conversion resulted in his biological family coming into a relationship with God, including his mother Lynn, who was a professor at LDS Church-owned Brigham Young University in Provo, Utah. We caught up with Micah while he was on the Adam's Road bus traveling with the ministry.*

**Eric and Sean: You described yourself as a "young Pharisee" when you were on your Mormon mission. What do you mean by that?**

Micah: Although I wouldn't have seen myself as such at the time, I was, in essence, a religious zealot. Much like Saul of Tarsus, I had a zeal for God, but that zeal was misplaced. I was ignorant of the righteousness of God through faith in Jesus Christ and I was seeking to establish my own righteousness by my works.

**Eric and Sean: What did the pastor tell you that caused you to eventually leave Mormonism?**

Micah: Pastor Alan Benson's approach to me was centered on two crucial elements: (1) love and (2) the Word of God. It wasn't really about what he told me, but rather what he challenged me to do. He told me to "read the Bible as a child." He had the profound wisdom and insight to point me to the source and allow God—through His Spirit and by His Word—to make the change in my heart. It was simply by reading the New Testament every day as a Mormon missionary that God opened my eyes to the immeasurable love He was offering me through Christ Jesus.

**Eric and Sean: Would you encourage Christians to use the "read the Bible as a child" approach that the pastor used on you?**

Micah: Absolutely. In fact, this is my favorite approach when ministering to anybody, Mormon or not. In Christianity, it can be all too easy for us at times to focus so much on history, apologetics, and the intellectual side of the gospel that we forget the greatest tool we have: the Word of God. As Hebrews 4:12 says, it is living, active, and sharper than any two-edged sword. In the end, we can't make someone believe, nor can we force that change to happen.

**Eric and Sean: Adam's Road is a musical group you cofounded in 2006 that travels around the United States and visits churches. You share your songs while providing the musicians a platform to give their testimonies. What has been the result with meeting people from all over the country?**

Micah: In 11 years we have performed more than 1,000 times in 42 states and 4 Canadian provinces. To the glory of God, we have seen many people, including Latter-day Saints, come to saving faith in the Lord Jesus Christ.

**Eric and Sean: The chorus to your song "I Would Die for You" says, in part, "For you to live I [Jesus] would die for you." If a Mormon asked you what you mean by this, how would you respond?**

Micah: Jesus died a substitutionary death for the sins of mankind on the cross of Calvary. He took our place, as our substitute, placing on Himself the penalty that we deserved. He paid in full the debt we owed to God because of our sins. Through His blood shed on our behalf, Jesus Christ offered His own life as a ransom for ours so we could be given the free gift of eternal life by grace through faith.

**Eric and Sean: You have come up with a bumper sticker phrase, "Jesus Is Enough." Yet a Mormon might argue he or she also believes in Jesus and point to how His name is a part of the LDS Church's title. How**

**would you explain the difference in how Jesus is viewed in Mormonism compared to Christianity?**

Micah: When I was a Mormon, I would have claimed that I believed in, trusted, and followed Jesus Christ. In reality, He was only a portion of what I believed I needed in order to be reconciled to God. As a Mormon, Jesus was just one of many pillars of my testimony. Now He is the Rock and the foundation of my faith. He's not just part of my testimony, He *is* my testimony! I know that my good standing with God is independent of any religious system, denomination, man, work, ordinance, or anything of my own merit. It is, however, completely dependent on Jesus Christ. There is salvation outside of Mormonism, but there is no salvation outside of Jesus Christ.

---

*See the testimony of Micah Wilder and other members of Adam's Road by viewing "Unveiling Grace: The Film," posted on YouTube by "Sacred Groves," March 6, 2011, https://www.youtube.com/watch?v=Dl0c5nl6u48.*

## SECTION 3

# Personal Approaches

When the apostle Paul traveled throughout the Roman world, he always knew his audience. When he was in a synagogue, for instance—and he was in plenty of those—he took out the Old Testament Scriptures and used these to explain his point. After all, Jews held to the veracity of the Scripture. However, if he were with Gentiles, he cited pagan poets to make a case for the Christian God against the pagan deities. See how he spoke to the scholars on Mars Hill in Athens, as recorded in Acts 17:16-34. To Paul, his audience mattered. As he stated in 1 Corinthians 9:22, "I have become all things to all people, that by all means I might save some."

Understanding our audience will help us choose the right approach. In chapter 9, Carl Wimmer—a former Utah state legislator—explains the repercussions he received after he and his family left the LDS Church. However, through patience and kindness the family was able to love their Mormon family members and reconnect their relationship, despite their differences in belief. Next, though some Christians might get scared or tongue-tied when Mormon missionaries come to their doors—some may even want to pull the curtains and hide behind the couch—Sandra Tanner explains in chapter 10 how it is possible to turn a missionary visit into a positive encounter, with the chance to share biblical Christianity with two young people who are usually very interested in spiritual things. By understanding a little bit about Mormonism and having a pleasant attitude, it's possible to reach out to the young men and women who ring your doorbell.

Because men and women are different, there are some tactics that might work for men but not for women. Thus in chapter 11, Becky Walker explains ways to approach LDS females and some approaches she has used to reach out to Mormon women. Then in chapter 12, Fred Anson takes a look at the Internet, which has become a twenty-first-century mission field, and provides ways to be a virtual missionary in chat room and social media formats without having to get out of the office chair.

Which individuals do you have in your life who require specialized approaches such as these?

9

# Sharing with a Mormon Family Member
## The Keeping-Good-Relations Approach

CARL WIMMER


### Summary

Leaving Mormonism is not easy, especially for those who have grown up in the LDS Church. When someone walks away from the Mormon faith to become an evangelical Christian, many relatives may consider the act to be egregious, even akin to leaving one's ethnic heritage. Yet former Mormons are still related to their LDS family members, and this presents unique challenges that must be faced with gentleness, respect, and patience.


### Writing a Difficult Letter

The day we dreaded had finally arrived. My wife Sherry and I, as nervous as we had ever been, sat staring at the computer and poring over each word to make sure the email to her parents was perfect.

"Dear Mom and Dad," it started. We then wrote a loving and beautiful memoir to her parents. It was the kind of letter any parent would be ecstatic to receive, except for one part: "Carl and I are leaving the LDS Church." I was not certain that sending an email was the right way to inform my in-laws that their only daughter had apostatized from Mormonism, but a recent incident forced our hand, and we were running out of time.

We ate Easter dinner with Sherry's family in 2013. Everything was fine until I rolled a four-wheeler on myself and was taken to the hospital by Sherry's younger brother. As the hospital staff removed my clothing to better assess my injuries, my brother-in-law noticed that I was not wearing my LDS temple garments, which "temple worthy" Mormons are required to wear under their clothes. He became one of the first people outside of my own home to learn the truth, though he agreed to keep it private until Sherry could tell their parents. We knew our secret with her Mormon family had come to an end.

Staring at that computer screen, we felt something like convicts on death row who were waiting for their last meals. Once the message was sent, we knew that a whirlwind was sure to follow. Sherry hit send. It was April first, otherwise known as April Fool's Day. Yes, God does have a sense of humor!

While the family revelation was finally complete, we had no idea how to deal with the public community as a whole. Because I served in the Utah state legislature and ran an unsuccessful campaign for the United States Congress in 2012, I had become a household name in Utah. There was a time when I practically could not even sneeze without a news article being written about me. While I thrived on the attention during my political days, my popularity had come back to haunt me.

My life as a Mormon had been far from perfect. John 12:43 was an appropriate description: I "loved the glory that comes from man more than the glory that comes from God." As I discovered soon after my run for Congress, I was nothing more than an LDS garment-wearing, temple-attending, tithe-paying, hypocritical Elders' Quorum president! For three hours every Sunday, I portrayed my best self, and then I would head home to set my dusty scriptures back on the shelf. I wasn't proud of my hypocrisy, but I simply didn't know how to change. Even if I could have, the willpower was not there.

A columnist from the largest newspaper in the state phoned me on October 10, 2013. It was a routine call, and he asked about local politics, which is right up my alley. But as our conversation drew to a close, he asked me a question that sent chills down my spine.

"So, I heard a rumor that you have left Mormonism. Is that true?"

I was speechless. I had become a Christian believer in late March 2013. Sherry followed soon after. Living in a small, rural, Mormon town, we had done an excellent job—or so we thought—of keeping our conversion private until we could come up with a plan to let everyone know. We now had less than 24 hours before the news would be blabbed to the entire world.[1]

In the weeks and months that followed, we made plenty of mistakes trying to evangelize our Mormon family members. We presumed they wanted to know what we had discovered and figured our information would be welcomed or, at the very least, considered. However, every attempt we made was met with a wall of either silence or defense, with an underlying tone of pity on our behalf.

As I've come to understand the Word of God more, my method of sharing the gospel with friends and family has taken a much different route. Though we realize that every situation is different, I've learned many biblical principles that can be employed with Mormon family members.

## A More Transparent Journey?

Many Christians who have left Mormonism express one common regret: *Perhaps it would have been better if we had walked slower with our families as we left Mormonism. Instead of hiding and revealing the conversion later, would it have been beneficial to bring them along with us as we studied and learned the truth?*

This is easier said than done within a Mormon culture that rewards a strong faith in the LDS Church and warns heavily against doubting. When devout Mormons begin to learn the truth about their religion, the cognitive dissonance is intense. Fear compels most to hide their questions and veil their research; this is a mistake.

I often wonder how things may have been different if Sherry and I had talked to her family earlier in our conversion process. Mormons are usually willing to help fellow congregants who are struggling, but as soon as a person takes the step to leave the "one true church," as Mormons call it, he or she is no longer to be trusted.

Would the information we were coming across—including problems with the Book of Abraham, the First Vision, Joseph Smith's polygamy, and the Book of Mormon—have been better received had we been more transparent as questioning Mormons? It's possible. But instead, we have never been able to share any of these things with certain family members; the conversation is completely off limits in order to keep the peace.

## Ways to Counter Frustration

I had a horrifying nightmare when I was a young child that I still remember in vivid detail. My mother had taken me to the local grocery store and we became separated. As I approached an aisle, two men were standing there looking at my mom and plotting how they were going to attack her in the parking lot.

I quickly ran to my mom to tell her that she was going to be attacked, but she would not listen to me. No matter how hard I tried and no matter what I said, she did not believe me and refused to heed my warning. I awoke in terror! I have never forgotten how frustrating it was to know something extremely important but to be ignored when trying to share it.

Fast-forward 30 years, and the frustrations I felt in that dream had become a reality. Sherry and I knew we were right. We spent many hours of intense research and could prove beyond any reasonable doubt that Mormonism was a religion based on falsehoods. It was so clear and obvious to us. We just *knew* it would be clear to our family as well if they would only listen. But they wouldn't.

We tried our best to have a conversation with our Mormon family members, yet nothing seemed to work. We reached out with emails, phone calls, and postings on Facebook. The more we pushed, the more our family recoiled. A few even blocked us on social media. The in-your-face, selfishly motivated approach was not working. We had lost sight of the godly process of rebirth.

It was a growth process until we learned how to become a positive witness to the ones we love the most. Based on our own experiences, let's consider some realistic ways former Mormons can reconnect with their families while not ignoring spiritual differences.

### *1. Understand the Process of Conversion*

The Bible compares the process of coming to a salvific relationship with Christ with being "born again." Jesus said in John 3:3, "Truly, truly, I say to you, unless one is born again he cannot see the kingdom of God." As Pastor David Earley points out,

> A birth is a process that culminates in an event. The event is recorded on a birth certificate with a distinct date and time measured to the exact minute. Yet the event of the birth is the product of a nine-month process we call gestation for the baby and pregnancy for the mother. Salvation is similar to birth in that there is usually a process often involving months or even years, leading to the moment the person gives his or her life to Christ.[2]

While Jesus can use various means to reach the lost, trying to short-circuit the process can lead to frustration. Feeling urgency for lost family members is a wonderful and godly attribute; but so often, in their zeal to lead loved ones to the truth, Christians can lose sight of how long a conversion usually takes.

I look back over the years of my life before I came to Christ and see how seeds were being planted, even though I had no idea it was happening. From attending Christian music concerts to the friendship of a few Bible-believing Christians, these seeds were watered by the Holy Spirit without my knowledge. The apostle Paul describes this process in 1 Corinthians 3:6-9:

> I planted, Apollos watered, but God gave the growth. So, neither he who plants nor he who waters is anything, but only God who gives the growth. He who plants and he who waters are one, and each will receive his wages according to his labor. For we are God's fellow workers. You are God's field, God's building.

We must understand that God's timing is more important than forcing the issue. It can take years of planting and watering before the chains that hold family members are broken. Patience is required.

### *2. Understand the Primacy of Loving Your LDS Family*

Love should be the primary motive when it comes to evangelizing family members. After all, we desire to show them the love of God, and His love is on display through our actions and words. What do they see when we preach of Him and defend His Word? Do our methods follow the teachings found in 1 Corinthians 13?

We should always be looking for opportunities to share the gospel message. In doing so, grace and respect must be extended, and we must never rush to make a point. It must be remembered that God's Word does not return void (Isaiah 55:11); He will give life to those seeds in His own time.

Keeping a healthy, respectful, and loving relationship with our family members is a key component that opens doors to opportunities for evangelism. Time after time I see families torn apart due to one of them leaving Mormonism. This division is exactly what Jesus talked about in Luke 12:51-53 when He said,

> Do you think that I have come to give peace on earth? No, I tell you, but rather division. For from now on in one house there will be five divided, three against two and two against three. They will be divided, father against son and son against father, mother against daughter and daughter against mother, mother-in-law against her daughter-in-law and daughter-in-law against mother-in-law.

Shortly after leaving Mormonism, Sherry had an opportunity to visit her brother's family who lives several hours away. She called her brother and told him that she would arrive in half an hour. He promised to relay the message to his wife who was at home with their young daughter. Sherry arrived during a rainstorm and knocked on the front door. Dogs barked inside, but no one answered. She continued knocking for several minutes and then chose a chair on the covered porch to sit while she waited.

Twenty minutes later, her sister-in-law finally opened the door and invited her in with no apologies. Sherry concluded it was part of the shunning that she had been experiencing in her family. But rather than responding with irritation or anger, Sherry immediately chose to forgive and decided to go out of her way to rebuild the broken relationships. She has faithfully sent gifts to her brother and sister-in-law for special occasions, including dropping off cupcakes as we passed through their town. These are small gestures, but these dedicated acts of kindness have displayed her genuine love for them and allowed her to regain the friendship she once had with them.

When division happens, it should not surprise us, yet it may be time to step back and make sure we adhere to the words about love written by Paul in 1 Corinthians 13. If we are following this biblical advice and are told to be quiet, we should comply as God leads while not giving up. Instead, we should focus on building the relationship in common areas while striving to live a life that displays God's unconditional love.

### *3. Understand the Power of Lifestyle Evangelism*

Paul said in 2 Corinthians 5:17 that, at conversion, a Christian becomes "a new creation," which is a genuine change that the Holy Spirit works in the lives of those who are born again. Jesus commanded in Matthew 5:16, "In the same way, let your light shine before others, so that they may see your good works and give glory to your Father who is in heaven."

It may take time, but as Christians let the light of Christ shine, family, friends and community members will be watching and taking notice. As new believers live their lives with Christ as their singular priority, others—including family—may begin to wonder what brought such a dramatic change in their lives.

After four years of patiently waiting, praying, and living a God-centered life, the Lord opened the door for my wife to engage in a conversation with her active Mormon father who had previously shut her down. They spoke about God, the gospel, and differences in their beliefs. Things that she had previously attempted to forcefully share with him came naturally through the Holy Spirit, who gave her a gentle direction as well as a recollection of Bible references. She was able to see her father's raw emotions of curiosity, concern, and doubt unfold before her eyes. Seeds were planted that day in a respectful, loving way.

Whether or not our family members are ready and open to conversation about faith or the gospel, it is always the right time to display the love of God through the way we live.

### *4. Understand the Priority of Prayer*

Sherry and I have prayed every single day for God to open the door to a conversation with her family. As we continually pray, those small opportunities are presenting themselves. Our daughter Jade had decided to start a prayer group at her high school. She printed off fliers, handed them out, and began inviting people to attend.

The pushback from some in the Mormon community was immediate. A few ripped up her invitations and piled them in the hallway. One city leader even got into the action by attempting to use his influence over my job to stop the prayer group at the school. While this was going on, our daily prayers for our Mormon family continued.

As providence would have it, we attended a family gathering at the home of my wife's parents. Even though they disagree with our decision to leave Mormonism, they remain interested in the lives of their grandchildren. We told them about the prayer group while describing the accompanying pushback from the community. Feelings of joy filled Sherry and me as her family defended Jade against those who were trying to interfere with their granddaughter.

If believers are humble and seek to glorify the Lord, God will listen. He may not answer when and how we want, but we can rest knowing that, in His sovereignty, God's perfect will shall be accomplished. Too often, I find myself thinking I really desire something in life, only to bring it to God as a last resort. Yet any godly desire cannot be considered a serious priority until it has been saturated with faithful and heartfelt prayer.

I do not know how many prayers we offered on behalf of my wife's family before her father was finally open to that one conversation, but I am convinced that it was the Lord answering the faithful prayers of my wife that led to him being open that day.

## Conclusion

On my introductory Facebook page, I write this: "A sinner saved by grace, with an unquenchable passion for the Lord Jesus Christ and for my family." I am amazed at how quickly God can work. The events from 2013—the discovery by my wife's family that we left Mormonism as well as the tell-all newspaper article—did create a giant wave—a tsunami, if you will—in our lives. Yet there is no doubt that it was God's clear orchestration for our lives that changed my family from the inside out while opening the door for me to reach out to others, including my family. We've seen great progress in the ongoing conversations with them. And I don't believe God is finished yet.

---

*Carl Wimmer (Gunnison, Utah) is a former Utah state legislator who ran for the US Congress in 2012. In 2017, he and his wife Sherry planted a church in his Utah town that has no Christian churches. Former Mormons who struggle with their relationships with Mormon family can contact him at carl@carlwimmer.com so he can pray for them.*

10

# When the Elders Come Calling
## The Missionaries-At-Your-Door Approach

SANDRA TANNER


### Summary

Mormon missionaries are sent throughout the world to declare that no church has the authority to extend the offer of eternal life except The Church of Jesus Christ of Latter-day Saints. With some training, Christians can compassionately engage these young men and women in conversations about the differences between the Bible and LDS teachings.


### Introduction

As a former Mormon, I have had countless discussions with both lay Mormons and church missionaries. I also hear from others who have their own experiences with Mormons. Recently an older Christian lady told me how she was approached by missionaries who wanted to know if she would like to learn about God's plan for her life and the gospel of Christ. She cheerfully responded, "Oh, I already know about that. I read my Bible every day. Isn't the gospel wonderful?" They wanted to set up a time to explain about God's plan of salvation as revealed by "modern-day" prophets. She kindly responded that she already knew God's plan and invited them to read the New Testament. When she wouldn't agree to future meetings, they quickly moved on.

What is the Christian's responsibility when Mormon missionaries knock on the door? And what should a Christian do to be an effective ambassador?

## About the Missionaries at Your Door

In 2016, the LDS Church sent more than 70,000 young Mormons aged 18 to 25 throughout the world to proclaim Joseph Smith and the "restoration" of Christianity. That year about 240,000 converts were baptized into the LDS Church.[1] These young missionaries are the primary method of spreading the LDS gospel.

Upon receiving their call to serve a mission, missionary candidates will attend the LDS temple ritual, usually for the first time, and begin wearing the special white temple undergarments. Missionaries typically spend about six weeks at the training center to receive basic training. The LDS mission experience is not only meant to convert potential members in the mission field, but also to teach the missionaries about their own faith.

The missionaries begin their service by attending one of the fifteen Missionary Training Centers located throughout the world, with Provo, Utah, representing the United States. Once they enter a training center, the missionaries are not allowed to see their friends and families until the mission is completed (two years for the men, eighteen months for the women). Missionaries are permitted to phone home twice a year (Mother's Day and Christmas) as well as contact their family by email throughout the year, though they are instructed to keep this communication to a minimum.

A common tactic used by the missionaries is to knock on doors. The question often comes up whether Christians should invite the Mormon missionaries inside their homes. Second John 10-11 has been cited as support by some Christians to not allow false teachers in their homes. The verses say, "If anyone comes to you and does not bring this teaching, do not receive him into your house or give him any greeting, for whoever greets him takes part in his wicked works." This passage has been misinterpreted. As Christian apologist Don Veinot has pointed out,

> Some Christians use this verse as a reason to not invite Mormons into their homes. But this stance ignores the passage's context. In the early church, churches met in homes. When Christian teachers arrived in a community, they looked for the home in which the faithful met. The Lord instructed the disciples to do this. In today's language, we would write, "Do not take them into your pulpit." It is a warning to not let false teachers into authority where they could mislead the unwary.[2]

Christians who invite missionaries into their homes do so to share the biblical gospel with them, not to support the growth of the LDS Church. For those who do invite missionaries into their homes, it is helpful to be aware of what the missionaries will teach and be prepared to provide solid biblical answers.

## The Missionary Lessons

Missionaries often focus their efforts on those who have recently moved into the neighborhood as well as the widowed and the lonely. These folks are generally more open to friendly visits, which will be more successful when a church member arranges a contact with a friend. The five lessons that the missionaries will give to an interested prospect are as follows:[3]

### *1. The Message of the Restoration of the Gospel of Jesus Christ*

According to Mormonism, God the Father and Jesus appeared to LDS Church founder Joseph Smith in 1820. They told Smith that the Christian church had gone into apostasy shortly after the death of Christ's apostles. This left nobody with authority to baptize people or ordain individuals to the priesthood. Smith claimed that he was chosen to restore the one true church and to translate the Book of Mormon, an ancient record of God's dealings with the ancestors of the American Indians.

### *2. The Plan of Salvation*

The Mormon view is that God, humans, and angels are all the same species. Heavenly Father and Mother are said to be humanity's literal parents in a prior existence. Through LDS priesthood and temple rituals, it is possible to reside with families for all eternity.

### *3. The Gospel of Jesus Christ*

One must be baptized by proper LDS priesthood authority to gain forgiveness of sin and the gift of the Holy Ghost. It is necessary to obey all church requirements to "qualify for eternal life." Eternal life is defined as living "forever as families in God's presence."

### *4. The Commandments*

These include keeping the Ten Commandments, paying tithes, abiding by the Mormon health code called the Word of Wisdom, regular participation in the temple rituals, and faithful obedience to the teachings of the LDS leaders.

### *5. Laws and Ordinances*

These include the rituals of Mormonism after baptism, such as ordination to the priesthood, temple marriage, temple work for the dead, and church service.

## The Doctrinal Differences

It can be confusing when missionaries use the standard vocabulary of Christianity and are not clear that they interpret these terms with radically different meanings. A Christian should never assume that the average Mormon understands terms such as *God*, *salvation*, *eternal life*, and *heaven* in a biblical way.[4] In order to help you be confident and prepared for these conversations, let's consider some of the differences between biblical Christianity and Mormonism.

### *Nature of God*

Joseph Smith claimed that he saw God the Father and Jesus Christ as two totally separate beings. Rather than trying to explain the Trinity when I talk to a young missionary, I like to focus on the basic nature of God the Father. Joseph Smith taught that God was once a mortal on another world ruled by another deity. Each god rose from mortality to immortality and earned the position of a god. The Father does not surpass the previous god but is forever under his direction. It is akin to an eternal pyramid system, or escalator, with each god answering to the previous god.

If the missionaries deny this teaching, ask if they have read Smith's sermons on God.[5] If Smith's doctrine of God is wrong, he falls under the condemnation of Deuteronomy 13:1-5. Ask how they reconcile Smith's doctrine of multiple gods with Isaiah 43:10-11 and Isaiah 44:6-8.

### *Total Apostasy*

Mormonism asserts that there had been a "great apostasy" of the Christian church. While the Bible speaks about people falling away from the truth, it never indicates that God's authority would be lost from the earth. Mormons often misuse 1 Timothy 4:1, which says that "in later times some will depart from the faith by devoting themselves to deceitful spirits and teachings of demons." Notice that the verse merely indicates how "some" would depart from the faith, not that there would be a *total* apostasy. Ask the missionaries, "How could there have been a total apostasy of the church when Jesus promised that 'the gates of hell shall not prevail against it'?" (Matthew 16:18). Point out how Jesus promised to remain even to "the end of the world" (Matthew 28:20).

Another problem is the Mormon teaching that John, one of Christ's 12 apostles, was told that he would remain on the earth to "prophesy before nations."[6] Besides John, three of the 12 disciples in the Book of Mormon were granted their desire to remain on earth, to "bring the souls of men unto me," until Christ's return (3 Nephi 28:6-9). If four apostles remained on earth, how could there have been a total apostasy?

Mormon missionaries also teach that the true church will have the same structure as Christ instituted, including 12 apostles. However, the Mormons do not conform to their own standard. They have three apostles in their First Presidency as well as their 12, thus making 15 apostles at the head of their church. Also, Jesus is the only high priest in Christianity (Hebrews 7:26), and deacons were to be mature men, not 12-year-old boys (1 Timothy 3:8-12).

### *The True Church*

Mormonism teaches that the Christian world is too divided to have the truth. Yet there have been more than a hundred different churches claiming Joseph Smith as their founder.[7] Many of these have totally different beliefs from the others. Obviously, LDS scriptures did not solve the problem of division. The biblical concept is that all believers constitute the church. In Ephesians 2:20-22, Paul explains that Christians are

> built on the foundation of the apostles and prophets, Christ Jesus himself being the cornerstone, in whom the whole structure, being joined together, grows into a holy temple in the Lord. In him you also are being built together into a dwelling place for God by the Spirit.

The question is not whether a person is a member of the right Christian church (denomination). Instead, an individual must trust in Christ's atonement to be made right with God.

### *The Need for a Prophet*

The missionaries will usually present the need for a "latter-day" prophet to guide the people of God. Ask:

- If the prophet is continually giving new revelation, how do you guard against false teachings?
- If your prophet were to give a revelation that differed from church teachings in the past, how would you determine which to follow?

Christians hold their ministers accountable to the Bible.[8] In Acts 17:11-12, the early Christians compared Paul's teachings with those in the Old Testament. The missionary may counter, "God has promised he will never let the prophet lead us astray." Then why is there a provision made in the Doctrine and Covenants 107:81-83 to replace a fallen prophet? Even Jesus warned about false prophets in Matthew 24:11, 24. Missionaries may appeal to Amos 3:7 to prove that God will always have a prophet leading the church. However, they have taken this verse out of context. God promised that He would not send judgment without giving a warning first through a prophet.[9]

If only the president of the LDS Church can receive revelation for the church, why were the books of the New Testament written by different people? Even Mormons agree that Paul was never the head of the church. Shouldn't the apostles of Mormonism be as authoritative as Paul? Yet Mormons often reject statements by their own prophets and apostles when they disagree with current teachings. Remind the missionaries that even though not all of Jesus's words are known, John assured in John 20:30-31 that enough is recorded to lead people to saving faith. As Jesus promised in Matthew 24:35, "Heaven and earth will pass away, but my words will not pass away."

If Mormonism is a restoration of original Christianity, then it needs to be demonstrated that original LDS teachings were deleted from the original Bible. However, no manuscript evidence shows revisions to the New Testament that eliminated cardinal doctrines.[10] Furthermore, the Scripture citations in the writings of the early church fathers show that there were no doctrinal revisions.[11]

### *More Than the Atonement Needed*

Mormon missionaries may claim that they are Christians by using the argument that they believe in Jesus Christ as their Savior. Yet what is the LDS definition of *saved*, Mormonism's view of Jesus, and its understanding of Christ's atonement?

According to Mormonism, because humans are gods in embryo, the fall of man brought mortality but not a sinful nature to humanity. While Mormons understand what it means to commit sin, they misunderstand original sin and the sin nature everyone receives at birth. The LDS atonement provided that all humans would be resurrected (immortality) but it did not provide everything a person needs to gain "eternal life" or "exaltation." To receive true salvation in Mormonism, a person must obey all of Mormonism's covenants and commandments, including being married for time and eternity in an LDS temple.

A distinction is made in Mormonism between being saved (resurrected to some level of heaven) and having eternal life (exaltation, godhood). An illustration of the Mormon concept of the atonement is presented in a parable by Apostle Boyd Packer.[12] Here a friend (likened to Jesus) pays off another man's huge debt. This was not a gift (i.e., the debt was not "forgiven"); it was a refinancing of the loan. The debt is now owed to the new creditor. Thus, Mormons do not see the atonement as a total payment for their sins, but rather as a transfer of the debt to a creditor whose terms were more acceptable. While Mormonism sees the atonement as necessary, it did not fulfill all that was required for eternal life. Apostle Packer's story is helpful in contrasting the Mormon concept of the atonement with that of the Bible.

When discussing grace with the missionaries, a good passage to bring up is 2 Nephi 25:23, which says that it is "by grace we are saved, after all we can do." Ask, "If grace only applies after all you can do, how do you know when you have done enough? Have you truly done *all* you could do?" If not, it appears that grace will not apply. The Christian, on the other hand, rejoices in grace (unmerited favor) as presented in the Bible. Mormonism teaches that almost everyone will be saved (resurrected) to one of the three kingdoms of glory. How can this be reconciled with Matthew 7:13-14, where Jesus taught that only those who follow Him would gain heaven? Mormonism appears to reverse the broad and narrow ways.

## Conclusion

Generally, missionaries will be able to detect if a Christian is speaking to them out of genuine concern and conviction or if the conversation is about winning a debate. As ambassadors for Christ, Christians should share about His redemption in the spirit of love.[13] When missionaries knock on the door, consider this a worthwhile opportunity to share the truth. Among other things:

1. Pray for wisdom and patience.
2. Be kind and respectful. If you had gone to share your faith at their door, how would you like to be received?
3. Ask them to come to dinner since missionaries are usually on a strict budget. Just having dinner with a Christian

family can be meaningful to missionaries who may not get many home-cooked meals.

4. Don't try to pose as a serious potential convert to evangelize. Instead, tell them that you are a Christian who would be glad to talk to them about the gospel while hearing their view as well. This gives you the opportunity to ask questions.
5. Think of your time together as seed planting—you plant, someone else waters the seed, and God gives the increase (1 Corinthians 3:6). It is not likely that you will convince someone to leave Mormonism for Christ in one sitting, but you may raise concerns and Scripture passages that they may want to consider.
6. Be prepared to share the evidences for the preservation of the New Testament, as Mormons are taught that it has changed so much and is not reliable.
7. Share about your relationship with God and how He has forgiven your sins, answered your prayers, carried you through hard times, etc.
8. Challenge the missionaries to read the New Testament.
9. Add the missionaries to your prayer list.

Several years ago I spent some time talking to a returned LDS missionary who was questioning his faith. As we discussed various Christian topics, I tried to encourage him to visit some of the local Christian churches. He responded, "I wouldn't step foot into one of those churches after the way they treated me at the door." Remember, you may be the only evangelical Christian that the missionaries have ever met. Your attitude and actions may be the determining factor as to whether they want to ever talk to another Christian again. It's an important responsibility, but I believe you can do this![14]

---

*Sandra Tanner is the great-great-granddaughter of second LDS President Brigham Young. After leaving Mormonism, she and her late husband, Jerald, dedicated their lives to documenting the errors of Mormonism and pointing people to Christ while writing dozens of books and articles on Mormonism. In 1983, they established Utah Lighthouse Ministry (www.utlm.org), an important source of information on LDS history and doctrine. The Utah Lighthouse bookstore in Salt Lake City is open six days a week.*

11

# Sharing the Truth with LDS Women
## The Compassion Approach

BECKY WALKER


### Summary

Because God created women to be nurturing and caring, approaches that emphasize compassion and understanding can go a long way in conversations with Mormon women who are so often consumed with being the perfect wives and mothers. Here are several types of outreaches to LDS women that have been effective and fruitful.


### Introduction

As many people know, Mormonism has created a unique culture. Typically, the goal of many LDS young girls and women is to become "Molly Mormons," which is a self-described nickname used by Latter-day Saints in reference to becoming perfect wives and mothers. But too often, these women are entrenched in taking care of their families while fulfilling church callings and trying to be on their best behavior at every hour.

On the outside, these women attempt to give the appearance that they have everything together. However, the truth of the matter is many are dying on the inside. With such a hard shell around their bruised hearts, what can ever break through this defensive wall?

The obvious and correct theological answer is that only a divine act can (John 6:44, 65), yet God chooses to use His people in His work. Unfortunately, believers who yearn to share truth with LDS women on a day-to-day basis can sometimes feel helpless. Though not all Mormon women display the same stereotypes, some insight into how most of them are raised will be helpful.

## Explaining the Differences

Before going further, let me first acknowledge that men and women are created differently, which is a fact supported by science. However, it must be understood that many of these women are led by their hearts (feelings). Good feelings are often thought to come from God while bad feelings originate with Satan. This does not mean that Mormon women cannot think critically, but there must be a reason to start the risky business of examining their faith. Reaching out with concern for these ladies, not with the goal of winning arguments, will be the most appealing approach.

In Mormonism, young girls are typically nurtured and trained to become fabulous homemakers when they grow up. The role of motherhood is highly esteemed as they are taught that their highest calling is to become a "mother in Zion."[1] With such an emphasis on homemaking, girls are not usually trained to do intense doctrinal study. They may have surface knowledge of Mormon teachings, but very few have really considered the distinctives of their faith.

Christians ought to be very intentional when they engage in faith-based conversations with LDS women. It must be understood that there are different definitions for almost all theological terms shared by Mormons and Christians, such as *God*, *Jesus*, *scripture*, and *salvation*. This can be confusing for the Christian trying to share her faith.[2] In fact, most Mormon women think what they and their Christian friends believe is basically the same. Because this misunderstanding is typical, it is important to explain that there *are* important differences, as many articles in this book emphasize. Perhaps a story to illustrate about the term *child of God* will be helpful here.

A Mormon friend and I were talking one day when she referred to the LDS teaching that "everyone is a child of God." Her reference was not limited to religious people; it included a celebrity in a news story who had made some bad life choices. She made her statement in a way that showed how confidently she thought that Christians believed the same thing. I got her attention when I said that I did not believe all people are "children of God."

Astonished, she asked, "You don't believe that? I thought all Christians believed that." By paraphrasing a few biblical passages, I explained that people must *become* children of God because they are born as "children of wrath." For example, John 1:12 says, "To all who did receive him, who believed in his name, he gave the right to become children of God." Meanwhile, Ephesians 2:1-3 declares,

> You were dead in the trespasses and sins in which you once walked, following the course of this world, following the prince of the power of the air, the spirit that is now at work in the sons of disobedience—among whom we all once lived in the passions of our flesh, carrying out the desires of the body and the mind, and were by nature children of wrath, like the rest of mankind.

The concept that everyone is *not* a child of God is offensive to Mormons because it does not sound very nice to them. This is a beautiful opening to a quick gospel presentation since it can be used to open a discussion on humanity's sinful condition.[3] It is only a miracle of God that causes a person to *become* a child of God. That was the opening of our conversation as we sat in her living room with our children playing around us.

These kinds of discussions can cause Mormon women to realize that there is something different about Christianity. After the above exchange, this same lady—both a neighbor and good friend—began to listen whenever our conversations turned to religious matters. She came to realize over time that I did not believe her religion was Christian, which really bothered her. She knew I loved her for who she was, but she was very concerned that I did not consider her a member of a Christian church. It's a delicate dance to "offend" a Mormon friend by explaining that we do not share beliefs, while still making her feel comfortable enough to let our kids play together in each other's homes and go on outings together.

It is important for Christians to remember to be patient and loving in these conversations; this was a process that took place over an extended period. My friend's husband eventually forbade her from spending any more time with me because our discussions were affecting her, but later she told me something showing that real seeds had been planted in her heart. Even though she was not allowed to spend any more time with me at a time right before her family moved out of state, she confided in me, "I can't tell you how many times I am walking around in my house having conversations with you in my head." This is the fruit of many discussions that all began when we simply discussed the differences between our faiths.

## Becoming Vulnerable with Others

Another factor in sharing truth with Mormon women is transparency and vulnerability. Most Christians don't realize the extreme emphasis the LDS Church puts on perfection. This is true for the entire membership, but it is greatly magnified for LDS women. They are weighed down with many jobs to do, such as keeping the perfect house and doing acts of kindness for others to be respected members of the church. This burdened life leads to great levels of anxiety and depression. Could this be one reason why Utah's residents are some of the biggest users of antidepressant drugs?[4]

Consider the story of a female friend I will call Penny. She was one of six siblings in a strong Mormon home. Her parents did everything they could to raise their children in all things Mormon. As Penny got older, she went through periods of time in her spiritual life where she vacillated between being an active member and going inactive. It was during one of those times of pulling back that she met and married a Christian man who didn't realize that Christianity and Mormonism were diametrically opposed. They ended up moving to San Antonio, Texas.

Penny began to meet some Christian friends who invited her to

Bible studies with them. Through attending Bible studies at various Christian churches, she observed something she had never seen before: transparency and vulnerability. As these women opened their lives and shared prayer requests while talking about life's real struggles, she could not believe how honest they could be about their problems. Mormon women rarely share in such a manner because they are expected to be happy and successful; if they have problems, they sincerely feel that there must be something wrong with them.

Seeing this display of love and openness caused Penny to have serious doubts about Mormonism. She prayed to God one day to know the truth, even if it meant that it would not affirm her church. God revealed Himself to her, and she has never been the same. It was extremely painful at first to realize that everything she had ever been taught was a lie, but she persevered and is now reaching out to many Mormons in her world, including her family.

## Reaching Out to Mormon Women

Because I have such concern for Mormon women, I have organized mission trips to specifically reach out to ladies who have been oppressed by their religion. One trip took place in fall 2012. First, we visited a polygamous community in northern Utah.[5] A group of a dozen women came with me to a community of about a hundred homes.

Two by two we knocked on the doors throughout the community, telling the women who answered that we had come from our homes in Texas to offer gifts to them and their children. We passed out roses, chocolates, children's Bibles, worship music CDs, and prayer request notebooks. In addition, we asked if we could pray for them. As can be imagined, there were many shocked expressions. Once they realized that they were not being solicited, the majority of those who answered their doors invited the Christian ladies into their homes. Inside, the needs of these ladies could be seen very clearly as they tried to manage the small children everywhere. As "sister wives" (women who are married to one man) came in and out of the rooms, it was obvious that a pecking order was in place.

A second purpose of this women's trip was to reach out to mainstream Mormon women. Twice a year the LDS Church hosts a women's conference attended by thousands of women at the Conference Center in Salt Lake City, Utah. Because women are known to cry a lot at these teaching sessions—perhaps because the expectations for perfection are so high that many feel defeated and unable to accomplish all that church leaders say must be done—we decided to hand out tissue packets along with business-sized cards inside.

The front of the card depicted a woman with her forehead against a wall in a posture of despair along with a bottle of antidepressant pills and the Salt Lake temple in the background. We put a Bible verse on the back and included a list of Christian ministry websites. These cards were placed into the small purse-sized tissue packets with a bow tied around each one. We prepared a total of 10,000 packets, although we found out later that the Conference Center seats 20,000 people and everyone who attends this conference is female.

Ladies from many different Christian churches helped put together these packets, which were shipped to Utah. Several Christian women in Utah decorated pretty baskets for use in distribution. A dozen Christian women and several men participated in the distribution. The men drove vehicles around the block, keeping the Christian volunteers supplied with the tissues as they handed them out to the women walking by on the public sidewalks outside the conference building. Amazingly, all 10,000 packets were distributed in just 90 minutes.

The Mormon ladies who received the packets were very grateful and took them eagerly. As our outreach continued, the Mormon security team discovered the cards that we had placed inside the packets. They began to take the packets away from the ladies at the security check stations, claiming they were "anti-Mormon" tissues. This angered many of the women. Some took the packets back from the security officers, saying the tissues were given to them as a gift.

Later, several Mormon women posted photos of the front and back of the cards on their blogs. Some noted how wrong it was for LDS security to take something that had been given to them as a gift. Others wrote about how awful *we* were. Either way, the card was being posted online and discussed. This gave our outreach even more exposure than any of us could have imagined, even reaching Mormons who didn't attend the conference. Although I was hurt that many of our gifts had been tossed into the trash, I realized that what Satan meant for evil, God used for good![6]

This outreach event the next year may be outside the realm of what most Christians will do to reach out to Mormon women around them, but the principles are valuable no matter the venue. It focused on the polygamous women and children of Colorado City, Arizona. This town is home to the Fundamentalist Latter-Day Saint Church (FLDS) led by Warren Jeffs, who is currently serving a life sentence in a Texas prison for sexual abuse of minors. Because a Christian presence had moved into the Colorado City community, we received word about how the FLDS people had suffered immensely under the control of this cult.

We decided to organize a team of Christian women to spend a weekend pampering the ladies of the community. The Christians who participated were makeup artists, hairdressers, massage therapists, skin care specialists, and manicurists. Our team also included art teachers, whose focus was working with the children and keeping them occupied in a creative way. The goal was to lift the responsibilities from these ladies for a brief time so they could feel beautiful while we could tell them how God sees them as such—despite how they have been neglected and abused by their husbands and their church.

The results were incredible. Bonding between the Christian and polygamist women took place and there was open communication. The gospel message was clearly communicated with many. Plus, some of the Christian women who participated could share the story of this trip with their Mormon friends. One Mormon friend of mine, who no longer talks to me about her beliefs, was willing to take and read our ministry newsletter that reported on the outreach.

I knew that reading the newsletter would plant seeds in her life because she would read the truth of how historic, authentic Mormonism is polygamous by nature. It was a fact that could not be escaped. Mormonism's polygamous past is a problem for most Mormons today who want to distance themselves from embarrassing times in their history. Discussing topics like Warren Jeffs and the FLDS brings them face-to-face with the awfulness of Mormonism's founder, Joseph Smith, whose behavior could be seen in a modern polygamist leader.[7]

I share this story about the Colorado City outreach to emphasize a few things. First, women need to feel loved before they will be willing to listen. If a Mormon woman thinks the Christian who is trying to share her faith doesn't care, no serious conversation can ensue. In addition, a tangible display of love will many times open the mind in a way no logical argument could. Christian evangelists should be prepared and equipped to share their logical arguments while understanding that the door to the Mormon's mind will stay closed unless love prevails.

Second, I want to point out that God can use creative ways to effectively reach the Mormon people. The idea of the Colorado City trip began percolating in my mind months earlier when I watched a Christian lady serve while on a mission trip to Utah. This friend is a professional hair and makeup artist who met and helped a Mormon woman with her hair. She didn't do it for money or fame. Her kind gesture was the start of an amazing conversation that would have never happened in any other way. The Christian cared for this woman's outside appearance, thereby unlocking the door to her heart.

Maybe these stories of service and loving Mormon women can help us realize the endless possibilities for those believers who are willing to be creative while serving and listening.

## Conclusion

Many Mormon women may not be interested in a systematic comparison of our worldviews, yet they need to know the unconditional love of the body of Christ. By opening the discussion in a softer manner, it is possible to expose them to nuggets of truth. It's the gentle, steady rain that seeps into the hardest ground, not the gushing torrential downpour that sweeps over the top, leaving destruction in its wake. Mormon women can be reached through thoughtful interaction and creative measures that could, by God's grace, forever change their eternal perspective.[8]

---

*Becky Walker (San Antonio, Texas) is cofounder of Evidence Ministries with her husband Keith Walker. Becky holds a one-year certificate from Emmaus Bible College as well as a bachelor's and master's degree in vocal performance from the University of Texas at San Antonio.*

12

# Preaching from an Asbestos Suit
## The Reasoning-with-Mormons-on-the-Internet Approach

FRED W. ANSON


### Summary

A twenty-first-century Christian does not have to live in a Mormon-dominated state to have positive conversations with Mormons. With discussion groups, Internet evangelism can be effective in causing Mormons to think through their faith and even consider clear reasoning. But watch out for land mines!


### Introduction

According to Acts 17, the apostle Paul waited in Athens for his co-laborers Silas and Timothy to rejoin him. Never one to be idle, Paul "reasoned in the synagogue with the Jews and the devout persons, and in the marketplace every day with those who happened to be there" (verse 17). Interested in what Paul had to say, they asked him in verses 19 and 20, "May we know what this new teaching is that you are presenting? For you bring some strange things to our ears. We wish to know therefore what these things mean."

Not long after, Paul stood on Mars Hill reasoning with the best and the brightest philosophers. According to verse 30, he declared that the only true God wants people to put away their idols and worship only Him. While the message hasn't changed, Mars Hill has. In fact, I maintain that Internet discussion boards are today's Mars Hill, a place where it's possible to openly discuss competing ideas. If this approach is used correctly, the Christian who engages nonbelievers on the Internet can make valid points to those who have never been challenged elsewhere.

## Prep Work

Like the Athenians of Paul's day, many Mormons are bright, articulate, and well trained in their worldview and religion. If there are any holes, gaps, or weak spots in the Christian's worldview or religious training, these deficiencies will be quickly exposed. This should be considered a gift of God! For example, I thought that I had a pretty good grasp of the doctrine of the Trinity until my first set of discussions with a Mormon.[1] Once this chink in my armor was uncovered, I made corrections. I am now able to explain Trinitarianism with some small degree of skill and finesse.

Another surprise was the realization that dialoguing with Mormons also means having to reason with agnostics, atheists, and skeptics. Actually, the biggest shock in sharing my faith with Mormons was how *often* they utilize atheistic arguments. This is because modern LDS culture has become increasingly atheistic in private while church members continue to confess theism in public. As one Christian researcher of Mormonism explains:

> The religion of Mormonism is hollowing out...there is a mass apostasy going on, intellectually and mentally speaking. People are leaving the LDS Church without leaving the LDS Church. Without asking probing questions, I can't assume any Mormon I talk to even believes in the existence of God or the resurrection of Jesus. Even the Mormons who aren't closet atheists are largely latent atheists (or agnostics) without knowing it.[2]

Often a Mormon's arguments are borrowed from well-known atheists and skeptics. To successfully engage, the Christian needs to understand current LDS theology and culture better than Mormons themselves do. Perhaps there is no better place to get accurate doctrinal information than the official church website (www.lds.org). This is the Christian's best ally since it is a source that cannot be disputed. However, the official church website is filled with whitewashed, spin-doctored, and largely incorrect accounts of Mormon history. This "official history" is not a small matter. As noted by two renowned journalists:

> There is a very real sense in which the [Mormon] church's history is its theology, and that not merely the supernatural events surrounding the church's beginnings with the Angel Moroni and the golden plates at Hill Cumorah. In a body that believes itself the recipient and expression of continuing revelation, it is everything that has happened to the church ever since. And just as creedal churches have official statements of faith, the Mormon Church tends to have official versions of sacred history.[3]

This means that one must go beyond the LDS Church website to learn what has come to be known as "New" Mormon history, which is much more honest and accurate when compared to the heavily propagandized "faithful" history officially taught by the leadership. A rich treasure trove of such resources is as accessible as an Internet search engine or bookstore.[4] It should be remembered that Mormonism is not relegated to an individual Mormon's private, unorthodox beliefs. Because Mormons may sincerely hold ideas that they don't realize contradict their church's leadership, it is important for the Christian *not* to tell them what they believe. Still, Mormons who hold unique beliefs *should* be pressed on *why* they disagree with official church doctrine.

It is also important to create and maintain research archives of useful material since many Mormons tend to repeat the same arguments. With this information readily available, one can make timely, powerful arguments that can be customized as needed. Further, the Internet is so dynamic that there's no guarantee that content available today will still be there when it's needed later. A person can create one's own research archive by placing a folder on one's computer and storing files there. These can include digital images, downloaded articles, eBooks, and other content that can be copied and pasted into a discussion board or email correspondence as supporting evidence for the arguments. Having these archives on cloud storage is even better since they can be accessed from all electronic devices. With these tools and the type of spiritual preparation that comes only through prayer, it's time to enter the forum.

## Welcome to Mars Hill—Please Watch Your Step!

Internet discussion groups exist so people can, as Acts 17:21 puts it, "spend their time in nothing except telling or hearing something new" and then debate it endlessly. Various forums are available on the Internet, including these that were active at the time of the writing of this book and, of course, are always subject to change:

- Mormonism Discussed: https://discourse.mrm.org
- B.C. & LDS (aka "Biblical Christians and Latter-day Saints"): www.facebook.com/groups/christian.and.mormons
- Mormons and Biblical Discussion Group: https://www.facebook.com/groups/659429537470202/
- Mormon Discussion (the "Celestial Forum" is recommended as a starting point): http://mormondiscussions.com
- Mormon Debate (start in the "Moon" forum): www.reddit.com/r/mormondebate

To get started, open a web browser and type in a link. Some groups allow the user to view the content without signing in first; however, most sites require the user to set up an account before commenting on existing discussions or beginning a new thread. It's very common for "newbies" to make a fatal mistake when entering a new Internet discussion group by saying too much too soon and too loudly. As a result, they may end up stepping on sensitive toes, making a bad first impression. That's why it's recommended to make a long, slow study of the group before contributing anything.

To start, it is important to read the group rules, which are there for everyone's protection, including yours. Second, it's wise to identify and acquaint yourself with the group's administrators. Doing so will build a foundation of resources in case problems arise in the future. Further, reading a few of their posts will provide a good model for how they expect members to behave in the group. Third, I recommend silently "lurking" for a while to get the feel for the group's culture while learning the various personalities on the board. Doing so will also answer the most important question of all: *Is this a place where I'm truly called?* If not, it's not a problem to quietly leave the group and move to the next one. Over time, it is possible to find a discussion board that is best suited to one's personality and gifts.

As a matter of fact, I've exited far more Internet discussion groups than I've stayed in. For example, I spent a lot of time in ex-Mormon groups when I first began because it seemed reasonable that former members would be a better source for information on Mormonism. But what I didn't know is that between 50-60 percent of Mormons who leave the LDS Church end up converting to atheism.[5] As a result, many of these ex-Mormons are openly hostile to theism in general and Christian theism in particular. They may be very angry, bitter, and profane while taking great delight in attacking theists of all flavors. Many ex-Mormons are quite open on these boards about their desire to disabuse *all* theists of their "psychosis." After a while, I found that I was only welcome in these groups if I kept quiet about my Christian beliefs and agreed to toe their atheist line. If I didn't, it was clear that I would be cyber-bashed into silence.

This leads to the subject of Mormon bashing, which can be defined as the use of derogatory language, put-downs, and mockery of Mormonism and/or the LDS Church. It is unfortunate that some Christians resort to these off-putting tactics. In some groups, the administrators are the worst of the bunch! This is completely unbiblical. Christians have been given a mandate in 2 Timothy 2:25 to correct their "opponents with gentleness. God may perhaps grant them repentance leading to a knowledge of the truth." Paul also wrote in Colossians 4:6, "Let your speech always be gracious, seasoned with salt, so that you may know how you ought to answer each person." And Peter explained in 1 Peter 3:15 how the Christian must "honor Christ the Lord as holy, always being prepared to make a defense to anyone who asks you for a reason for the hope that is in you; yet do it with *gentleness and respect*" (italics added).

The way I apply the principles embedded in those passages is to use even-toned, scholarly language in every argument, reply, and comment. I sometimes fail, but I still *know* what the Master expects of me nonetheless. Unfortunately, some Mormons do not feel the need to return the favor. It is not uncommon to be on the receiving end of a string of insults, personal attacks, condescension, fight baiting, mockery, or worse.

For many Mormons, anyone who fails to speak about their religion and culture in absolutely glowing, positive terms is an "anti-Mormon" and, therefore, an enemy of the "only true and living church" on earth. Most Christians are shocked that they would be so villainized just for disagreeing with Mormonism, but for these Latter-day Saints, this is war! When this happens, the Christian's calling is clearly stated in 1 Peter 3:9: "Do not repay evil for evil or reviling for reviling, but on the contrary, bless, for to this you were called, that you may obtain a blessing."

When attacked, it's important to assume an even *more* scholarly tone. Staying focused on a particular topic is crucial because there will be some who will want to "rabbit trail" the discussion into the weeds and then constantly change the subject so that nothing gets accomplished. While remembering the command to be respectful and gentle, when this happens we need even *more* logic, *more* reason, and *more* evidence. Reasoning with Mormons on the Internet requires a thick skin and utter dependence on God. This approach is *not* for the fainthearted or thin-skinned. Anyone who is called to this type of ministry will need an asbestos suit.

## Preaching from an Asbestos Suit

With the prep work complete, it's time for the initiatory post or comment. In framing an argument, it's best to focus on the top five issues that surveyed former members have said were the reasons they abandoned the LDS Church:

- Doctrine/theology
- Church history
- Joseph Smith
- The Book of Mormon
- Lost trust in the church leaders[6]

I recommend stealing a page from Socrates's playbook and framing arguments in the form of questions. This is done for reasons that Os Guiness explains well:

> Questions...are powerful for two reasons. First, they are indirect, and second, they are involving. A good question will never betray where it is leading to, and it is an invitation to the listener to pick it up and discover the answer for him- or herself. This constructive use of questions is often traced back to the great Greek gadfly Socrates, whose probing questions stung his generation into thinking, and exposed the illogic and complacency of their unthinking.[7]

For example,

- If I want to challenge the Latter-day Saint's faith in the Book of Mormon, I might ask, "Here's a link to Biblical Archaeology Review's list of its Top 10 discoveries of the year. What were the top Book of Mormon archaeological discoveries this year?"[8]
- If I want to challenge the faith-promoting version of Mormonism's history, I ask, "If Joseph Smith and his associates didn't have a profit motive, why did they try to sell the copyright for the Book of Mormon in Canada?"[9]
- If I want to challenge their faith in church leaders, I could ask, "Why does the LDS Church donate less than 1 percent

(0.7%, actually) of its annual income to charity while the United Methodist Church gives about 29 percent?"[10]

- If I want to challenge Mormon doctrine or theology, I'll ponder, "How can Mormons claim to believe in monotheism when their church teaches that Heavenly Father, Jesus Christ, and the Holy Ghost are three separate gods?"[11]

When making an argument, it's vital to provide credible supporting evidence. *This is not optional.* Whenever possible, this evidence should originate from official LDS Church sources by utilizing the church's website and manuals along with LDS scripture. The burden of proof is on the one *making* the claim, so the more easily verifiable one's evidence is, the stronger the assertion will be. Nevertheless, it's likely that any argument—no matter how strong, cogent, or persuasive it might be—will result in attacks upon the person who is delivering the evidence rather than the evidence itself. This is an *ad hominem* (Latin for "to the man") logical fallacy that fails to directly address the argument.

Never forget that many Mormons use emotional reasons to remain in their church, despite any amount of logic, reason, or evidence. As one former Mormon put it, "As long as people want the Mormon Church to be true, more than they are willing to face the possibility that it is not, they will not entertain evidence or reason. Delusion becomes a choice."[12] Past experience has shown that five to ten quality contacts are needed before the Mormon will even begin to question the church. (I can't *prove* this statement, but it does ring true in my experience with Mormons.) And even then, it may take several more years with many more contacts before the person will finally leave. While those who share their Christian faith may never know which contact number they are, it really doesn't matter. As the apostle Paul reminds us in 1 Corinthians 3:7, "So neither he who plants nor he who waters is anything, but only God who gives the growth."

## Conclusion

Because reasoning with Mormons on discussion boards can be difficult, time-consuming, heartbreaking, and surrounded by almost constant acrimony, I'm often asked, "Why do you do it?" Sometimes I wonder that myself. Then, once in a while and out of the blue, a Mormon will tell me privately how he or she is having *real* doubts about Mormonism due to something that was presented on the Internet. When that happens, all the insults, rancor, endless effort, frustration, and bruises to personal pride melt away. It may not be easy, but it's worth it. With that, I'll see *you* on Mars Hill!

---

*Fred W. Anson (Lake Forest, California) is the founder and publishing editor of the Beggar's Bread website (www.beggarsbread.org), which features a rich potpourri of articles on Christianity with a recurring emphasis on Mormon studies. Fred is also the administrator of several Internet discussion groups and communities, including several Mormon-centric groups.*

# Spotlight

## BRODY OLSON

*Although the LDS Church no longer advocates the practice of polygamy (one man married to two or more women) in this lifetime, the arrangement still takes place with many polygamist groups scattered throughout North America. Perhaps no group is better known than the Fundamentalist Church of Jesus Christ of Latter-Day Saints (FLDS), which is based in the southern Utah/northern Arizona cities of Colorado City and Hildale. Leader Warren Jeffs has been in federal prison since 2006 and is serving a life sentence for his crime of marrying multiple underage girls. Brody Olson and his wife Liz minister to this polygamous community.*

**Eric and Sean: Can you explain the purpose of your ministry?**

Brody: In 2012 we moved to Colorado City to minister to the Mormon fundamentalists who were exiting the FLDS church. Their extreme sensitivity and loath for organized religion suggested a more practical "bridge-building" approach that displayed the Jesus whom we ultimately wanted to verbally share with them. We partnered with a help organization to provide emergency assistance to exiting families. Not wanting to foster codependency, we started a thrift store and community center where people could learn to help themselves and their own community. In the meantime, we established a Bible study with people who were interested in learning more about the Bible and going deeper in their relationship with Jesus.

**Eric and Sean: Although the FLDS people do not belong to the LDS Church, would you say sharing your faith with them is similar to sharing it with mainstream Mormons?**

Brody: While there are some obvious similarities in theology, preunderstandings, and traditions, the FLDS are very reluctant to engage in religious discussions on any level. Conclusions to theological matters are not the results of deductive reasoning but divine communication through a bona fide prophet.

**Eric and Sean: Is it possible to share the gospel with polygamous people?**

Brody: Yes. However, it is important to make the distinction between "polygamous" and "FLDS" people. Mormon polygamists are scattered throughout many communities, especially in Utah, and their level of openness to gospel discussions varies. The FLDS people are largely inaccessible and are very averse to gospel conversations. They believe in their religion because it's all they've known. Most have never been challenged to think otherwise. Gospel topics tend to reveal their ignorance and may result in shame. Expository living, not preaching, on the part of the Christian will likely yield more meaningful gospel discussions.

**Eric and Sean: Give a highlight of a recent encounter you have had with a polygamist.**

Brody: Recently a man argued that Christianity is too easy. He felt that a simple confession of belief would yield a superficial faith followed inevitably by hypocrisy. I described that saving faith in Jesus demands life transformation; otherwise it devalues the gift as well as the giver. I used the rich young ruler [Mark 10:17-27] as an example of one who undervalued Jesus and highlights the real difficulty in following Him.

**Eric and Sean: We have heard that polygamous women and children do not talk to strangers. How do you interact with them?**

Brody: FLDS women are indeed very shy. The best method I've found is to bring a baby. The women have not been having children since late 2012 because the prophet (Warren Jeffs) commanded them to stop having conjugal relations with their husbands, so it's a great way to break the ice.

**Eric and Sean: What is an approach that you have used to help the people learn to trust you?**

Brody: We have provided a plethora of community building and children's activities. These provide venues for meeting the children as well as the parents. It has served to display a heart of service and not condemnation toward them. We are intentional in trying to gauge people's interest in the gospel from discussions we have during these outreach events.

**Eric and Sean: You have had many out-of-state, short-term mission teams, including some organized by Christian schools, come from all over the United States to help you in your ministry. How does that work?**

Brody: Not only do the short-term missionaries get excited about missions, but also the missionary is tremendously blessed. In my years of working with mission teams, I have realized that their presence not only provides accountability, but they promote creativity.

*If you would like to receive the Olson's newsletter, contact them at brody.olson@gmail.com.*

## SECTION 4

# Invitational Approaches

Everyone has been invited to a special event—whether it was a senior prom, the wedding of a friend, or a dinner. Remember how you were made to feel important as your presence was requested to honor the one who made the invitation. There is nothing better than to know you are "somebody" and have someone pay attention to you and your needs.

In a similar way, Christians have the chance to present an invitation to their Latter-day Saint friends and family members by offering to engage in an honest conversation about something that ought to matter more than anything else: spirituality and truth. Evangelism is not about a "project" or "crossing an item off the list." It's about getting to know other people, hearing what they have to say, and engaging them as a fellow human. This attitude and using the right approach can go a long way.

First, Aaron Shafovaloff believes that some Christians who want to reach out to Mormons make things more complicated than they ought to be. In his "keep-it-simple" approach described in chapter 13, he outlines ways to utilize questions to get to know the person better and share multiple "Jesus stories" to make a connection. In chapter 14, Dr. David Geisler and Brian Henson use the acronym "LISTEN" to show how to make a Mormon most comfortable in any conversation.

It all begins by making the Mormon feel important through the validation of hearing what they have to say. Next, Dr. Lynn Wilder—who at one time was a professor at LDS Church-owned Brigham Young University—talks about how to successfully use questions to guide a conversation and deal with important issues. Finally, Dr. Bryan Hurlbutt—a Christian pastor in Utah—explains in chapter 16 how inviting Mormons to the Christian's church services can help break stereotypes and show that the LDS Church does not have a monopoly on community and church.

13

# Engaging in Gospel Discussions
## The Keep-It-Simple Approach

AARON SHAFOVALOFF


### Summary

It is possible for Christians to present the gospel to Mormons without having much background knowledge of Mormonism. While it is helpful to understand the teachings of this religion, using questions can be an effective tool, opening opportunities for correcting common misconceptions Mormons have about Christianity and sharing stories about Jesus from the four Gospels.


### Introduction

Since 2007, I have regularly shared my faith with Mormons in downtown Salt Lake City, Utah. Temple Square is the number-one tourist site for the entire state of Utah. It is the heart of the city and home to Mormonism's most prominent temple. Other believers join me to hand out pamphlets and newspapers while we occasionally do open-air preaching[1] on the public streets surrounding the city-block square. This has been a wonderful place to share the gospel.

Most of what we do is conversational evangelism. Typically about half of those with whom we speak are tourists and nearby convention attendees while the other half are Mormons visiting the temple, strolling through the grounds on dates, or walking to classes at the nearby LDS Business College. I spend most of my time asking simple questions and sharing well-known stories about Jesus, even with deeply committed Mormons.

It is beneficial to have a working knowledge of Mormon doctrine and understand how many Latter-day Saints think. In fact, I try to stay conversant with Mormonism. Although I have a full-time job as a computer programmer, I regularly read LDS manuals, theology books, and LDS General Conference talks. I interact with Mormon apologists while helping train other Christians in sharing their faith. Based on my experience, one does not need to know a lot about Mormonism to plant meaningful seeds and provide a clear gospel presentation.

## Starting a Conversation

Mormons believe they are already genuine Christians—the best kind. They remind me of the Jews that Paul spoke about in Romans 10:2 since "they have a zeal for God, but not according to knowledge." They believe in a false god as well as a false gospel. I critically engage these issues, but I avoid doing this prematurely in conversation. First, it's important to know the Mormon by asking some introductory questions, including these:

### *"Did you go on a mission?"*

For those who are committed Mormons, especially men, this is a great start and will generally cause their eyes to light up. A mission is a special, formative time of life in their lives. It helps the Mormons begin speaking about themselves. If the person did go on a mission, here are possible follow-up questions:

Where did you serve your mission?

What are some highlights of your mission?

Perhaps they did not go on a mission. It's important not to embarrass them, as serving a mission is a cultural expectation. Alternative questions work, such as:

### *"Where did you grow up? Did you ever have any born-again Christian friends there?"*

If the person lives in a highly Mormon population (Idaho, Arizona, Montana, and especially Utah), this question is a reminder about how unreached our Mormon neighbors are. Many Latter-day Saints have never had a meaningful relationship with an evangelical Christian. If they have had such a friend, I like to ask:

### *"Did you ever talk about God together? What did you discuss?"*

I want to help the Mormon introduce a topic we can talk about. We can work with it, build on it, and use it to share the gospel. These questions help us understand the person's background. One of my favorite direct questions is:

### *"Have you ever heard a born-again Christian explain the gospel?"*

Many Mormons have never had a simple summary of the gospel presented to them. If they say they have heard the gospel from an evangelical Christian perspective, ask,

### *"What did they say?"*

Listen to see if the Mormon understood what was presented. Now you have something to work with. If the person says he or she has never heard a clear gospel presentation, ask,

### *"May I explain it? It would only take me a few minutes."*

The answer is usually yes! This is the perfect opportunity to share the basics of the biblical message without having to get into LDS doctrine.[2] After a few minutes, I am able to get a sense (typically from body language) for whether I should continue or gracefully end the conversation.

In addition to having never heard a clear gospel presentation, most Mormons lack a basic understanding of Christian doctrine. They have not sufficiently considered Christian beliefs before finding them lacking. Rather, many of their disagreements with Christian theology are the result of an inaccurate understanding. When a topic comes up, I like to ask,

### *"Have you heard the born-again Christian explanation for _____?"*

This question can help mitigate the temptation to quarrel or to correct unkindly. There is a time and a place for debate, strong refutation, and even rebuke. Apollos "powerfully refuted the Jews in public" (Acts 18:28). But while there are times for this, the general biblical pattern is to show kindness and patience in teaching and correcting. Paul wrote in 2 Timothy 2:24-25, "The Lord's servant must not be quarrelsome but kind to everyone, able to teach, patiently enduring evil, correcting his opponents with gentleness."

When evangelizing Mormons, it is important to present support from the Word of God. There is an easy way to do this. Ask,

### *"May I show you a verse from the Bible on that subject?"*

Read the verse slowly while providing an opportunity for participation. Prompt the Mormon to complete a sentence or read aloud a key word. Ask basic reading comprehension questions afterward. Give the person time to reread the passage.

As you offer explanations and share verses from the Bible, the Mormon may feel defensive or nervous about any tension that the conversation might initiate. Out of this anxiety, and because of Mormonism's own claim to be the most authentic form of Christianity, many Latter-day Saints will want to minimize the differences between Mormonism and biblical Christianity. "We believe that too" or "We agree with that" are common responses, even when you're describing distinctively evangelical doctrines that clearly contradict Mormon teaching. To help bring clarity to muddy waters, ask,

### *"What would you say are the biggest differences between Mormonism and evangelical Christianity?"*

Listen to the differences they list. Often the Mormon will use phrases such as "modern-day prophets," "the Book of Mormon," or "being with families forever." While important topics, these don't come close in significance to the most important issues. I will often reply, "Thanks. What else?" until they list a doctrinal topic that would be helpful to talk about or until they ask in return, "What would *you* say are the biggest differences?"

These questions give me the chance to better learn about the individuals while seeing if they have an accurate understanding of what Christians believe. I will let them introduce a topic on their own and offer helpful explanations where their understanding is lacking. Starting a conversation is the hardest part, even for those of us who are experienced. Our hearts race too. But it usually only takes a few minutes before we are talking about something profoundly gospel related.

## Correcting Common Misconceptions

Just as we cannot assume what individual Mormons believe,[3] so too should we avoid assuming that they have an accurate understanding of the basics of Christianity. Misconceptions are low-hanging fruit—opportunities to provide helpful explanations. The following is a simple list of truths that can be shared with Mormons, each of which corrects a common misconception:

- The typical Christian church teaches the inevitability of a morally changed life for those who believe in Jesus. The forgiven are transformed.
- Christians believe in the resurrection of the body. The historic Christian teaching is that the body is important and will be renewed.
- The New Testament has been reliably preserved and is faithfully translated from the original Greek. Any major modern English translation can be trusted. If there are any significant "textual variants," they are typically noted in footnotes.[4]
- A particular denomination is not a Christian's religion, as those who belong to other denominations are considered

to be a part of the same broad Christian family. Many Christians may not even be aware of the denomination with which their church is associated!

- The unity of Christians across the globe is not because of an organization. It is a shared trust in Jesus.
- Feelings and spiritual experiences are important to Christians. We feel deep emotion and a profound connection to God over songs, prayers, Scripture, and special experiences. Our feelings are fallible, but they are still important.
- While Paul sometimes paid his own way, he otherwise insisted that Christians pay their local pastor-teacher (1 Timothy 5:17-18; 1 Corinthians 9:9; Galatians 6:6). Most pastors are underpaid and live on a tight budget. They are busy studying the Bible, counseling people, and dealing with needs in the congregation.
- The Council of Nicaea did not debate over whether the Godhead is three separate deities or whether the Father was an exalted human. It was about the divinity of Jesus. The Trinitarians held that Jesus was fully divine. The Arians instead held that Jesus was a created, inferior being.
- The Trinity does *not* teach that the Father, Son, and Spirit are one person. It affirms that they are three persons in relationship. For a Trinitarian, it is therefore no surprise that Jesus prayed to the Father.[5]

## Sharing Stories About Jesus

I once heard a foreign missionary explain that his work was quite simple: he learned and shared a lot of "Jesus stories." He had a list of all the parables, miracles, and teachings of Jesus on his refrigerator. He taught them to his children. He looked for ways to share them as a story. That sounds suitable for unreached peoples—for Muslims, Hindus, and Buddhists—but what about for Mormons?

While Mormons have some familiarity with the Gospels, very few can answer the basic question, "What did Jesus teach?" It is our mission to teach them—or at least stir them up—by helping them connect the dots.

Sharing Jesus stories isn't just about sharing new information. It is about revisiting and delighting in the stories. No matter how Mormons respond, there is joy in sharing the words and works of Jesus. This is how God encourages faith in Jesus. John 4:41 says that "many more believed because of his word." John 8:30 adds, "As he was saying these things, many believed in him."

Where can you start? I suggest that you be prepared to share stories about the authority of Jesus Christ. Perhaps the most common topic for Mormons to stress is that of "priesthood authority." Mormons believe that Jesus authorized apostles by the laying on of hands. When this comes up, I simply ask,

*"Where did He do that?"*

They flip through their pages, but this teaching is not there. At this, I expand the question:

*"How would you say Jesus typically showed His authority in the Gospels?"*

Whether or not they provide an example, I follow up with this:

*"May I share a Jesus story with you?"*

I suggest familiarizing yourself with Matthew chapters 8 and 9, which are packed with examples of Jesus demonstrating His authority. Among other things, Jesus tells

- a storm to be quiet (8:23-27)
- thousands of terrified demons "go" and they drown in water (8:32)
- a paralyzed man, "Your sins are forgiven" (9:2). To show He has the authority to pronounce this, He also says, "Rise, pick up your bed and go home" (9:6)

Sharing these stories with as many details that you can remember helps prime a listener for understanding the immense power of Jesus. The Roman centurion featured in Matthew 8:5-13 tells Jesus, "Lord, my servant is lying paralyzed at home, suffering terribly." Jesus replies, "I will come and heal him." The centurion provides a profound understanding of the nature of the authority of Jesus:

> Lord, I am not worthy to have you come under my roof, but only say the word, and my servant will be healed. For I too am a man under authority, with soldiers under me. And I say to one, "Go," and he goes, and to another, "Come," and he comes, and to my servant, "Do this," and he does it.

Jesus responds with amazement. The centurion is correct. Jesus did not even need to be in the same room, perform a ritual, or touch anyone. As with the storm, the paralytic, and the casting out of demons, all He had to do was "say the word." If time permits, share as many of these stories as you can remember. Let the Mormon see you glow as you share and treat His words as priceless and crucial to your life and faith. Since Mormons often know bits and pieces from these stories, you might prompt them to participate. When sharing a story, pause and let them finish a sentence. Or you can prompt them, "And then Jesus said..."

A wonderful way to end these stories is to ask,

### *"After He resurrected from the dead, how did Jesus authorize His apostles to preach, teach, and baptize?"*

Whether or not they remember, open up the passage and review it with them. Cite the last paragraph of the Gospel of Matthew:

> Jesus came and said to them, "All authority in heaven and on earth has been given to me. Go therefore and make disciples of all nations, baptizing them in the name of the Father and of the Son and of the Holy Spirit, teaching them to observe all that I have commanded you. And behold, I am with you always, to the end of the age" (Matthew 28:18-20).

Again, all Jesus had to do was say the word. This is a wonderful segue to the good news of the gift of eternal life. Jesus promises in John 5:24:

> Whoever hears my word and believes him who sent me has eternal life. He does not come into judgment, but has passed from death to life.

His work on the cross is finished. His words have infinite authority. Who can compete with that?

## Challenging Mormons to Know the Words of Jesus

I challenge Mormons to pick one of the four Gospels and devote themselves to the study of it. Cursory knowledge will not suffice. I encourage them with a few key texts that cite Jesus in John 15:

- Verse 1: "I am the true vine, and my Father is the gardener."
- Verse 2: He promises that those who bear fruit will be pruned by the Father to bear *more* fruit.
- Verse 3: "Already you are clean because of the *word* that I have spoken to you."
- Verse 7: "If you abide in me, and my *words* abide in you, ask whatever you wish, and it will be done for you."

Jesus says in John 6:63, "The words that I have spoken to you are spirit and life." Earlier we saw how Jesus commanded the believers to make disciples by "teaching them to observe all that I have commanded you" (Matthew 28:20). This can't be done without knowing His words. And it is disingenuous to recommend this to others without having done it ourselves.

The words of Jesus have supernatural power. Obeying them provides a durable foundation. Jesus said in Matthew 7:24, "Everyone then who hears these words of mine and does them will be like a wise man who built his house on the rock." And as Jesus said in Matthew 24:35, "Heaven and earth will pass away, but my words will not pass away."

## Conclusion

This approach is simple:

1. Ask questions to see if the Mormon understands the gospel.
2. Help introduce topics for conversation.
3. Offer to provide an evangelical Christian explanation for any misunderstandings or disputed topics.
4. Familiarize yourself with "Jesus stories" and share them.

Knowing about Mormonism will eventually help you better communicate with your Mormon neighbor. But that knowledge can come later. You can start doing the above today.

---

*Aaron Shafovaloff (South Jordan, Utah) is a regular evangelist at Temple Square, an elder at the Mission Church in South Jordan, Utah, a volunteer with Mormonism Research Ministry, and the founder of www.Theopedia.com.*

14

# LISTEN
## The Conversational Approach

DR. DAVID GEISLER AND BRIAN HENSON


### Summary

Instead of becoming defensive and ending up in endless arguments, it is possible to have productive conversations with Latter-day Saints. It may take an adjustment, but by following the LISTEN approach, the Christian evangelist can be more productive and share Christianity in a loving way by creating a more receptive atmosphere.


### Introduction

Perhaps you've had a couple of people come to your door who claim to be Christian but hold an unorthodox perspective.[1] In your conversation, you rush to let the individuals know what is wrong with their views. You may even articulate in a brilliant fashion why those views are dead wrong. But what typically happens after encounters like this?

If a person isn't ready to hear everything you have to say, you'll likely never see them again. May we suggest that if you have had an experience like this, it could be a sign that you need to consider a different approach. Jesus Himself understood this dilemma. He confessed to His disciples, "I still have many things to say to you, but you cannot bear them now" (John 16:12).

Many times, we "win" an argument with Mormon friends or neighbors, but then they begin to avoid us because we use an argumentative approach. I (David) remember a conversation I had with a Mormon bishop from Washington who sat next to me on a plane. My approach with him was soft and nonthreatening. To my surprise, before he got off the plane, he confessed to me that I was the first evangelical Christian he had ever talked to who wasn't, in his words, "in my face."

I also left him to wrestle with a question that he struggled to answer, but the question was worded in a way that didn't make him unnecessarily defensive. Furthermore, by walking a mile in his shoes, so to speak, I was able to get him to hear and think about an issue that challenged his faith, but I did it without an argument.

## A Different Approach

My experience with the Mormon bishop highlights an important paradigm shift that we may need to make in our conversations with Mormons. To begin with, we should think from their perspective. Perhaps we should ask ourselves, "What problems might Mormons have with our traditional Christian faith?"[2] You may have heard the proverb, "Never criticize a man before you walk in his shoes." This is especially good advice for witnessing to Mormons. Once we understand their questions and concerns more clearly, we can offer answers from a correct Christian perspective.

We also need to learn how to both listen better and talk *less*! As Christians, we have been taught from our youth that we are responsible to proclaim the gospel. Unfortunately, this leaves us at times with little reason to listen. But if we truly believe that these people are victims of the enemy (2 Corinthians 4:4), maybe we should really listen and earn the right to be heard. We also need to truly love them, as Christ taught (Matthew 5:44).

We should also learn how to ask the right questions with the purpose of clarifying their beliefs and gaining a greater understanding of why they believe what they believe. We need to ask questions in a way that doesn't make the Latter-day Saints unnecessarily defensive, leaving them with no desire to continue the dialogue. With these concerns and cautions in mind, let us suggest an approach that may be fruitful in witnessing to Mormons using the acrostic LISTEN, which is an abbreviated version of the "Conversational Evangelism" approach advocated at Norm Geisler International Ministries.[3] The acrostic LISTEN[4] stands for the following ingredients to this approach:

Learn Their Story

Invest Time in Them

Search for Gaps

Throw Light on the Conversation

Expose the Gaps

Navigate in the Conversation

Let's briefly look at each ingredient in more detail and suggest some applications that can help us in our conversations with our Mormon friends.

## LISTEN

Sometimes we as Christians are unaware that the most important way to build bridges with Mormons is to hear what they have to say. If we listen carefully, we might glean what they actually believe and have a better idea how to help them take a step closer to the cross. By listening first, we communicate that we want to win them over, not just win an argument. My (David's) experience with the Mormon bishop left me with the impression that most of those evangelical Christians with whom he spoke were somewhat argumentative. This kind of approach is rarely productive. A better approach would be to first ask a Mormon what he or she believes and listen intently rather than argue against positions a Mormon is *supposed* to believe.

For example, I (Brian) will ask someone what he or she believes about God. Very rarely does someone say that God used to be a man, as Mormonism's leaders have taught. That is why we have to listen beyond the label and not assume that in today's mix-and-match religious culture all Mormons hold to all the beliefs of traditional LDS teaching.

Again, the most important thing we can do in our first encounter with a Mormon is LISTEN.

### *Learn Their Story*

If our purpose in a conversation is not just to listen well enough to tear down someone's beliefs, perhaps we might see a different outcome. In an initial encounter, our listening should be directed at *learning their story*. Too often we only listen in order to find a chink in the armor, a weakness we can exploit to prove how wrong Mormonism is. What we should focus on first is learning about the Mormons' spiritual journeys that led them to where they are today. We can ask thought-provoking questions like these:

- Why is your faith so important to you?
- How does your faith help you cope with difficult times?
- How does your faith help you resolve the tension you may sometimes feel that you don't meet your own personal standards of how you should live?
- How does your faith help you to achieve a sense of purpose and meaning in your life?

If we spend more time getting to know the Mormons with whom we have contact while learning what's important to them, certainly we will have a better idea of the deeper questions we can ask. But this can only take place after we have *earned* the right to be heard.

### *Invest Time in Them*

To learn about our friends and their spiritual journeys, we must spend quality time with them. Many faithful Mormons have spent time during their missions knocking on our doors and sharing their faith with us. Shouldn't we return the favor and invest time *in them*? Remember that Jesus was a friend of many unbelievers (Matthew 11:10; Luke 7:34); He knew these people well! Jesus also spoke to the crowds in a way that kept their attention even over long periods of time. In the same way, the more we get to know the Mormons who live in our area on a personal level, the more open they may be to continue the conversation. Furthermore, if we do see them as victims of the enemy and *not* our enemy, maybe we should at least rethink any initial urge to get rid of them quickly when they come to our door!

### *Search for the Gaps*

Once we take the time to really listen to our Mormon friends, learn their stories, and invest time in their lives, our next step can be more fruitful. When we search for the gaps in their beliefs, we are looking for contradictions, outright errors, or areas where their beliefs lack a satisfying or coherent answer. By this, we don't mean that the moment we detect any gaps, that we immediately point them out! We may not be at a point where we should be asking penetrating questions.

Asking the wrong questions at the wrong time is like walking through a minefield, not knowing where the landmines are placed. Certainly we should ask God for wisdom (James 1:5) to make sure our approach is gracious and "seasoned with salt" (Colossians 4:6). But please remember that some people may not be motivated to change their beliefs until they see that the foundation on which they are resting is not strong enough to hold them up. This in turn may provide the motivation for them to take steps away from their current beliefs. But before we surface these gaps, it is important that we first learn to "hear"[5] and recognize the gaps ourselves.

The gaps in the beliefs of your Mormon friends may include their incomplete criteria for truth, the lack of archaeological evidence for the Book of Mormon, or perhaps the belief that God could have once been a man, as both Joseph Smith and Brigham Young taught. You may also find that some Mormons agree with what a Mormon prophet says, but some may not. Make a list in your mind of these gaps while listening very carefully with a discerning spirit. No matter how many gaps you may hear, at this stage it may be more helpful to hold back any questions you may have.

### *Throw Light on the Conversation*

Some Christians, in their encounters with Mormons, ask questions too quickly about the gaps in their beliefs. Can you imagine if we acted the same way with our loved ones, trying to settle a disagreement by pointing out all the things they say that don't make sense to us? This is a recipe for disaster! Similarly, if the focus of our conversation with our Mormon friend is to merely run through a grocery list of things we find contradictory or offensive about what the LDS Church teaches, our first encounter with them may be the last!

That is why it is so important that whatever gaps we may hear, that we tuck away those potential questions and focus on *throwing light on the conversation* by clarifying their beliefs. We can do that by simply asking them questions such as, "What do you mean by...?" We cannot overemphasize how important it is to learn to ask that simple question, especially with those who hold non-Christian beliefs.

Mormons use many words that we may need to clarify with them.[6] For example, it may be helpful to ask Mormons to define terms like *grace*, *faith*, *Jesus*, *Heavenly Father*, *heaven*, *works*, and *Scripture*. I (Brian) have discovered over and over that a Mormon will say they are saved by God's grace through faith in Jesus, just as we do. But they mean something different by these terms than what I as an evangelical Christian understand them to mean. That is why defining the terms (asking, "What do you mean by [blank]?") is so very important.

You might ask clarifying questions about the nature of God, such as:

- Do you believe the Son of God is eternal? Is He all-powerful?
- Is the Son of God all-knowing in His divine nature like the Father?
- Is God the Father eternal, infinite, all-knowing, and omnipresent?

### *Expose the Gaps*

The next step is to raise their doubt by asking thought-provoking questions. We can use certain words in our questions to minimize the possibility that someone will become unnecessarily defensive. Here are a few phrases you may want to keep in mind no matter what kind of questions you ask, which I (David) find actually work well with almost anyone:

> I am curious to know...
>
> Would you agree...?
>
> Have you ever considered...?
>
> Did you know...?
>
> How is it possible...?

Let's give a few examples of questions you can ask your Mormon friends using these phrases:

- I am curious to know if you think that man's real problem is that we don't work hard enough to achieve a better state. Or is it that we have fallen short of the standards of a holy and righteous God?
- Would you agree that our beliefs should never contradict what the Bible teaches?[7]
- Did you know there are some discrepancies between the teachings of Mormonism and the Bible?[8]
- How is it possible to have an infinite progression of gods? To explain our own existence, don't we have to start with an eternal being that is the first cause of everything?

The downside of using thought-provoking questions like these is that they could raise red flags in their minds and end your conversation. That is why it is so important to cultivate the fine art of asking the right question in the right way at the right time.

### *Navigate in the Conversation*

One way we can make sure our questions to Mormons have the

greatest impact is to keep in mind the three D's of Conversational Evangelism: Doubt, Defensiveness, and Desire. We want to ask questions that surface their *doubt*, minimize their *defensiveness*, and create a *desire* to hear more.

For example, to help Mormons see some of their gaps yet desire to continue a conversation, I (Brian) will first explain to Mormons that there is evidence to God's existence using arguments like the cosmological, teleological, and moral arguments.[9] Then I'll explain how we can use history, archaeology, fulfilled messianic prophecies, and the historicity of Jesus's resurrection to argue for the truth of the Christian faith. Since Mormons also tell me they believe the Bible is true, they usually welcome hearing the arguments for the Bible.

I'll also ask them if they think the Mormon scriptures have the same amount of evidence. When they begin to say, as they often do, "I feel they are true," I'll ask why they think that God would make it so that the Bible can be grounded with reason and evidence, but the Mormon scriptures cannot. In doing this, I am creating a desire in them to hear about apologetics (since they believe they are Christian), while at the same time helping them surface doubts about Mormonism. Keeping the three D's in mind when speaking with a Mormon may increase the likelihood that they will want to continue the conversation at another time.

## Conclusion

To summarize the conversational evangelism approach, the Christian will want to begin by *listening to the Mormons*, *learning their story*, *investing time in them,* and *searching for the gaps* in their beliefs. Only once these steps have been completed should questions be asked to *throw light* on the conversation and clarify their beliefs. The final step then is to *navigate the conversation* using the 3 D's (Doubt, Defensiveness, and Desire). Here we want to probe further and ask thought-provoking questions that *expose the gaps* in a way that surfaces *doubt* yet minimizes any potential *defensiveness*. We also want to ask questions in a way that creates *desire* on their part to continue the conversation!

In today's world, this indirect approach could be especially helpful when speaking with those who have never given themselves permission to question what they have been taught and may be reluctant to engage in a meaningful exchange of ideas. The LISTEN acrostic can lead toward a step in the right direction.

---

*David Geisler (Indian Trail, North Carolina) is the cofounder and president of Norm Geisler International Ministries and adjunct professor at Southern Evangelical Seminary. He coauthored* Conversational Evangelism: Connecting with People to Share Jesus *(Eugene, OR: Harvest House) with his father Norman Geisler. David is a graduate of Dallas Theological Seminary (ThM/MABS) and Southern Evangelical Seminary with a DMin in apologetics.*

---

*Brian Henson (Matthews, North Carolina) is the director of youth apologetics and evangelism for Norm Geisler International Ministries (NGIM). He received a master's in biblical archaeology degree from Wheaton College (2001) and earned a second master's degree in Christian apologetics from Southern Evangelical Seminary (2011). Brian teaches Bible classes at Charlotte Christian School. His* Grounded *video training series for youth can be found at www.ngim.org.*

15

# Authentic, Humble Dialogue with Mormons
## The Columbo Approach

DR. LYNN K. WILDER

### Summary

Too often, well-meaning Christians attempt to tell Latter-day Saints what Mormons believe and what they *should* believe. A better strategy is to ask thoughtful questions so Mormons can explain their personal beliefs, discover what the Bible says, and ponder the differences. The well-informed biblical Christian who listens carefully creates ample opportunities for authentic and humble conversation with Mormons.

### Introduction

After our family left Mormonism, many Latter-day Saints who were struggling with a variety of faith issues began to contact us.[1] Now in ministry, we introduce Mormons questioning their faith to the biblical Jesus; we also help Christians understand how to offer the gospel of grace to Mormons. Our love for the LDS people is personal, and our purpose is to free anyone in bondage to any form of religion by introducing them to a relationship with Jesus Christ. The approach we find to be effective is to introduce Mormons to specific passages in God's Word in friendly conversation, allowing them to discover when a passage conflicts with LDS teachings. In this approach, asking the right questions is key.

## Who Are the Latter-day Saint (LDS) People?

If you have a desire to talk with Mormons, my first recommendation is to *know your audience* so you can love them. Remember, no set of attributes fits everyone in any group, but the following traits may be helpful in better understanding LDS culture and people:

*Conservative followers.* Because Mormons follow their church leaders devotedly and trust that God places these men in their positions, they tend to be good followers. These are capable folks who believe their living prophet speaks for God and their church is the only true church. There are many laws, ordinances, and commandments to follow. Mormons are likely conservative traditionalists in politics, although not always. Temple-worthy Mormons are also moderate in appearance since their temple garment underwear must remain covered.

*Pleasant proselytizers.* The outward behavior of most Mormons typically includes being polite, pleasant, and proselytizing. Mormons consider themselves Christian and may judge others based on how "Christlike" they act. Mormons are also loyal to their church and family. Many converts to Mormonism come out of biblical Christianity and may have previously believed in Jesus, though they may not be familiar with what the Bible says about who He is or what He teaches. They deeply cherish sharing their LDS faith.

*Family values.* Latter-day Saints value traditional marriage and gender roles. In the US, they have larger-than-average families (a third more children)[2] and are highly involved in their children's activities.[3] Family is important since the definition of "eternal life" in the LDS Church means the family unit will live together forever.[4] Marriage can be for this life as well as the next if a "worthy" couple is sealed together in a temple. Since the faith requires works to earn eternal life and possibly reach the status of godhood, Mormons are often quite industrious and may be exhausted in their striving toward perfection. This is an opportunity for Christians to be a safe haven for them and pray with them over their challenges.

## Landmines

The Christian who hopes to be successful in LDS evangelism needs to be aware of what Pastor Jim Catlin calls "landmines."[5] These are things that ought to be known about Mormons to avoid offending them and closing their ears to the biblical gospel of grace. Here are two to consider:

*LDS dislike contention.* Most faithful Mormons are honored to talk about their faith and their church—unless they sense persecution. They can be sensitive to what they perceive as attacks on their faith. According to 3 Nephi 11:29 in the Book of Mormon, Jesus says that the spirit of contention is of the Devil. Therefore, Mormons sometimes see someone who presents anything that opposes their church's beliefs as being contentious, or from the Devil. They will not want to feel pushed or cornered. This is a tricky landmine; if you step on it, there is a good chance the conversation will be over. This is marked by the Latter-day Saint defaulting to reciting a personal testimony that goes something like this: "I know the [LDS] church is true. I know Joseph Smith is a prophet of God. I know the Book of Mormon is true," and so forth. These testimonies stress allegiance to the church organization and leaders rather than Jesus.

*LDS offer milk before meat.* Mormons will not always answer direct questions or admit that their church teaches a particular belief. This is a principle known as "milk before meat" that is found in Doctrine and Covenants 19:22. It says in part that "they cannot bear meat now, but milk they must receive." Typically, missionaries try to commit their investigators (those who are considering converting to Mormonism) to baptism in three or fewer visits. Explanations about what is required after joining the church usually come *after* baptism. It is normal for Mormons who are sharing their faith to avoid the deeper doctrines while telling listeners only those things that can be easily accepted. Stepping on this landmine by trying to converse about deeper doctrines before a good relationship is formed might be offensive and end the conversation. Stick to Jesus and His Word.

While many Christians wrongly assume that Mormons are experts in their faith, this is usually not the case. They will certainly know the basics of what their church teaches—these have been drilled into them from an early age. Yet some may still be deciding what they believe. If a Mormon invites a Christian to talk about God, this is an appropriate occasion to show kindness and respect, offer food and drink, and listen intently to what they believe. Avoid the temptation to tell Mormons what they believe, as it is better to let them tell you. Inquiry about a Latter-day Saint's faith is usually welcomed, but you might begin with, "Do you mind if I ask you a question about your faith?"

Subsequent discussion is an opportunity to gently set up a dilemma using scripture that begs exploration. In conversation, turn naturally to the Word of God. An excellent resource for discussion topics and related scripture is Adam's Road's "LDS Doctrine Topical Guide" or the "Quick Doctrinal Comparison" found in the back of *Unveiling Grace.*[6] We suggest not reading passages *to them.* Instead, have them open their own King James Version of the Bible and ask them to read the passage out loud. Then ask what they think. Allow them to be the experts on their own faith. By selecting biblical passages that are different than the beliefs they are taught, you are setting up a dilemma that will require investigation and resolution—perhaps not at that moment, but at a later time.

## How the Columbo Approach Can Work with Mormons

Greg Koukl, the founder of the ministry Stand to Reason, first introduced the tactic known as the "Columbo tactic." Named after the 1970s detective TV series *Columbo* starring Peter Falk, Koukl explains how the police lieutenant arrived at each episode's murder scene sporting unkempt hair and a rumpled trench coat.[7] The approach is simply to ask thoughtful, targeted questions while using Columbo's trademarked "Do you mind if I ask you a question?" Koukl writes:

> The key to the Columbo tactic is to go on the offensive in an inoffensive way by using carefully selected questions to productively advance the conversation. Simply put, never

> make a statement, at least at first, when a question will do the job.[8]

The Columbo approach involves genuine and innocent inquiry to stimulate thinking. Since Mormons can be easily offended, asking questions to address topics in conversation is an effective way to be nonthreatening. Of course, Jesus used questions in a brilliant fashion. In the same way, the Columbo approach is never meant to be disingenuous but is a tool to use to avoid landmines that offend while allowing the Holy Spirit to draw people to Him through the Word. Asking specific questions can guide the conversation to stay on one topic at a time while avoiding tangents.

## Sample Columbo Questions for Seven LDS Teachings

The pattern is this:

1. The Mormon explains personal beliefs on a topic. Listen closely and ask clarifying questions.
2. Turn to a passage of Scripture that challenges that LDS teaching. Hand them the Bible, or ask them to turn to their own, and read the passage out loud. Then ask them to please explain what they think it means.
3. Ask, "How have you reconciled what the Bible says with what the LDS Church teaches since they are opposite?"

Here are some examples of how this approach can be used with particular LDS doctrines.

### *Great Apostasy*

Mormonism teaches that God's authority left the earth not long after the death of the apostles. This "Great Apostasy" is one of the first principles taught to potential converts by LDS missionaries. When the missionary brings up this topic, a possible response could be:

> I'm confused because of something I read in the Bible. You say Jesus's church went into apostasy and He therefore

> failed to establish a church that would endure through the centuries, right? Could you please read these words of Jesus and explain what you think He meant?

Look up Matthew 16:18 where Jesus said, "I tell you, you are Peter, and on this rock I will build my church, and the gates of hell shall not prevail against it." Here Jesus Himself refutes the idea of a Great Apostasy. I once asked a missionary to read this scripture out loud and tell me what she thought it meant. As she read it, her face turned red as she had no idea how to explain it. I prayed she would return to her apartment and open her Bible to investigate if Jesus *really* said that and why He would.

### *The Word of God*

Mormons usually are not convinced of the reliability nor the sufficiency of the Bible since they have been instructed to trust the Bible only "as far as it is translated correctly" (Eighth Article of Faith) and additional scripture is needed. According to 1 Nephi 13:28-29 in the Book of Mormon, "plain and precious things" were removed from the Bible. To Mormons, biblical Christians have *part* of the truth but need the "*fullness* of the gospel."[9] Evidence that the Bible is both reliable and sufficient may need to be part of the conversation.[10] Reference Matthew 24:35, where Jesus said, "Heaven and earth will pass away, but my words will not pass away." When a Mormon expresses any doubt about the Bible, ask:

- Do you believe the words of Jesus in the Bible?
- What do you think He is saying in this passage?
- Do you believe He is able to keep the right words together through the ages or did man corrupt them and remove important teachings?
- Is additional scripture necessary?

If you have an opportunity to present the historical, geographical, and archeological evidence for the Bible in conversation, it could be new information for them.

### *Jesus*

Mormonism's version of Jesus is different from the biblical Jesus in significant ways. One main difference is that, unlike in Mormonism, the biblical Jesus has been God from the beginning (John 1:1) and is a person belonging to the co-eternal and co-equal Trinity.[11] The Bible is clear that He did not earn His status as deity nor was He created, but He has always been God. In addition, Mormonism teaches that each member of the Godhead is separate (three gods). Hebrews 13:8 says that Jesus is the same yesterday, today, and forever. The biblical Jesus is unchanging, yet the LDS Jesus progressed/changed to earn His status as deity. Ask:

- Who is Jesus to you?
- According to this scripture, does He change?
- What did He do for you?

Mormons often claim that Jesus is their Savior. If they say this, ask:

- From what did Jesus save you?
- If He is your Savior, when is the last time you prayed to Him?

Forgiven Christians believe that Jesus saved them from their sins and they therefore have eternal life. First John 5:13 says, "I write these things to you who believe in the name of the Son of God, that you may know that you have eternal life." Further, Mormons are not allowed to address Jesus in prayer, but Christians have the privilege of praying to Him directly. How is it possible for Jesus be your Savior but you're never allowed to talk to Him?

### *The Cross*

To the Christian, the cross symbolizes eternal life provided through the death and resurrection of Jesus. According to 1 Corinthians 1:18, "The word of the cross is folly to those who are perishing, but to us who are being saved it is the power of God." Ask:

- What does the cross mean to you? (May I tell you what it means to me?)
- Considering what the Bible says about it, how have you reconciled the fact that the LDS Church does not use the symbol of the cross?

### *Grace*

Let the Mormon define grace, which he or she may describe as an enabling power that helps one keep God's commandments. However, Ephesians 2:8-9 says, "By grace you have been saved through faith. And this is not your own doing; it is the gift of God, not a result of works, so that no one may boast." Ask:

- If grace is a free gift and sufficient for eternal life, how did you come to the conclusion that temple works are necessary to earn eternal life?

### *Office of High Priest*

The Jews had only one high priest at a time; the Bible claims that Jesus is now this high priest. As Hebrews 7:28 says, "The law appoints men in their weakness as high priests, but the word of the oath, which came later than the law, appoints a Son who has been made perfect forever." Mormons have thousands of high priests "after the order of Melchizedek." If the topic of priesthood authority comes up, ask:

- Why does the LDS Church have thousands of high priests when God appointed only one in the Jewish temple and Jesus now is that one?
- Once Jesus died and the temple veil was torn, was there a need for multiple high priests?

### *Temples*

The LDS Church has built many dozens of temples throughout the world for its people to do religious ordinance work for both the living and the dead. Although the main purpose in the biblical temple was to sacrifice animals on behalf of the sins of the people, Latter-day Saints learn new names and special handshakes in Mormon temples while making covenants and even participating in ordinances for the dead.

- What is the purpose of the LDS temple?
- Would you say these temples are like the Jerusalem temple described in the Old Testament?
- If the Bible describes only one temple and it had to be in Jerusalem with daily sacrifices and special feasts, how did you conclude that so many different temples are needed?

## Conclusion

Regardless of the topic, be sure to have a firm grasp on the differences between biblical and Mormon teaching. This will involve study on your part to understand the doctrines taught in Mormonism and to familiarize yourself even more with biblical content. As you are in conversation, weave in your own testimony of the living Jesus and testify how He has transformed your life. Give examples of answered prayer and evidence for how He has worked in your life. Share His gospel of grace.

Since Mormons rely on feelings and experience in matters of faith, they may be willing to hear your testimony. So be prepared to share it. Understand that the Word's results may be slow and plodding since there are so many contrasting teachings to address, but be patient and trust God. He appears to be on the move with the many Mormons leaving their faith for such a time as this.

---

*Dr. Lynn K. Wilder (Fort Myers, Florida) is a former Mormon and Brigham Young University professor who currently teaches at Florida Gulf Coast University. She and her husband, Michael, founded the ministry Ex-Mormon Christians United for Jesus (www.unveilingmormonism.com). She has authored five books, including* Unveiling Grace: The Story of How We Found Our Way Out of the Mormon Church *(Zondervan, 2013), and is the coeditor of* Leaving Mormonism: Why Four Scholars Changed their Minds *(Kregel, 2017).*

16

# The Power of a Simple Invitation
## The Come-and-See Approach

DR. BRYAN HURLBUTT


### Summary

When the Samaritan woman encountered Jesus in John 4, she told everyone she knew to "come" and "see" (verse 29). In the same way, Mormons can be invited to see what an authentic relationship with God looks like through the example of Christian believers who gather in a local church body with a commitment to passionate worship.


### Introduction

Perhaps the most overlooked evangelistic opportunity with Mormons is also the simplest. What if we just invite them to church? However, such an approach is too often looked down upon. Christians are often made to feel that they are copping out. "Oh, so you didn't share Christ with them but just invited them to church?" says the pious Christian with a smile. Is this really the case? There may be much more available in a simple invitation to the worshipping community of God.

### An Invited Woman's Invitation

Life with Jesus is infectious. Perhaps this is seen most vividly in John 4 when Jesus meets a Samaritan woman at a well of great significance in both Jewish and Samaritan history. What ensued from that meeting is a vivid picture of what it means to meet the Savior.

The nature of Jesus's cross-cultural engagement with this sinful woman has been well chronicled. The two were separated by gender and by socioreligious culture. As a Jewish man, He ignored societal norms by conversing with a Samaritan (half-Jewish/half-Assyrian) woman. Her astonishment at His forthrightness is apparent in her response to His request for refreshment. "How is it that you, a Jew, ask for a drink from me, a woman of Samaria?" she asks in verse 9. Jesus seizes on the setting at the well to press her with a picture of "living water" as a metaphor for the perpetual refreshment that comes to those who receive what Jesus has to offer. She struggles to grasp His invitation to this new kind of life.

But the conversation begins to change when He exposes how she has sought to fill up the hole in her soul through repeated relationships with a number of men. His recognition of this fact clearly makes an impression on her. After Jesus discloses to her who He really is, she heads out to tell others about Him in verse 29. "Come, see a man who told me all that I ever did," she says. "Can this be the Christ?" In response to encountering Jesus, she immediately invites others to meet Him too. Her wonder at this man at the well who identifies and addresses her wounds cannot be contained.

When humans meet God, their lives are exposed. They are seen for the chaos and confusion that they are. This is at once both exhilarating and excruciating. This woman finds herself captivated by Him and is amazed at His ability to see into the hidden recesses of her life. That amazement and wonder leads her to give others the same opportunity. Jesus's revelation of Himself stirs her to want others to have a similar experience. Her words *come* and *see* are a simple invitation to an encounter that ends up being anything but simple.

## Following in Her Footsteps

This woman doesn't stand alone. After encountering Christ, we too can invite others to share in our experience. Without question, one of the great privileges of the Christian life is to invite others to encounter the One who has brought us into the experience of the life-giving joy of His kingdom. Sometimes we tend to overthink when it comes to evangelism. We feel a pressure to know all the answers, have a presentation nailed down, and be prepared to give a winsome personal invitation for sinners to turn their lives over to Jesus.

Yet the reality is that Jesus has already done the work through His death on the cross and through the empty tomb. Additionally, the spiritual heavy lifting is accomplished as the Holy Spirit opens eyes to the gospel. There should be very little pressure on us. We are simply called to invite people to come and see.

While this invitation is simple, it is by no means benign. Instead, it is loaded with power. Inviting someone to view the sunset is not filled with performance. All the work is done by nature of the thing being observed. The wonder is not in the witness but in the object of awe. We invite people to gaze upon God. We invite them to savor the Savior. We invite them to be caught up in the King of kings. Gospel witness is, by its nature, not a compelling or clever method of witnessing but a direct invitation to experience the majesty of God in Christ.

While apologetic arguments surely do have an important value, something deeply embedded in LDS history and its origin opens the avenue for the power of a simple invitation.

## Two Different Visions

This key is hidden in two contrasting theological visions. One finds expression in the First Great Awakening in American church history and the other as an outcropping of the Second Great Awakening. Eighteenth-century pastor Jonathan Edwards was a figurehead in the First Great Awakening and is regarded by many as the greatest theologian in American church history. For Edwards, everything revolved around the glory and majesty of God. The creation, including a now-fallen and broken humanity, was called to bring glory to God. We exist for God, and He upholds all things to bring glory to His name. This theme is apparent in Edwards's writings:

> All that is ever spoken of in Scripture as an ultimate end

> of God's works is included in that one phrase, *the glory of God*...The refulgence shines upon and into the creature, and is reflected back to the luminary. The beams of glory come from God, and are something of God and are refunded back again to their original. So that the whole is of God, and in God, and to God, and he is the beginning, and the middle and the end.[1]

In this Christian vision, revelation, creation, and the daily fabric of life all resolve to the glory of God. In short, man exists for the glory of God.

At contrast with Edwards's vision is the vision of LDS Church founder Joseph Smith, who is, in many ways, an ideological child of the culture that produced the Second Great Awakening. Smith was reared in the western portion of upstate New York in the early- to mid-nineteenth century. This area, along with parts of central New York, became known as the "burned-over district." It received its nickname from the Second Great Awakening evangelist Charles Finney in the first half of the nineteenth century who saw the area as so saturated in evangelism that there was nothing left to get lit on fire for the gospel. Smith was far from alone in spurring a new religious movement out of the spiritually oversaturated soil.[2]

Smith's new movement was characterized by something quite different from Edwards's theology. In fact, from the standpoint of an overarching theological vision, it was the exact opposite. God's existence paves the way for man's exaltation. As fifth LDS Church president Lorenzo Snow said, "As man is, God once was; as God is, man may become."[3] The ultimate glory of man sits as the focal point in Smith's religion. The entire point of human life is centered on a process of exalting humans. It is at the forefront of LDS marriage, family life, and temple work. In a very real sense, Mormonism's version of God exists for man's personal glorification. Moses 1:39 in the Pearl of Great Price states, "Behold this is my work and my glory—to bring to pass the immortality and eternal life of man."

Consider the following quote from Smith as recorded in a church manual:

> The first principles of man are self-existent with God. God himself, finding he was in the midst of spirits and glory, because he was more intelligent, saw proper to institute laws whereby the rest could have a privilege to advance like himself. The relationship we have with God places us in a situation to advance in knowledge. He has power to institute laws to instruct the weaker intelligences, that they may be exalted with himself, so that they may have one glory upon another, and all that knowledge, power, glory and intelligence which is requisite in order to save them in the world of the spirits.[4]

The theological visions of Jonathan Edwards and Joseph Smith could hardly be any more divergent. Why does this matter so significantly? Succinctly put, a theological vision paves the way for our conceptualization of just about everything in our spiritual lives. It determines whether we live for our exaltation or for God's glory, and whether we worship God as a distinct and holy being or consider Him a being of the same species as ourselves who paved the way so we could become like Him.

It directs whether our communal life with our church families and our participation in corporate worship is focused on the majesty of God or on progressing toward levels of personal and familial glory. These are two very different visions with two entirely different textures of what constitutes the purpose of the church and what establishes the aroma of local church worship.

## Corporate Worship as an Aesthetic Apologetic

Christian worship is about the glory of God. It can be understood as both the opportunity to express our awe and wonder to God as we behold and ponder His glorious character as well as a corporate opportunity to be formed by that vision of His glory. In that sense, we are both longing for God and learning from Him. But it is no static or stoic enterprise. Instead it is passionate and captivating. As David wrote in Psalm 108:1-5:

> My heart is steadfast, O God! I will sing and make melody with all my being! Awake, O harp and lyre! I will awake the dawn! I will give thanks to you, O LORD, among the peoples; I will sing praises to you among the nations. For your steadfast love is great above the heavens; your faithfulness reaches to the clouds. Be exalted, O God, above the heavens! Let your glory be over all the earth!

This passion for God and His character to be lifted up should pervade the spirit of the Christian's worship. This passion can be intoxicating and enthralling. It is the kind of celebration that is intended to call others into it and enrapture them as well. The intention is to make those outside of God's family look with quizzical intrigue at the emotional and spiritual investment of God's people.

One Sunday our church celebrated a parent/child dedication for a young family who had just given birth to their third child. This is always a wonderful time for attendees to invite people in their relational circle to celebrate the occasion with them; this couple used the celebration as a relatively innocuous outreach to their LDS friends and relatives.

As the officiating pastor, I shared a few words with the family and the church before I prayed over the child. Additionally, the parents, under the father's leadership, had crafted a statement of dedication regarding their intent to raise their child in Christ. As the service continued, our worship leader and band led us in exuberant songs to our God and King. It was nothing novel and was simply what happens in gospel-teaching churches all over the world on a weekly basis.

As we sang, a child of one of the Mormon families looked around at the congregation and then looked up at his uncle, whose child was being dedicated. "It looks like these people actually want to be here!" he exclaimed. Out of the mouth of babes! He had picked up on a contrast from his regular experience as a child in the confines of the local LDS ward, fully captivated by the sight of people who were wrapped up in the joy of proclaiming the glory of God!

The disparity that exists between a practical theology driven by the glory of God versus one driven by the glory of man bespeaks its own apologetic to the world. It is a type of aesthetic apologetic where the beauty of God does the work. A dear friend of mine who came out of Mormonism used to play in a worship band at our church. He coined my favorite description of a worship leader's job when he said, "We are just called to take people to the edge of the cliff and say, 'How's the view?'"

I love that assessment! The tour guide's job isn't to steal the show; instead, it is to point people to what constitutes the show, namely the grandeur and wonder of exalting the King. When we worship, we are touring the character of God, declaring His gospel, and celebrating His rightful place as the sovereign Ruler over all.

Celebrating this view of God together with full hearts leads others to conclude that something unusual is happening. This intriguing hook into passionate worship creates tremendous opportunity for future discussion, incites questions, and establishes a sense of what Christian community is centered on. It usually takes time and plenty of processing when Mormons come to faith. Introducing them to a passionate community of believers can begin a journey of amazing transformation.

## What Now?

Here are a few ways to use this extremely simple approach with your LDS friends and family. First, take the initiative to extend an invitation. Explain how you would love to share the most precious part of your week with them. Apply no pressure and don't push; just ask. If they decline, accept that and ask how you can pray for them. Wait a year and ask again. You never know what God has brought into their lives that might cause a different reaction the next time you offer. If they accept, let one of your pastors know that they are coming. You don't want them to be mobbed, but you do want people to connect intentionally with them.

Second, while our church in Utah cares deeply about accurate theology and presenting a clear exposition of the Word of God, we have a rule: those on the platform don't use the word *Mormon* or any form of it. We simply want to put God on display as we worship together. Mentioning Mormonism on Sundays risks making visitors uncomfortable or possibly causes a church to be labeled "anti-Mormon." This may not have the same significance in a less LDS-dominated culture; however, there is wisdom in generally being aware of labels that could close people off to the nature of the intended message, no matter where our churches are.

Third, give your guests a preview of what they can expect so they aren't caught by surprise. For instance, let them know what is expected in the attire of your church. Mormons are typically used to dresses for ladies and ties for men. Don't let them guess. If your church has a band with drums, tell them. And prepare them for what to expect in the sermon.

Fourth, don't apologize for your church's culture. The passionate worship of God yields no regret. Part of the necessary process for your Mormon acquaintances is experiencing something different and possibly even awkward. Let the oddity be your companion in engaging them and let it be a robust catalyst for conversation.

Finally, be prepared for an invitation for you to attend a service at their local LDS ward. If they do invite you, don't sweat it. Attending one week with them might open a huge opportunity for ongoing relationship and dialogue, possibly paying eternal dividends. Tell your pastor or church leader about what you are doing, make sure you and your family are spiritually equipped for the visit, and ask your church family for prayer support.

## Conclusion

The woman at the well in John 4 parlayed her encounter with Christ into an invitation for others to experience the same. This is the heartbeat of true Christianity. We fall in love with the One who has identified us, loved us, healed us, and given us hope. Then we extend an offer to others who need all the above, just like us, and let God encounter them. The simple invitation is powerful because we are entreating them to witness a vision of God in His glory and hear from His Word.

He alone can save, but He can use you to introduce people to a compelling vision of Him and to acquaint them with a community in which He may be found.

---

*Dr. Bryan Hurlbutt (South Jordan, Utah) is the lead pastor of Lifeline Community in West Jordan, Utah. He received his bachelor's degree in religious education from Davis College in Johnson City, New York, his master's degree in theology from Dallas Theological Seminary, and his doctorate of ministry from Talbot School of Theology. He authored* Tasty Jesus: Liberating Christ from the Power of our Predilections *(Resource Publications, 2013).*

# Spotlight

## SHANE JONES

*Smack in the middle of the state of Utah is the small town of Ephraim, which is home to Snow College. It's estimated that about 80 percent of the 5,000 students belong to the LDS Church. Across the street from the school is the Solid Rock Cafe, a former house that has been transformed into a coffee/hang-out spot for students. Shane Jones and his wife Kim manage this shop where many students make it a habit to visit regularly throughout the school year, even though Mormons are not supposed to drink coffee.*[1] *We caught up with Shane between orders of espressos and lattes to find out more about this ministry.*

**Eric and Sean: So why would Christians place a "coffee" shop across the street from a college that is mainly attracting an LDS audience?**

Shane: It does seem odd to choose a coffee shop as a tool for ministry to the LDS, doesn't it? We recognize that if Mormons are questioning their church, many times one of the first rebellious acts they will commit against the authority of the LDS Church is drink coffee. This is a sign that a person is willing to question and think "outside the box." Since the coffee shop culture allows people a comfortable place to hang out and talk about all kinds of topics, including religion, it has been our goal to create a safe space for spiritual dialogue and relationship building.

**Eric and Sean: Do many Latter-day Saints come in?**

Shane: Some Mormons are fearful of our establishment and what we stand for, but many who come in enjoy the caffeine-free drinks as well as the other menu items and activities such as open-mic events. Others come out of curiosity or to challenge us. Of course, most of our relationships are built with those who are struggling with Mormonism or who don't belong to the LDS Church.

**Eric and Sean: Your ministry uses college interns. What is the goal in having these folks as a part of your ministry?**

Shane: Student interns are a crucial part of our coffee shop ministry. The applicants we consider are strong believers who have a minimum of two years of college experience and are between 20-25 years old. Their commitment is from 1 month to 11 months. We want to serve our student interns by equipping them for various forms of evangelism, one of those being the coffee shop ministry, and send them into the world as prepared, passionate ambassadors for Christ. These young people are able to connect with students at a peer level and pursue relationships at a deeper level because they better understand the thinking of their own age group.

**Eric and Sean: What kinds of conversations take place here?**

Shane: A dialogue usually starts with a lot of relationship building where we discuss "life" (family, classes, pastime activities) while allowing the Holy Spirit to guide the conversation in a spiritual direction. We also have a lot of dialogue with those wanting to learn more about coffee, and surprisingly enough, those conversations often lead to discussions about faith.

**Eric and Sean: What advice would you have in sharing your faith with a younger Latter-day Saint?**

Shane: For one, the younger generation can sniff out a "sales job" in a second. If you don't know what you're talking about or don't have an answer, they will respect you more if you are humble enough to admit it and get back with them after you have researched. Humility and sincerity go a long way. In addition, ask a lot of investigative questions and be quick to listen. Do not be thinking about what you will say next while they talk. And be willing to find a common ground even if you differ in religious beliefs.

**Eric and Sean: Do Bible studies happen here? If so, how do those go?**

Shane: We have had our larger college group Bible studies in the cafe during open hours. Many times, coffee shop patrons who are not part of the study are listening. We also have one-on-one studies with a variety of people.

**Eric and Sean: There is a Bible museum in this place located in different rooms, with the artifacts from the Holy Land in glass cases. What is the purpose of having these here?**

Shane: We use 500-year-old manuscripts, 2,000-year-old coins, and a 3,000-year-old brick from the wall of Jericho, among other items, to show how ancient civilizations coincide with biblical stories. The evidence for the Bible is much better than what can be used to support the Book of Mormon story.

## SECTION 5

# LDS Event Approaches

Whether it's a neighbor, friend, coworker, or family member, talking to a Mormon whom the Christian already knows is probably the most effective evangelism possible. After all, if the Christian has an already-established relationship with the Latter-day Saint, the hard part of getting to know each other and building a factor of trust is already accomplished. But what if you don't have a Mormon with whom to interact? Answer? Begin to throw out chum—in fishing, this is excess bait—to attract attention and initiate a conversation.

There is plenty of different "bait" to use when evangelizing in public waters, which is often called "stranger evangelism." Even though you probably have never met that stranger on a public street, this is a way to interact and possibly get into a conversation. The techniques discussed in this section might provide some "outside the box" ideas. Of course, the goal is not to trap anyone (as bait does), but rather to find creative ways to open up conversation with Mormons who wouldn't typically be interested.

First, some may think that standing on a public street corner and proclaiming the truth about God and the gospel is too confrontative, but as Andrew Rappaport explains in chapter 17, this can be a very powerful method if it's done in the right way. In chapter 18, Sharon

Lindbloom explains how handing out newspapers at public events can be very informative and even lead to one-on-one conversations. And the information in the paper can have an effect on both the curious Mormon and non-Mormon alike.

Next, Randy Sweet and I (Eric) explain in chapter 19 how giving away books written by an LDS president provides the opportunity to interact with hundreds and even thousands of people at public events, causing many to consider this leader's ideas that are, quite frankly, nothing less than impossible to follow. Finally, Rob Sivulka describes ways in chapter 20 to advertise his apologetics website by holding a sign to gather the attention of drivers and passersby and get hundreds of additional visitors to view his site. Indeed, chumming can work, especially if it's distributed with a little ingenuity.

17

# Let Your Voice Be Heard
## The Open-Air-Evangelism Approach

ANDREW RAPPAPORT


### Summary

The words *street preaching* often conjure up the image of screaming evangelists shouting arrogantly through bullhorns at their opponents. While some may give a bad name to open-air evangelism, it is possible to efficiently and lovingly share the gospel in public if humility, not pride, is the main motivation.


### Introduction

At the annual Mormon Miracle Pageant held in 2016, I watched a man standing on a public street with many Mormons walking by as he condemned them for the sin of homosexuality (not an issue most Mormons struggle with). As he was talking to someone afterward, I saw a woman waiting to speak with him. I asked if I could answer any questions she had. "Are you with that street preacher?" she asked.

When I responded that I was not, she informed me that she was a Christian who wanted to chastise the man for preaching on the street. While more than a hundred Christians were using a variety of strategies to evangelize thousands of Mormons, she felt that this one strategy of publicly calling people to repentance was wrong.

Many Christians would agree with this woman. It is true that some people do not do public preaching (or, as I will put it throughout this article, "open-air evangelism") well, seemingly motivated by pride and not love or passion for the lost. However it can also be done right! When I told this woman that I planned to proclaim the gospel publicly, she was not happy. In fact, she said that if I did, she would stand in front of me and warn the bystanders that I was not a Christian. If they wanted a pleasant conversation, she would invite them to talk to her. I asked if she would at least listen to what I would say before she condemned me for my approach. She agreed to give me 30 seconds.

I stood on a box and told those who were listening how much I loved them and how I wanted to give them the truth of Jesus Christ. I pleaded with them to repent of their sin. I cried out that many of them were probably far more moral than I am, yet I added that morality cannot make anyone right with God. What people heard that day was the gospel of Jesus Christ from a man who was willing to look foolish because he cared where they would spend eternity.

As I stepped down, the same woman approached me. *Here it comes*, I thought to myself, fully expecting a tongue-lashing. Instead she requested forgiveness. She told me she had never heard anything like what she just witnessed. She then thanked me and apologized three more times.

The manner of delivery made all the difference. The other man preached condemnation, but it was probably not the message these people needed to hear. Instead, I proclaimed the truth by allowing the gospel to be the only offense.

## Answering Objections to Open-Air Evangelism

Like the woman I met at the pageant, many people perceive open-air evangelism as an outdated method to communicate the gospel. While respected apologist Greg Koukl is committed to training Christians to have confidence with clear-thinking skills to tackle any situation, he has stated that he is not a fan of this strategy.[1] However, he also admits that it can be done right, pointing to the examples of California evangelist Ray Comfort[2] and me.

What are some reasons for the negative impression so many Christians may have? Perhaps they associate such an approach with loud-mouthed evangelists screaming condemnation in arrogant pride to bystanders who are not listening or, even worse, getting angry. Those who have attended the General Conference sessions in Salt Lake City, Utah, held two weekends every year may have observed certain street preachers who angrily condemn those Latter-day Saints streaming past while making their way into the LDS Conference Center.

In the past, some of these evangelists have even antagonized the Mormons by taking special LDS undergarments or their unique scriptures and desecrating them. One evangelist tied a chain to the three combined scriptures, throwing the book to the ground and dragging it around, to the dismay of faithful Mormons who watched.

Some see drawing opposition from or disagreement with unbelievers as ungodly. But Jesus, Paul, and many others in the Bible practiced open-air evangelism, even when those to whom they spoke disagreed! The most successful open-air evangelism includes opposition, as many people will gather around to hear a conversation taking place between an evangelist and potential hecklers. That dynamic can be used to share the gospel, shut the mouths of the ignorant, and provide biblical answers to challenging questions.

Other Christians may perceive this approach as "intolerant" because it involves telling others their views are wrong. But Christians should not allow their culture to affect biblical methods of evangelism. I would never claim that it is the *only* successful approach. Evangelists use many strategies; this book demonstrates that we should not limit ourselves (or others) to only one method. Open-air evangelism is appropriate and can be successful when it is done well. In fact, I can share the gospel with more people in one hour of open-air evangelism than when I hand out gospel tracts or do one-on-one evangelism.

## Why Do Open-Air Evangelism?

If the culture disapproves of open-air evangelism, why should we do it? Because it is an example given in Scripture. Like many other things in the Bible, God commands that the gospel is proclaimed publicly. The Greek word for *preach* is used 61 times in the New Testament and means to proclaim or announce publicly so people can hear, as described in Matthew 4:23; Mark 6:12; Luke 8:1; and Acts 9:20.

As a regular open-air evangelist in New York City, I often see people who will listen for hours to open-air evangelism, but once someone hands them a gospel tract or tries to start a conversation, they walk away. Many people are fearful or just private and don't want to have to defend their view of spiritual things in a public place. While they might not accept the gospel message that night, there is a chance they could hear the gospel preached clearly, maybe even for the first time. If God's Word does not return void, as Isaiah 55:11 says, there is value in publicly proclaiming to everyone that there is hope even for the hopeless.

## How *Not* to Do Open-Air Evangelism

We cannot discuss open-air evangelism without addressing the common errors. The greatest hindrance to open-air evangelism is pride. A simple search of YouTube reveals that many open-air evangelists appear arrogant in their presentation. To help keep pride in check, open-air evangelists should be part of a local body of believers. The local church is the means God instituted for evangelism, including open-air evangelism, and an authority in a person's life gives them the trait of submission. The goal in open-air evangelism should never be to win an argument or embarrass an unbeliever. Instead, we should always seek to share the gospel, doing whatever we can to remove ourselves as an offense.

I have two goals when I do open-air evangelism. The first and most important goal is to share the gospel. Secondly, I want to conduct myself in such a way that one unbeliever will tell another unbeliever to stop talking so they can listen. I want unbelievers to respect my behavior (Titus 3:1-7; James 2:13; 1 Peter 1:15,17; 2:12) as I proclaim a biblical gospel message in a manner that does not betray my message. The Christian's conduct must match the gospel message. We do not do open-air preaching to proclaim ourselves but to declare Christ.

## How to Do Open-Air Evangelism

I believe there are three elements of ambassador evangelism:

1. Disarm the defenses of the unsaved
2. Disarm our own defenses
3. Use the law

### *Disarm the Defenses of the Unsaved*

Salvation is a personal subject. Therefore, a person is bound to get defensive in a discussion of where he or she will spend eternity. But a defensive person is not open to discussion; he or she seeks to defend a position rather than understand someone else's. A defensive person is hard to persuade, but the evangelist can disarm people with politeness and humor.

It is important for the evangelist to be polite even when the hecklers are heated up. One way to do this is look individual agitators in the eye and refer to them by their names. (Learn their names at the very beginning and offer to shake their hands while giving them your name.[3]) Additionally, I hope to have an observer in the crowd publicly tell a heckling unbeliever to be quiet so he or she can hear what I have to say.

The evangelist must also keep in mind that any evidence used to show how Mormonism is not the same as biblical Christianity can turn the nicest Latter-day Saint into a bulldog. "What, are you saying we're not Christian?" someone might complain. "What makes you better than we are? We are Christians too." A natural reaction when someone disagrees is to use a raised voice in response, which can easily end up turning into a shouting match and makes the Christian the biggest loser in the eyes of the public. The better approach is to keep calm and remain polite, which allows the evangelist to disarm an objector's defenses as well as maintain the crowd. As Proverbs 15:1 puts it, "A soft answer turns away wrath."

Humor is another tool that can lower the defenses of the unbelievers so the Word of God can pierce their hearts once they are listening. It can make the conversation more enjoyable for all who stay and listen. Those with whom you dialogue may remain skeptical and hard-hearted.

But others may be watching closer than you would ever know, especially with larger crowds. Humor even allows the open-air evangelist to appeal to the crowd if a heckler acts rudely.

In the past, I made the mistake of poking fun at other people, offending some observers. But very few people get offended when I make fun at myself. This approach has been beneficial, and many nonbelievers have told me that I do not seem to be the typical Christian they expected. They apparently anticipate believers to be full of themselves. Making myself the butt of my own comments communicates that I am humble, which makes me a better ambassador for Jesus Christ since my method is not viewed as prideful. When I laugh at myself, it relaxes the person to whom I am speaking and opens up the discussion in a way that otherwise could not have been possible.

### *Disarm Our Own Defenses*

Evangelists can also struggle with defensiveness, so we need to disarm our own defenses. A powerful means to calming our defensiveness is to ask excellent questions. Greg Koukl provides four uses of questions:

1. To gather information
2. To get off the hot seat
3. To reverse the burden of proof
4. To exploit a weakness in someone else's argument[4]

If we are going to ask well-placed questions, we must first learn the importance of good listening, which can serve two critical purposes. First, listening is an important means of gathering information. Second, listening earns respect. An evangelist who thoroughly and attentively listens to someone's arguments often earns the right to ask the other person to do the same.

It is possible to get defensive when someone challenges us with a question. What should be done if the evangelist doesn't know the answer? Of course, there is nothing wrong with admitting we don't know every answer to every question a Mormon might ask. Using a question in response shifts the burden of proof while providing a way to get more information from the other person. Most often the person making the challenge has not even thought through the issue enough to have an answer in defense of their claim.

Once at Union Square in New York City, a man named Jason challenged me with the statement, "God cannot exist because there is evil in the world." In order to show him how God must exist, I asked how he would explain evil without God. He had never thought of that before, so I was able to explain that evil is the absence of good, and the nature of God defines good. Questions not only shift the burden of proof but help us understand the issue.

### *Use the Law*

The difficulty in evangelism is not "getting someone saved"; it is "getting someone lost." Most people think that they are "good" and do not need a Savior. It is easier to get people to see their need for a Savior after exposing them to their sinfulness before an all-holy God. The purpose of God's law is to expose the inability of people to attain to God's standards and, thus, highlight their need for a Savior who can forgive all their sins. According to Romans 1 and 2, God has written His law on the hearts of all people; therefore, no matter where we go and no matter whom we talk to, we can always use God's law to expose our need for Christ without having to use language that only Christians understand.

Someone without a church upbringing may not understand terms such as *sinner*, *repentance*, and *washed in the blood of the Lamb.* And even with Mormons, the same terms might be used, but with much different meanings. Yet everyone has a God-given conscience, which we can use to help people see what sin looks like before a holy and just God. Getting the sinner to understand this will help bring a person to true repentance and turn them from sin to Christ.

A simple way to do this is to ask questions using the Ten Commandments. For instance, ask if the person has ever lied, stolen anything, or used God's name in vain. Point out that lying makes someone a liar while stealing creates a thief. Church attendance will not fix this predicament. About 160,000 people die every day. Ask, "If you were one of those today and were to face the judgment throne, would you be found innocent or guilty by God's standard?" A temple recommend does not work in the Mormon's favor.

The advantage of using the law with open-air evangelism is that nobody can complain that the evangelist is being judgmental; after all, the law is the standard—the mirror for people to judge themselves. When the unbelievers in the crowd complain that evangelists are being judgmental, Christians can boldly announce that they did not judge. They merely allowed the person to judge themselves by God's law (James 1:22-25).

## Evangelists Are Ambassadors for Christ

To be effective at open-air evangelism, it is vital to remember that, above all, Christian evangelists are ambassadors for Christ (2 Corinthians 5:20) and must be marked by humility and love. It must be kept in mind that everything done in Christ's name reflects back to Christ. As His ambassadors, Christians must act like Him and not like the world. Those who are listening should see that the Christian in the open air has true compassion for them, even if listeners do not believe the Christian message.

## Conclusion

It is typical to be nervous about standing in front of a crowd of people and proclaiming God's Word. Even though I have been using this approach since 1992, I still feel nervous every time. But we must overcome our fears and obey what the angel of the Lord told the apostles in Acts 5:20: "Go and stand in the temple and speak to the people all the words of this Life." So go, stand, and speak in the open air, and rely on God for the results.

*To see some examples of Andrew in action, go to his YouTube channel (StrivingForEternity) and look under "Open Air Evangelism."*

---

*Andrew Rappaport (Jackson, New Jersey) is the founder and president of Striving for Eternity Ministries (www.Striving*

*ForEternity.org). Andrew received his master's degree in theological studies from Calvary Baptist Theological Seminary and is the author of* What Do They Believe? *(Owosso, MI: One Million Tracts, 2015) and* What Do We Believe? *(Owosso, MI: One Million Tracts, 2017).*

18

# Extra! Extra! Read All About It
## The Newspaper Approach

SHARON LINDBLOOM


### Summary

Newspapers have informed the public's opinions for centuries. As an accepted and familiar form of communication, a well-done publication distributed at Mormon events can serve as a very effective evangelism tool. With enough space to include information on a variety of topics, this something-for-everyone handout approach impacts many lives for Christ.


### Introduction

It's never wise to set boundaries for God. I learned that lesson a long time ago on a hot August day in Nauvoo, Illinois.[1] Visiting the town to tour historic Mormon sites, I had spoken to a dozen Mormon tour guides while hearing inspiring heroic tales of early Mormon settlers and watched the rousing *City of Joseph* musical pageant presented by the LDS Church. All around me, Mormons were swooning over the faith-promoting stories that seemed to be the very fabric of Nauvoo.

Heartbroken over the eternal fate facing these dear Mormon people who were not only following but *adoring* a false prophet, I suddenly knew that God was calling me to serve Him in reaching these lost ones for Christ. In a flood of joy and enthusiasm, I answered, "Yes, Lord! I will go wherever You want me to go! Um...except...please don't ask me to hand out tracts to strangers."

Before I left Nauvoo two days later, having been invited to join the Nauvoo Christian Visitors Center in its annual summer outreach, I was standing on the street handing out Christian newspapers to the Mormon tourists. Thus began my ministry to Mormons, a ministry that has been punctuated by tract and newspaper distribution outside many Mormon proselytizing events.

## What Is the Newspaper Approach?

This evangelistic outreach tactic begins by simply offering a specially prepared newspaper to passersby, but it isn't intended to end there. Ministry via a single newspaper might continue for minutes, hours, or even years! The primary goal is to get the carefully written newspaper into the hands of people who need the information it contains. Therefore, most often (in the context of evangelizing Mormons) it is done in an area or at an event where a high concentration of Latter-day Saints is expected. After distributing the material, evangelists move on to discussion, sharing contact information, and hopefully, a long-term relationship of trust.

## The Newspaper

Outreach newspapers are most effective if they are designed for the specific event and audience they are intended to reach. A newspaper prepared for a temple open house outreach will be somewhat different than one prepared with visitors to Temple Square in mind.[2] This uniqueness keeps a handout fresh and pertinent to each event.

The newspaper format allows an abundance of information to be shared because there's something for everyone inside. For example, Mormonism Research Ministry has published a four-page newspaper designed to be used at Mormon temple open house events.[3] In addition to a comparison chart of Mormon teachings versus biblical teachings, this paper contains challenging articles addressing such issues as the nature of God, eternity, the virgin birth of Christ, Mormon temples, the biblical temple, the Book of Mormon, and much more.

This variety is excellent because every person's journey out of Mormonism is unique. For instance, during his customary morning reading of the Book of Mormon, my friend John was struck by the mention of horses—dating to a time in history when there were no horses in the Americas.[4] This raised a question in John's mind, starting him on a research path that eventually ended his LDS Church membership and led him to Christ. Another friend who had already "heard all the Christian arguments against Mormonism" was given an outreach newspaper that included a list of foundational LDS doctrines missing from the Book of Mormon. Disbelieving the newspaper, Kathy searched the Book of Mormon to find the doctrines of three degrees of glory, eternal marriage, eternal progression, preexistence, and baptism for the dead. Discovering that those critical doctrines were not in her faith's primary book of scripture, Kathy began her own years-long journey away from Mormonism to Jesus.

In addition to including information on *individual* topics that will strike a chord with any Mormon reader, an outreach newspaper presents so *many* different problems within Mormonism that these can have a cumulative effect on readers. A Latter-day Saint might shrug when learning Joseph Smith had more than one wife, but it's not as easy to dismiss nearly 40 wives, including those who

- were as young as 14 years of age;
- had living husbands; and
- were related to another Smith wife (mother/daughter/sister).[5]

One other very important element every outreach paper should include is contact information noting the ministry or person who has prepared it. This not only provides the recipient a follow-up resource, but also makes it clear that the criticisms are not from an anonymous source.

## The Story Below the Fold

While the focus of outreach at an LDS event is evangelizing Mormons, curious people who are not members of the LDS Church—or those investigating this religion with an eye toward joining—often attend LDS pageants or temple open houses. In fact, the Mormons view these public events as proselytizing opportunities. Therefore, any Christian outreach at an LDS event involves reaching this people group as well. A good outreach newspaper will not only challenge Mormon heresies but also expose them to uninformed non-Mormons while, of course, presenting the gospel to all.

When distributing Christian newspapers outside the Preston England Temple in 1998, our outreach team met Michael, a lapsed Catholic from Ireland. For eight years he had been seeking God through the Bible, but at that time was reading the Book of Mormon. Though he was inspired by the book of Alma, Michael was skeptical about Mormonism, so he traveled to England to see what this Mormon temple had to offer. As we spoke with him on his way to the temple tour, he allowed us to pray for him. Months later we received a letter from Michael that read,

> Thank you, again, especially your guidance and advice concerning the LDS Church. I did not enjoy my visit to the Temple; it did nothing for me. The only good thing that came out of this is that I met you...Thank you for making the book of Romans alive to me again.

## The Delivery

Latter-day Saints have grown accustomed to being approached by critics of Mormonism. Therefore, some are unwilling to accept anything that is not published by their church. Christians must be creative to convince Mormons that an outreach newspaper is valuable. One way to encourage Latter-day Saints to "read all about it" is simply approaching them with a smile and a kind greeting, a cheerful countenance, or even a playful attitude. When we're friendly and enjoying our outreach work, Christians are perceived as nonthreatening and approachable.

This happy attitude influenced an LDS woman in St. Louis who saw Christians passing out newspapers outside the temple. Chris didn't get a paper and didn't stop to talk, but months later she recognized me in Nauvoo, Illinois. This time she stopped long enough for me to give her my contact information. Months went by before Chris called. Because she was having doubts about Mormonism, she felt that I was approachable. This story has the best of all endings: The Lord brought Chris to new life in Him.

Sometimes friendliness by itself isn't enough to generate interest or overcome suspicions. I've found it helpful to tell people what I'm handing out. I'll say something like, "This is a free Christian newspaper I'd like you to have," or "This is a gift for you from [the ministry that is sponsoring the outreach]." Another approach is to pique interest by telling people a bit about what's in the paper. "Here is a Christian paper that compares LDS doctrines to the Bible," or "Did you know that LDS temples and the biblical temple have completely different purposes? Read about it here!"

When a newspaper outreach is underway at an LDS event, some Mormons will attempt to hinder the distribution of the Christian materials. This is something to be aware of and to guard against. Obstruction tactics take many forms, including posted signs over prominently placed trash cans, friendly requests from security guards that visitors toss their papers, requests for extra copies of the paper for nonexistent "friends," blocked access to foot traffic, and conversations meant to distract Christians from distributing papers. Sometimes these obstruction tactics work, but they can also backfire.

During the Christian outreach at the Preston England temple, LDS security guards began to take newspapers out of the hands of those who had picked them up before entering the temple grounds. "You're not allowed to bring that paper in here," visitors were told. Not surprisingly, this ploy irritated visitors, many of whom returned, seeking out the Christians to request replacement papers. "I wasn't going to read it the first time you gave it to me," one ruffled man said. "Now I *want* to read it!" Temple security stopped using this obstruction tactic later that day.

Sometimes traffic patterns, municipal ordinances, or inclement weather make reaching people on a sidewalk very difficult. Thankfully, traditional door-to-door newspaper delivery in surrounding neighborhoods works well, too. As a "silent evangelist,"[6] a newspaper can still impart its message when left on a doorstep or tucked into the screen door. The main evangelistic objective of this approach is to provide as many people as possible information that will challenge false beliefs while also presenting the gospel. This can be accomplished both face-to-face or by acting as a "paperboy."

### Extra! Extra!

Periodically, someone who has accepted an outreach newspaper will come back after a few minutes to talk about it. It's important that the Christian understands what the newspaper says and, ideally, knows how to further address each topic it contains if given this fantastic opportunity. These return encounters might begin in a negative way, with the Mormon saying something like, "This is garbage! It's just filled with lies!" With a soft word, the Christian can set a better tone for the ensuing discussion. Possible responses include, "What's in this paper that has upset you?" or, "What did you read that you believe is a lie?" Once a specific concern has been identified, it can be addressed, hopefully beginning a long and friendly conversation.

This was proven true while I was distributing papers at the 2002 Winter Olympics in Salt Lake City. An LDS man approached me with a paper he had received from someone else and told me it was deceptive. "How so?" I asked. Bob didn't like the way the facts were presented in an article discussing the death of Mormonism's founder Joseph Smith. After I acknowledged (but didn't agree with) his concern, the conversation moved on to other more important topics.

Bob and I discussed Mormon history, archaeology, the Book of Mormon, and finally the doctrines surrounding eternal life. I shared my great love of Christ and my deepest desire of spending eternity with Him. But Bob believed eternity with Christ was just the "appetizer" before a fine meal; personal Godhood was the "main course" that he anticipated. Though we didn't come to agreement, Bob and I parted ways cordially.

An hour later he came back to continue our discussion. He had highlighted the outreach newspaper, marking all the things he didn't like. We reviewed each one before eventually saying our friendly good-byes. I don't know what happened to Bob, but I know he read every word of that newspaper—and he heard God's amazing gospel of grace.

## The Late Edition

Once an outreach newspaper has been delivered, the paper may be promptly tossed in the garbage, read and dismissed out of hand, or even stuck in a drawer and quickly buried under bits and pieces of daily life. Though it might *look* like that is the end of an outreach paper's ministry usefulness, looks can be deceiving. The paper that is thrown away still displays its headlines for those who glance into the trash bin. I have seen Mormons fish these discarded newspapers out of the garbage and sit down to read them.

The paper that has been read and dismissed has done its job. It has imparted challenging information about Mormonism as well as a gospel message. These things can't be unlearned. That information can and often does come to mind over and over again, pressing for answers. Meanwhile, the paper that is carelessly thrown into a drawer is just biding its time. Someday someone will pick it up and decide its fate. Keep it, read it, or toss it? The pictures and headlines will plant seeds in any case. In some cases, this "late edition" of an outreach paper or tract will have a monumental impact on its readers.

Katrina was a dedicated Mormon wife and mother. As she cleaned out a dresser one day, she found a Christian tract that she had received years earlier outside a Mormon pageant.[7] She casually flipped open the tract and read Joseph Smith's own words:

> I have more to boast of than ever any man had. I am the only man that has ever been able to keep a whole church together since the days of Adam. A large majority of the whole have stood by me. Neither Paul, John, Peter, nor Jesus ever did it. I boast that no man ever did such a work as I. The followers of Jesus ran away from Him; but the Latter-day Saints never ran away from me yet.[8]

Katrina was stunned. *Surely*, she thought, *a prophet of God would never say something like that!* She ran to her bookcase and found the book cited in the tract. Quickly scanning the page, she stopped dead in her tracks. Joseph Smith's unbelievably boastful words were confirmed. And in a church-published book, of all places!

In a daze, Katrina picked up the Christian tract again and read it from cover to cover. When her husband came home, she gave *him* the tract. Over the next few months Katrina and her husband checked the references of each citation included in the pamphlet. They talked to their bishop and friends. Nobody could soothe the unrest they felt. Katrina and her husband spent much time in prayer, finally understanding what they must do.

The tract challenged them with this: "The Word of God never asks what you have done with Joseph; instead it asks: *What will you do with Jesus?* Here are four keys to help you find true Christianity for yourself, based on what God says in the Bible."[9] Katrina, her husband, and their children all came to understand that Joseph Smith was a false prophet and that Mormonism was not of God. They surrendered to Christ and now serve God as Christians!

## Old News Is Still Good News

In summary, advantages of this approach include:

- Information written for the specific audience
- Photos and headlines that impart immediate (though limited) information
- Information on many topics
- Enough variety to present something of interest for nearly everyone
- Cumulative effect of challenging details
- Recipients taking the information with them
- Follow-up discussion points
- Contact information for long-term discussions

To make the best use of this evangelism strategy:

- Always be prayerful.
- Keep the main thing the main thing: Distribute the material.
- Be kind, approachable, and happy.
- Describe what is being distributed.
- Tell people the origin of the newspaper.
- Know what is in the paper and how to further address its assorted topics.
- Listen to, recognize, and address the concerns of recipients.
- Hand-deliver to people's doorsteps (make sure it won't blow away!).
- Always be ready to provide a reason for the hope that is in you (1 Peter 3:15).

## Conclusion

When I began in ministry three decades ago, I had no idea how effective handing out newspapers could be. All I knew was that I was scared and intimidated by the stonewalling of the very people I longed to reach with the gospel. They didn't want my handouts, they didn't want my questions, and they didn't want my God. But God wanted them—and still does. Christians are told in 2 Timothy 2:24-26:

> The Lord's servant must not be quarrelsome but kind to everyone, able to teach, patiently enduring evil, correcting his opponents with gentleness. God may perhaps grant them repentance leading to a knowledge of the truth, and they may come to their senses and escape from the snare of the devil, after being captured by him to do his will.

We have our marching orders. May God grant Mormons repentance leading to His glorious truth.

*Sharon Lindbloom (Eden Prairie, Minnesota) has been involved in Christian missions to Mormons since 1987. After serving for nearly two decades as director of a Minnesota-based outreach ministry to Mormons, Sharon joined the staff of Mormonism Research Ministry (www.mrm.org), where she has served since 2006. She writes a regular column that can be found at http://www.mrm.org/category/in-the-news.*

19

# *The Miracle of Forgiveness*
## The Free-Book Approach

ERIC JOHNSON AND RANDY SWEET


### Summary

Those who attempt to distribute Christian tracts and free information about Mormonism at public events often get rebuffed. But what if material written by an LDS General Authority is offered? While it may puzzle the Mormon, offering free copies of *The Miracle of Forgiveness* can be an effective method for Christians who want to engage in conversations on the topic of salvation.


### Introduction

Individual Mormons are encouraged to have personal testimonies. However, they are specifically taught that they should not believe doctrines that contradict the leaders of their church, who are called General Authorities. These leaders are crucial for this "restored" church because Mormons believe they are divinely ordained by God Himself. As Apostle L. Tom Perry told an October 2003 General Conference audience, "It is contrary to the economy of God for any member of the Church, or any one, to receive instruction for those in authority, higher than themselves."[1] James E. Faust, a member of the First Presidency, stated in that same

General Conference, "Revelations from the prophets of God are not like offerings at the cafeteria, some to be selected and others disregarded."[2]

If the Mormon leaders are placed on the earth to reveal the mind of God, what they say ought to be taken seriously by all Latter-day Saints. While some members may not personally agree with their teachings, these men are supposed to be empowered by God to give authoritative teachings, not mere theories or opinions. Understanding where the power originates with this church provides a backbone to the approach described in this chapter.

## A Book of Debate

During late summer of 2014, we decided to try something new at the Ogden temple open house event. On the first day of the outreach, we had brought along eight copies of *The Miracle of Forgiveness*, a book that was originally penned in 1969 by then-Apostle Spencer W. Kimball. A few years after it was published, Kimball became the church's twelfth president.

Some background to the book is necessary for anyone wanting to try this approach. According to Edward Kimball, Spencer W. Kimball's son, there had been 1.6 million copies of *The Miracle of Forgiveness* printed in 17 languages as of 1998.[3] While very popular, the book has also bristled many followers who disagree with Kimball's hardline stance on the necessity of keeping all of God's commandments to have any hope to be exalted in the celestial kingdom as gods and goddesses. One online petition from 2013 argued,

> The Miracle of Forgiveness contains nondoctrinal and incorrect information that is not taught by or practiced by The Church of Jesus Christ of Latter-day Saints...As with the cessation of publishing of Mormon Doctrine (1958), we, the undersigned, ask that you cease publishing this book.[4]

Perhaps it was criticism like this that finally caused the Mormon publisher, Deseret Book, to stop printing the book in hard-copy format in July 2015 after 47 years of continuous publishing![5] Still, church leaders and official publications have praised this work. In the April 1995 General Conference, Apostle Richard G. Scott taught, "In *The Miracle of Forgiveness*, Spencer W. Kimball gives a superb guide to forgiveness through repentance. It has helped many find their way back."[6] A decade later, Scott hadn't changed his opinion, stating in the October 2004 General Conference:

> When needed, full repentance will require action on your part. If you are not familiar with the classic steps to repentance, such as confession and abandonment of sin, restitution, obedience, and seeking forgiveness, talk to a bishop or study a source such as President Spencer W. Kimball's masterly work *The Miracle of Forgiveness*.[7]

Compliments for the book come from other church leaders as well, including Seventy Bruce C. Hafen:

> Some of us make repentance too easy, and others make it too hard. Those who make it too easy don't see any big sins in their lives, or they believe that breezy apologies alone are enough. These people should read President Spencer W. Kimball's *The Miracle of Forgiveness*, which reviews many sins of both commission and omission. And while forgiveness is a miracle, it is not won without penitent and strenuous effort.[8]

If the book cannot be considered reliable, as its critics advocate, the LDS Church had the perfect opportunity to distance itself from it in a 2006 church manual that all members were supposed to read in 2007. Titled *Teachings of Presidents of the Church: Spencer W. Kimball*, the editors for this manual referenced *The Miracle of Forgiveness* in the historical summary and cited the book 22 times in chapter 4, which was titled "The Miracle of Forgiveness."[9] In the church manual's endnotes, *The Miracle of Forgiveness* is quoted 69 times, which makes up an incredible 12 percent of all citations found in the manual! In addition, a copy of the book sits directly below Kimball's portrait in the

Church History Museum, which is located across the street from Temple Square in downtown Salt Lake City.

## Giving Away the Book

Holding up a copy of the book as people walked by us on the corner of a public street near the temple, I (Eric) proclaimed, "A free copy of Spencer W. Kimball's *The Miracle of Forgiveness* to anyone who will read it." We found that most Mormons—especially those who were born before 1980—owned the book or at least had seen it. The offer of a complimentary book written by an LDS prophet had given us a platform from which to engage those walking by.

For the rest of the afternoon, we further developed our spiel that went something like this:

> Free copy of *The Miracle of Forgiveness*. President Kimball wrote this book as an apostle, the same position of authority as Peter and Paul. He then became the twelfth president of the church who maintained the accuracy of the book, and it has been recommended several times at General Conference.

We noticed that passersby would listen and were often intrigued. That day we gave away three or four copies, a small investment for the dozen or more conversations that took place with those who were curious about this strategy.

As we drove home, we stopped by several Deseret Industries (DI) thrift stores—owned and operated by the LDS Church—and bought a half dozen more copies. Since then, it has not been unusual to walk into any DI store in Utah and Idaho and find three or four copies costing no more than two dollars each. We estimate that, between 2014–2017, we have purchased a total of more than five hundred copies and handed these out at a variety of LDS events.

For example, with huge crowds passing by us as they walk to the biannual General Conference outside Temple Square, we typically give away 40 or more copies in just a few hours! Each copy has our favorite sections highlighted and includes a copy of an 8.5 x 11-inch back-to-back tract that we wrote.[10] Also included is a "million-dollar bill" with Kimball's portrait on the front.[11] In 2015, we purchased the URL www.TheMiracleofForgiveness.com and posted additional information on this site.

Meanwhile, the number of conversations that happen because we offer a free LDS book makes this strategy invaluable. It has become our personal favorite tactic in public evangelism at Mormon events.

## Conversations on the Street

As mentioned in the introduction to this section of the book, in deep-sea fishing, chumming is taking bits of broken fish or anchovies and throwing them into the water to attract sport fish. The bits of food attract the fish, making them want to bite anything in the area in a way they otherwise would not. In spiritual terms, giving away a free book is spiritual chum.

Over the next few outings, we expanded our approach. For instance, we produced a two-sided, handheld poster featuring a picture of the book on both sides while advertising "Free Book!" Holding up this sign allows those approaching from a distance to see what we're offering. As we invite people to receive a copy as they pass by, we get three common reactions:

1. *They ignore the offer:* This happens about 85 percent of the time. Still, many are listening. Can you imagine the conversations that occur after families get out of our earshot? "Mom, why are they giving away a copy of *our* leader's book?" Or, "Honey, don't we have a copy of that at home? Maybe we should read it."

2. *They request a free copy:* This happens about 1-2 percent of the time. Before handing a copy to a Mormon, we explain that we are evangelical Christians who think every Latter-day Saint should have the opportunity to read this important book. All we ask is that they read it.

3. *They tell us they already own the book:* This happens the rest of the time and is our favorite response. When they say they have read it, without missing a beat, we say, "Wonderful. Are you doing what Kimball said you should do?" There are three typical responses:

   - About 50 percent ignore this question.
   - About 40 percent say no or of course not.
   - About 10 percent say yes.

Of course, there's not much we can say to those who ignore the question. For those who say that they are not following Kimball's teaching, we usually compliment the respondent and say out loud for everyone to hear, "It appears he/she *really has* read it!" It is a confirmation that nobody can do what Kimball said must be done: keep *all* the commandments *all* the time. Meanwhile, those who reply to the question in the affirmative usually do so in a joking manner, as it's not uncommon for the claimant to flex his/her muscles. We then remind the person how Kimball responds to the question "Doesn't that take a superman?" He writes on page 286 that "We are commanded to be superman" before quoting Matthew 5:48 ("Be ye therefore perfect…").[12]

Matthew 5:48 is also cited on pages 208-209 under the subtitle "Repentant Life Seeks Perfection":

> Eternal life hangs in the balance awaiting the works of men. This progress toward eternal life is a matter of achieving perfection. Living all the commandments guarantees total forgiveness of sins and assures one of exaltation through that perfection which comes by complying with the formula the Lord gave us. In his Sermon on the Mount he made the command to all men: "Be ye therefore perfect, even as your Father which is in heaven is perfect" (Matt. 5:48). Being perfect means to triumph over sin. This is a mandate from the Lord. He is just and wise and kind. He would never require anything from his children which was

> not for their benefit and which was not attainable. Perfection therefore is an achievable goal.

Almost all Latter-day Saints who respond admit that they are not keeping all the commandments. With that, they often give one of the three following excuses to deflect the problem.

### *"I'm trying."*

The most popular comeback is "I'm trying" or "I'm doing my best." However, the commands given by God are doable, as Kimball says on page 164 of his book. He relates a fictional conversation between an army officer and a soldier. The officer orders the soldier to take a message to another officer. Three times the soldier promises he will "try," "do the best" he can, and "do it or die." Each time the officer reprimands him, concluding, "Now, the request is a reasonable one; the message is important; the distance is not far; you are able-bodied; you can do what I have ordered. Now get out of here and accomplish your mission." Kimball explains on pages 164-165:

> *Trying Is Not Sufficient.* Nor is repentance complete when one merely tries to abandon sin...To try is weak. To "do the best I can" is not strong. We must always do *better* than we can. This is true in every walk of life.

### *"That's why we have repentance."*

Kimball references Doctrine and Covenants 58:43, which says, "By this ye may know if a man repenteth of his sins—behold, he will confess them and *forsake* them" (emphasis added). Saying that repentance is efficacious only when the sin is not repeated, he teaches on pages 324-325:

> Your Heavenly Father has promised forgiveness upon total repentance and meeting all the requirements, but that forgiveness is not granted merely for the asking. There must be works—many works—and an all-out, total surrender, with a great humility and "a broken heart and a contrite spirit."

> It depends upon you whether or not you are forgiven, and when. It could be weeks, it could be years, it could be centuries before that happy day when you have the positive assurance that the Lord has forgiven you. That depends on your humility, your sincerity, your works, your attitudes.

Toward the end of the 369-page book, Kimball references Alma 13:11-12 and explains on pages 354-55 that

> repentance which merits forgiveness...is that the former transgressor must have reached a "point of no return" to sin wherein there is not merely a renunciation but also a deep abhorrence of the sin—where the sin becomes most distasteful to him and where the desire or urge to sin is cleared out of his life.

An LDS Church manual uses a citation by Kimball to explain how repentance means not doing the sin again:

> But President Kimball warned: "Even though forgiveness is so abundantly promised there is no promise nor indication of forgiveness to any soul who does not totally repent....We can hardly be too forceful in reminding people that they cannot sin and be forgiven and then sin again and again and expect repeated forgiveness" (*The Miracle of Forgiveness*, 353, 360). Those who receive forgiveness and repeat the sin are held accountable for their former sins (see D&C 82:7; Ether 2:15).[13]

While an attitude of not wanting to sin again is an *admirable* goal, it is not *realistic*. Even the apostle Paul struggled with sin, writing in Romans 7:15, "I do not understand my own actions. For I do not do what I want, but I do the very thing I hate."

### *"I can do it later."*

Many Mormons assume there will be a chance to repent after death. Kimball disagreed. He quotes Alma 34:32, which says, "This life is the time for men to prepare to meet God; yea, behold the day of this life is the day for men to perform their labors." Writing on page 10 of his book, Kimball explains how "*the time to act is now, in this mortal life.* One cannot with impunity delay his compliance with God's commandments." On page 210 he proclaims, "As I have indicated previously, the time to do this is now, in mortality." Referring to a quote from Joseph Smith, Kimball explains on page 248, "*While in this probation* and *in this life* certainly mean the period of our mortal lives." On page 249, he speaks of those who "procrastinated the day of their preparation" by saying,

> The Lord's program is unchangeable. His laws are immutable. They will not be modified. Your opinion or mine does not alter the laws. Many in the world, and even some in the Church, seem to think that eventually the Lord will be merciful and give them the unearned blessing. But the Lord cannot be merciful at the expense of justice.

Kimball lays out an impossible goal.[14]

## Conclusion

How well does this strategy work? One Latter-day Saint who read the book we provided says that it caused him to leave Mormonism. We know others who have been greatly troubled by what they read in this classic work. The tactic does not require you to give the book away. Instead, the Christian could read a copy and highlight important quotes.[15] Then tell your Latter-day Saint friends that you have some questions about Kimball's book. Go to TheMiracleofForgiveness.com for more ideas.

If the Mormon disagrees with Kimball's words, ask, "Wasn't Kimball a prophet, seer, and revelator? If this book can't be trusted, what else did Kimball say that should no longer be considered true?" These questions put the Latter-day Saint in a precarious position, especially since many passages found in the LDS scriptures as well as citations from Mormon leaders seem to support Kimball's message.[16] Shouldn't that be even more bothersome to Latter-day Saints?

---

*Eric Johnson (Sandy, Utah) ministers full time with Mormonism Research Ministry (www.mrm.org). He has coauthored* Answering Mormons' Questions *(Kregel, 2012) and* Mormonism 101 *(Baker, 2015) with Bill McKeever. He has also penned* Mormonism 101 for Teens *(MRM, 2016). Eric received his master's of divinity from Bethel Seminary San Diego in 1991 and spent nearly two decades in secondary and college education.*

---

*Randy Sweet (Sandy, Utah) volunteers at Mormonism Research Ministry. He regularly evangelizes at a number of outreaches, including LDS summer pageants around the United States as well as at Temple Square, the biannual General Conferences in Salt Lake City, Utah, and various temple open house events. His wife, Carol, is in charge of the MRM prayer ministry.*

20

# Website Advertising
## The Sign Approach

ROB SIVULKA


### Summary

How is it possible to grab the attention of Mormons who are attending their church's General Conference sessions or on their way to any of their other gathering places? What if there were a way to plant a seed in the mind or put a pebble in the shoes of those who may be questioning their faith to encourage them to do further research online? Holding up website signs is one option for an effective witness.


### Introduction

At the end of 2011, LDS Church Historian and Recorder Marlin Jensen admitted that those in the Mormon leadership were aware that members were "leaving in droves." The primary culprit, he said, was what they were finding on the Internet. "My own daughter," he added, "has come to me and said, 'Dad, why didn't you ever tell me that Joseph Smith was a polygamist?'" For the younger generation, Jensen acknowledged, "Everything's out there for them to consume if they want to Google it."[1]

Consequently, I value public advertising for my two websites—MormonInfo.org and JosephLied.com—for two primary reasons.[2] First, since I am a full-time Christian missionary in the state of Utah, I certainly desire to see Mormons leave this organization and be steered toward biblical Christian churches. I love Mormons and am concerned for their spiritual welfare.

Second, I advertise my sites so more people will become inoculated from joining the LDS Church. I love everyone else enough to warn them about the errors of Mormonism. While there are many reasons people convert to this religion, they are less likely to do so when presented with a more complete picture of what it is about. To make my point, the Mormon missionaries would never say the following to someone on the other side of the screen door:

> We are Christians...except we hold that our Heavenly Father is a man who became exalted to Godhood by following some other god before Him. In fact, there is not a God anywhere who literally created all things. Each god had to get a wife (or perhaps wives) and become sealed to her (them) in a temple ceremony and then spiritually birth humans in a spiritual kingdom. Then those spirit children are sent to another planet (in our case, Earth) to be born with more tangible bodies of flesh and bone to prove their own worthiness and return to their God someday. As such, every child has the potential to become gods of their own worlds and start the cycle all over again for their own spirit-children, from whom they will receive exclusive worship.[3]

I could give many other examples, but I think my point is clear.[4] Once they receive the appropriate information, those with a biblical Christian background may (but not always) be repelled. Such a full-disclosure policy at least provides a reason or two for reconsideration.

Of course, people typically strive to obtain full information when dealing with temporal things. For example, I once considered purchasing a truck from a smooth-talking private owner. On the surface, everything seemed right. Before the purchase, he allowed me to take the vehicle to a trusted friend who is a mechanic. He said everything was fine except for one major problem: the axle was insecure. It was not only dangerous, but it would require an expensive repair.

People don't always appreciate getting correct information; when I told the seller about this detail, he began to act rudely. I have been approached on the public streets on many occasions and dismissively told that the information on my websites is nothing more than "anti-Mormon." A common complaint is, "You wouldn't listen to a Ford dealer tell you all the problems with Chevys."

To the contrary! In fact, because I am open-minded, I'll check out other resources that have taken the time to do the necessary research. In effect, my website is the *Consumer Reports* for checking out the claims of Mormonism. Shouldn't Latter-day Saints or "investigators" (those who are considering joining the LDS Church) put more time into verifying a spiritual decision that is for eternity than researching a can opener or even an expensive car?

There is nothing wrong and everything commendable about being as objective as possible, especially in the most important decisions of life. Unfortunately, today's Mormon leadership discourages investigators from hearing all sides prior to making their decision.[5] Brigham Young University professor Robert Millet teaches Mormons to give investigators "the milk before the meat."[6] Nonetheless, consider the words of Brigham Young, who said, "Our doctrine and practice is, and I have made it mine through life—to receive truth no matter where it comes from."[7] He also said in a flamboyant way, "Take up the Bible, compare the religion of the Latter-day Saints with it, and see if it will stand the test."[8]

One may think these two primary reasons for sign advertising should suffice. Yet many well-meaning Christians, including some former Mormons, needlessly worry about offending LDS sensitivities. Some Christian leaders, as well as other Christian friends, have expressed their reservations of my methods. They have called my methods sensationalistic and destructive to the friendly relationships they have been cultivating with Mormons over the years. These Christians think we can "attract more flies with honey rather than vinegar," as the old saying goes, and that the "shaking the beehive" (the state symbol of Utah) will produce a lot of angry bees. One author and friend of mine wrote me this:

> I admire your devotion to the Christian cause; however, [I] have always felt that you come on too bombastically with signs that, for example, say "Joseph Smith lied." I respectfully suggest that that method is not going to win converts at all. It immediately puts Mormons on the defense. You need something more invitational that will produce congenial dialogue.[9]

My friend may have a point if my sign simply said, "Joseph Smith lied." The only information conveyed with that is what I personally think of Smith. In that case, why should anyone else care? However, my sign displays a website—JosephLied.com—and as such, it conveys more information than simply my attitude toward Smith.

But let's assume that JosephLied.com is really what was meant. In that case, why must congenial dialogue be the priority rather than giving the masses something they won't forget to look up later in the comfort of privacy? While I am for friendly dialogues and lifestyle evangelism, should these approaches hold the monopoly on all evangelism? This person's priority need not be mine. Finally, the idea that my "method is not going to win converts at all" has happily proven untrue, as I will soon demonstrate with real testimonies.

## Do Website Signs Work?

Occasionally I drive by a local pizzeria that hires someone to stand on the sidewalk next to a busy street. He plays air guitar—technically on a cardboard-cutout guitar with the pizza company's name on it—and dances like a madman. Some observers might say he is rather obnoxious while others may dismiss him with laughter. Why does the owner pay this man to do this? For the same reason millions of dollars are expended on 30-second Super Bowl ads. Advertisers know a memorable spot in front of a large crowd will have a huge payoff.

Furthermore, many memorable ads are controversial; controversy sells. People will talk about it, keeping the attention on the product. Some may not like the sales pitch and might even be repelled, but others will at least consider the product, including those who were initially repelled.

Just like the pizza sidewalk salesman, a person who holds a Christian website sign on a busy street is involved in "sales." While holding up my sign, I don't need to be silly. But I can smile, wave to the passing cars, and politely greet bystanders, encouraging them to do further research by visiting the site. My very presence at a Mormon event, such as a temple open house (which sometimes lasts three or four weeks preceding the opening of newly built or remodeled temples), may cause someone to take another look at a religion that many consider mainstream.

Holding signs for crowds is a head-scratcher for some. Yet as Jesus says in Matthew 10:16, "Be wise as serpents but innocent as doves." Common sense needs to play a major role in any strategy. Just as the pizza salesman probably doesn't play his air guitar in front of his family or friends, I don't stand outside my relatives' or neighbors' homes holding a website sign. As Solomon put it in Ecclesiastes 3:1, "For everything there is a season, and a time for every matter under heaven."

The assumption that website signs are not effective is simply mistaken. Using Google Analytics to check the stats, I find that the number of visits to my websites typically skyrockets wherever I hold up my sign. For example, I went to the Hartford, Connecticut, temple open house from October 12 to 18, 2016. From October 1 to 11, the analytics showed only 3 visits to my website from Connecticut; in the surrounding states of Massachusetts and New York, there were only 4 and 17, respectively. However, during the short duration of my trip, there were a total of 1,393 visits from Connecticut, 228 from Massachusetts, and 394 from New York! During this time, Connecticut produced more hits than any other state. Yes, advertising does work!

## Testimonies for This Approach

Over the years, I have collected numerous testimonies that have encouraged me to continue doing what I do. Here is one such example:

> Rob, this is awkward to say, but I just wanted to thank you for your evangelizing efforts...Don't ever give up or get discouraged! After all, it was a picture of you holding

> the sign JosephLied.com that started my search, though I really just wanted to know why you were so angry with the Mormons.[10]

It is not unusual for people who see my sign to file the names of the sites away until they are open enough to begin researching. Some seed germinates faster than others, and some trees bear fruit much sooner than others. And some may take many years. I recall someone taking eight years to tell me that they saw me outside the Newport Beach Temple in 2005! This person looked it up at the time and put it on the mental shelf. Sometime in 2013 that shelf came tumbling down, and the person thanked me for planting the seeds of truth.

Another former Latter-day Saint said that he wanted to talk to me at an LDS event but his friends wouldn't let him. When he got home, he looked at the site and stated how "God opened my eyes to the truth about Mormonism." He later became a Christian! Keep in mind that the site name "JosephLied.com" is not easily forgotten, and for those who see the lighted sign, it literally burns on the retinas!

Some have seen me advertising and have written to simply thank me for helping them leave the LDS Church, even getting their names removed from the membership role. But others seeing my sign have thanked me with tears for helping them remove the blinders and now really getting to know the Savior.

## Justifying Offense

As if these notes aren't enough, some still claim that my strategy is nothing more than a pragmatic approach, which means that even if it works, it may still contradict clear biblical commands. Some Christians fear offending LDS sensitivities and the risk of being disrespectful.

While I understand their concerns, these critics forget how controversial Jesus was along with His disciples. There is a reason Jesus was beaten and crucified after all. Besides the religious leaders of His day, Jesus offended many people, including His disciples and members of His own family. While He was "a friend of sinners," this never kept Him from telling others the truth in the loving way they needed to hear it.

The apostles were threatened and beaten for their stand with Christ, even dying for proclaiming the controversial message of Jesus. Acts 24:5 and Philippians 1:13-17 show how Paul caused riots and was jailed for the defense of the gospel. Second Corinthians 11:16-33 explains how the apostle was beaten and stoned on several occasions (some of which are documented in the book of Acts) for speaking the truth.

We must not forget the biblical commands for the watchman to warn (Ezekiel 33:2-6), to "go therefore and make disciples of all nations" and "teaching them to observe all that I [Jesus] have commanded you" (Matthew 28:19-20), to "contend for the faith that was once for all delivered to the saints" (Jude 3), to "destroy arguments and every lofty opinion raised against the knowledge of God" (2 Corinthians 10:5), and to "preach the word...reprove, rebuke, and exhort, with complete patience and teaching" (2 Timothy 4:2). We minimize God's Word when we are not faithfully teaching it. Every day I am teaching and warning people all over the world through the Internet.

The late Walter Martin, a pioneer in researching cults, famously said, "Controversy for the sake of controversy is sin, but controversy for the sake of truth is a divine command." He also said,

> Controversy is part and parcel of the Christian heritage. You cannot escape it if you really want to serve Jesus Christ. The only way you can avoid controversy as a Christian is never to say anything except that which people want to hear. No one wants to hear they're lost. No one wants to hear there is eternal judgment. No one wants to hear about meeting Christ as the Judge instead of the Savior; yet this is precisely what the Church is committed to preaching.[11]

Unfortunately, the critics of this approach are often willing to allow this politically correct culture to unduly influence them. This mindset prioritizes everyone to get along at the expense of truth. While people are walking quietly on their broad road to eternal separation from God, this attitude is wholly unbiblical. Both elements of Ephesians 4:15 always need to be kept in mind: "speaking the truth in love." Using website signs in evangelism has not only worked for me, but is also very much in line with the biblical mandate found in the Great Commission: going out into all the world and sharing the gospel message the lost so desperately need.[12]

## Conclusion

I won't argue that we should *always* win unbelievers over with words. In fact, 1 Peter 3:1 gives an example of the believing wife winning her unbelieving husband without using a word. I also won't argue that "anything goes" in our evangelistic tactics. First Peter 3:15 is clear that we are to be gentle and respectful relative to God's standards, not *merely* others' emotional standards. With that said, using website signs in evangelism to Mormons is a legitimate means of bringing others to Christ and can be used by anyone who wants an effective way to share the truth.

---

*Rob Sivulka (West Jordan, Utah) is president of Courageous Christians United based in West Jordan, Utah. He holds four degrees in biblical and theological studies, philosophy, and philosophy of religion and ethics from Biola University, Talbot School of Theology, and San Diego State University. He has also studied at the University of Oxford, the University of Strasbourg, and the University of Utah.*

# Spotlight

## STEVE DEALY

*Just down the block from the Nauvoo (Illinois) temple lies the Nauvoo Christian Visitors Center (NCVC), a ministry managed by Steve Dealy. He has been involved with Christian ministry to Mormons for more than two decades.*

**Eric and Sean: Why is Nauvoo an important city for the Mormon people?**

Steve: Nauvoo was a Mormon boomtown of the early 1840s. Situated on a horseshoe bend of the Mississippi River, it served as a refuge for the Latter-day Saints following a time of intense conflict with the people of Western Missouri. Today it is considered the "Jerusalem" of the LDS faith because it was here where Joseph Smith completed his earthly mission. Nauvoo represents a short, pivotal season of peace and prosperity for Smith in which he completed laying the foundation of the young Mormon faith. Within six years of its meteoric rise, the Mormons abandoned Nauvoo.

**Eric and Sean: What is the purpose of the center you run?**

Steve: In the 1980s, a group of Christians opened the Nauvoo Christian Visitors Center (NCVC) in the historic Mormon village as an information and ministry center. Today it continues to serve as a voice for biblical Christianity. Unlike the other visitors centers already in operation in Nauvoo, the NCVC was created to present an evangelical Christian perspective of Nauvoo and its important religious history. A nineteenth-century storefront was purchased to house the center located just two blocks from the rebuilt Mormon temple that opened in 2002. Today it serves as a voice for biblical Christianity in a town that is very Mormon oriented. Tourists are able to pick up maps and sight-seeing information as well as Christian literature, music, books, and DVDs. We also show educational and gospel films.

**Eric and Sean: Do you get many Mormon visitors?**

Steve: About half the visitors are Mormon. Some drop in quickly to use our restroom or ask for directions and restaurant recommendations. Most accept a free copy of our evangelistic *Nauvoo Times* newspaper. Those who take the time to view our displays and resources often ask about our beliefs. Many come to Nauvoo expecting that everyone will be fellow LDS believers who hold to the same doctrines and a faith-promoting history of the town's Mormon past. Because we make ourselves accessible, we get the opportunity to have many spiritual and fruitful conversations with Mormons.

**Eric and Sean: Tell us about a recent encounter you had with a Mormon.**

Steve: Once an elderly LDS woman came to the center at about 1:30 in the morning as I was preparing for an open house scheduled for the next evening. She knocked on the door in desperation because her husband had fallen ill after they had arrived the day before. The town was shut down for the night and I was the only person she could find to ask for help. She had no cell phone or knowledge of how to find a hospital. I called the ambulance before she led me to their apartment where they allowed me to offer a prayer for his recovery. As I knelt by his bed, I overheard her tell her husband, "He's a good person." He was taken to a nearby hospital and his condition was diagnosed as dehydration. The next day, this dear couple came back to help me clean and prepare for our open house. He was feeling much better and thanked me for the prayer, but at that time they did not know I was not LDS. It turns out that he had not been feeling well upon his arrival to Nauvoo and a Mormon had given him a "blessing," saying that God would be sending him "angels." She told me that I was one of the angels that God had sent to help them. Although many Mormons in the town told them not to trust me, they saw me in a completely different light!

---

*If you are ever in Nauvoo, Illinois, stop by and see Steve. The NCVC is located at 1340 Mulholland Street, and their phone number is 217-453-2372.*

# SECTION 6

# Salvation Approaches

As the other chapters have discussed, there are many aspects to evangelism. These include:

- Getting to know the Mormon
- Hearing what the Mormon has to say
- Understanding where the person is coming from
- Answering questions
- Asking our own questions

Now we've come to a place where we can talk about salvation and how it is possible to come into a relationship with God and Jesus as described in the Bible. Because it's impossible to give good news without first explaining the "bad news," Joel Groat shares in chapter 21 how to deliver the bad news (sin) in a way that shows how all people fall short of God's glory. Some don't want to wear a life preserver until they understand the consequence for those who don't wear them is drowning. In chapter 22, Dr. Loren Pankratz—a Utah pastor—talks about grace and what it really means. Unless this concept is understood, a Mormon will attempt to earn God's favor yet never be able to do it.

Next, John Kauer explains in chapter 23 what the word *imputation* means and shows how forgiveness of sins can come in no other way than a complete trust in the Jesus described in the Bible. Finally, Keith Walker ends the book by describing how to explain that nobody can do what Mormonism requires, using a few passages from unique LDS scripture. Mormon scriptures themselves are a powerful tool in showing the impossibility of anyone succeeding at the Mormon gospel.

21

# When Being Good Is Not Good Enough
## The Awareness-of-Sin Approach

JOEL B. GROAT


### Summary

Many Mormons see themselves as basically good people and are generally unaware of the sin chasm between them and God. When we come alongside them as fellow sinners worthy of eternal death (Romans 3:23; 6:23), we can both avoid an adversarial interaction and help them see their only hope of eternal life is exchanging their huge load of sin for the perfect righteousness of Jesus. This can only be obtained on God's terms as a gift and never on the merits of their good works.


### Introduction

The woman on the phone was unhappy and made me aware of her displeasure in very clear terms. She had just read an article in our ministry newsletter that critiqued Mormonism. She told me she knew that her church, The Church of Jesus Christ of Latter-day Saints, was true and that she was confident of her belief.

I felt prompted to ask her how much she struggled with sin. Her reply was quick and decisive: "I'm doing fine; I hardly ever sin at all." Realizing that I might never speak to her again, I asked, "When you pray during this next week, would you be willing to ask Heavenly Father to show you any sin you might have?" She replied without hesitating, "Why would I want to pray a thing like that? There would be nothing to see anyway."

Her reply saddened me, but it highlighted something that I've found common among Mormons—a superficial view of sin. This view significantly affects how Latter-day Saints understand forgiveness, guilt, and grace, and it is an obstacle to conviction and true repentance.

## The Problem

The LDS religious system does an admirable job of encouraging its members to avoid sin, especially the serious and readily noticeable sins like murder, sexual immorality, and apostasy. The church places an accompanying emphasis on the many necessary requirements for members to prove their worthiness. A teaching manual lists more than a dozen commands for keeping the Sabbath day holy. It also provides at least fifteen specific requirements for "exaltation" along with the admonition that "the time to fulfill the requirements for exaltation is now."[1]

It can inflate a person's pride to associate sin with mainly grave offenses while abiding by a checklist of externally good behaviors. This self-righteousness hinders many people from accepting *grace only* through *faith only* for salvation.

It is easy to miss this works-based aspect of LDS culture and think our main goal in evangelism is to divest the Mormon of Mormonism so he or she can "turn to Jesus and be saved." But if we think this way, we may miss opportunities to engage relationally with Mormon people. When we attack using devastating arguments as weapons that disprove the LDS religion, we could destroy a person's connection to his or her faith and ignore the deeper spiritual need. There are no winners or losers in evangelism; we should avoid paradigms that are more about "subduing the enemy" than sharing the grace and love of Jesus.

There are potential dangers in depending on information and winning arguments to prove our point. For one, it is possible to become frustrated, angry, and argumentative during the conversation. And if we "win," we run the risk of becoming prideful, arrogant, and even condescending. I have cringed when hearing fellow believers boast about how they sent the Mormons packing by "ripping apart their arguments" or "putting them in their place." Is it really a victory to win the battle for the argument while losing the war for the soul?

## The Solution

If the eternal state of the soul is the priority, a good starting point is embracing our own inability to bring about the change in heart a person needs to move from error to truth. It comes by admitting how powerless humans are to bring about their own regeneration and spiritual transformation while humbly seeking God's divine intervention on their behalf. This removes the pressure to "win" and frees us to share, regardless of how we, or our message, are received. The Mormon must be seen as a person who is a fellow bearer of the image of God rather than the enemy.

Only when this happens will our Mormon friends be in a position to realize that sinfulness starts in the heart and that no amount of good works could possibly offset the sin that separates all people from God. Our objective, then, is to help them see how focusing on externals can cause people to miss the seriousness of sin in their lives, which can keep that person from a right relationship with God.

## The Goal

The goal is to help Mormons discover the biblical view of human sinfulness for themselves. To do this, we must establish common ground to connect with them as fellow fallen humans who need Jesus. Once their self-awareness has been heightened, they can pray and ask God to show them their own spiritual need in light of His holiness. We aren't teaching or lecturing; rather, we are directing them by using questions so they can discover their true spiritual state from God's perspective.

## The Opener

One straightforward approach is to ask the Mormon if it's important to keep the commandments. Commandment keeping is an integral part of the LDS system and is understood to be essential for eternal life. This question, therefore, is familiar and nonthreatening. Most likely the response will be an emphatic *yes*. This is a perfect time to tell the story of the rich young ruler who came to Jesus asking about how to obtain eternal life.

## The Progression

Go to Matthew 19:16-22 and read the account, pointing out that this man was seeking eternal life. From here a series of questions, such as the ones below, can allow the Spirit to teach through the pages of the Bible. (Note: The order these questions are used does not matter.) Take the time to listen carefully to the answers.

- *Did the young man think he was doing well? Upon what did he base his confidence?* The young man thought he was fulfilling his duty by keeping the commandments of God.
- *What are the Ten Commandments?* These are found in Exodus 20:1-17; turn here if the person is struggling to come with all of them to help them avoid embarrassment.
- *What did Jesus teach about keeping these commandments?* Read Matthew 5:21-22, 27-28. Let your friend see that successful commandment keeping begins in the heart... and that is where commandment breaking starts as well.
- *What does God want from His saints?* Contrast the external commandment keeping with the internal. Psalm 51:6 says, "Behold, you delight in truth in the inward being, and you teach me wisdom in the secret heart." Jesus said in Matthew 12:34: "You brood of vipers! How can you speak good, when you are evil? For out of the abundance of the heart the mouth speaks."
- *Did the young man have an inward or outward righteousness? Had he truly kept all the commandments?* Stay here for as long as necessary to identify the real problem of the rich young man—he had substituted external commandment keeping for true purity of heart.

- *Was God impressed with the rich young man?* The answer, most emphatically, is *no*.

## Getting Personal

Up to this point, the discussion has probably been comfortably impersonal. But hopefully you have established common ground with a mutually agreed-upon understanding of these passages. Rather than sparring, this conversation allows a Christian and a Mormon to pursue truth together. Now it's possible to become more personal with the following questions while remembering to listen and remaining open to how the Holy Spirit can direct the conversation.

- Do you think you have ever been like the rich young man?
- Do you think being unrepentant can hinder our relationship with God? Can it keep us from closeness to God?
- If you sincerely ask God to show you the sin that might be hindering your relationship with Heavenly Father, do you think He would show it to you so you could confess it?
- Have you ever asked God to show you your own sinfulness and waited quietly for an answer?

This might be the perfect opportunity to share your own personal testimony. Like many of us, Mormons are attracted to personal stories of moving spiritual experiences. Explaining how you felt when you returned to God after a time of confession and repentance can have a profound effect on the listener. Maybe even share a time when you were like the rich young ruler, so the Mormon knows this is an issue you have worked through personally. This might even prompt them to share their story. If so, please don't dismiss or negate this experience simply because they are Mormon. The goal is to establish common ground; whether they realize it or not, they may demonstrate that an experience with the Holy Spirit is not limited to Mormons.

These personal questions can help lead you to that last question: *Would praying for God to show you your sinfulness be something you would seriously consider doing?* If the answer is yes, encourage your friend to do it that night and to come back another time to share with you what God has shown him or her. You could even volunteer to do the same.

## Taking the Sum of Our Sins

Another way to heighten awareness of sin is to ask Latter-day Saints what separates human beings from God. Or, are they even aware of how much sin stands between them and God? Most have no idea. Feel free to use a piece of paper to demonstrate the math and help a Mormon understand the following point.

> *Let's say a child starts sinning at age five and from five to nine years old only commits four sins per day. Is that a reasonable amount?*
>
> Have some fun with this dialogue. For example, I'll share that my kids were pretty good, but they could accumulate three sins in three minutes at bedtime.
>
> *So, four sins per day times five days per week (we're giving nights and weekends free from sin) equals 20 per week multiplied by 50 weeks in a year (two weeks a year vacation from sin) equals 1,000 sins per year. From ages five to nine a child will accumulate approximately 5,000 sins.*
>
> *From ages 10-14, let's agree that more sins will happen—after all, these are the junior-high years. Let's make it eight sins per day.*
>
> I've never had anyone say eight sins a day was too many, but I've had people say that eight was far too few.
>
> *So, 8 sins each day times 5 days a week (yes, we are still giving weekends sin-free) is 40 sins per week multiplied by 50 weeks (junior high kids need vacation too) equals 2,000 sins per year. In this five-year period, a child accumulates 10,000 sins. That may sound like a lot, but let's not dwell on that for now.*
>
> *Now for the teen years—ages 15 to 19—eight sins per day just seems far too few. My kids could burn through eight sins before*

> *lunchtime. And these are usually more serious sins. With that in mind, let's use 16 sins per day for this epoch in their lives.*
>
> *So, 16 sins per day, five days per week—yes, I know teenagers sin far more on the weekends, but we're still giving them weekends sin-free—that's 80 sins per week. And teenagers will never stand for losing their two weeks of vacation, so we are still at 50 weeks, which comes to 4,000 sins per year. During this five-year period, about 20,000 sins have been committed.*
>
> Pause—let that sink in.
>
> *So that's 35,000 sins accumulated before age 20. If we go another five years, we've added an additional 20,000 sins, which brings us to 55,000 sins by age 25. Now, do you think that is an exaggerated or unrealistic assessment?*

Again, I want to be clear: In many years of using this illustration with Mormons of different ages, church positions, and ethnicities, *nobody* has ever challenged the way I counted the sins!

With that, ask a few key questions:

> *Do you think this is also true of you? I know it's true of me.*

After getting an affirmative answer, I ask:

> *How many of those sins have you confessed? How many of them do you even remember so you could confess them? And is it possible you have sinned and didn't even know it, making it impossible to repent?*

Silence here is your friend. Pray that it sinks in.

## Follow-up Conviction with Questions

A Christian friend in Peru asked me to speak to his elderly LDS mother. I was prompted by the Spirit to walk through the sin-counting exercise with her. She was over 80, so when the sum hit 55,000 by the age of 25, she said quietly, "*Estoy condenada*" (I am condemned). This is where we want the Spirit to bring people—to a place where they feel the weight of their own sin.

From here, the conversation can go any number of directions, but I try to ask some variation of these questions:

- *With that much sin on your account, do you think you could ever do enough good works to tip the scales in your own favor?*
- *If God the Father is perfect, and we need to be perfect to be worthy to live in His presence, can we ever hope to do enough to offset a life of accumulating sin?*

Depending on the answers to these questions and the openness of the person, I may ask,

- *If there were a way you could get rid of every sin you've ever committed or ever will commit so you could stand perfect before Heavenly Father, would you want to know it?*

Unless I get a clear and convincing *yes* to this question, I won't share the gospel. But if the Mormon is open, I explain how God is willing to take every sin that a person has committed and trade them for the perfect righteousness of Jesus. Key verses that highlight this exchange are 1 Peter 2:21-25; Isaiah 53:6; and 2 Corinthians 5:17-21.

Regarding the elimination of all their sin, I have had Mormons tell me how they were forgiven when they were baptized into the LDS Church. While this is a Mormon teaching about a person's status at the time of the baptism, other doctrines make it clear that the only way a Mormon can receive forgiveness of sins after his baptism is through *repentance,* which involves confession, forsaking, restitution, and keeping the commandments.[2]

The goal is to make a person aware of the pervasiveness of sin and the affront it is to a holy God. Jesus told the story of the Pharisee and the tax collector who went to the temple to pray in Luke 18:9-14, concluding that it was the tax collector, not the Pharisee, who went home justified (a term meaning "declared righteous") when he cried out, "God, be merciful to me, a sinner!"

Forgiveness, justification, and eternal life can only be obtained as *gifts*—freely given by God and freely received by believers in faith. True faith is in the character of the Giver (God) and the trust that He will do what He said. It is important at some point to help the Mormon realize that any attempt to use commandment keeping to *earn* God's acceptance and forgiveness is an act of *unbelief*. In fact, it is an affront to God the Father who has already paid for the gift with the blood of His Son Jesus (Titus 3:3-8; 1 John 1:7-10).

I've used the following example to illustrate the offense of earning or paying for a gift: Suppose my millionaire aunt gave me a new car. I'm grateful, so I tell her that while I could never hope to pay her back, I'll do her yardwork every Saturday for the next ten years and pay her ten dollars a week. The car is such an expensive gift, how could I possibly take it for free? I ask the person, "Would my aunt appreciate that my actions seem to be more of an act of repayment rather than mere gratitude for her gift?"

In the course of discussing awareness of sin with our Mormon friends, we may find it appropriate to ask related questions such as the following:

- *Could we ever do enough to have God owe us anything?*
- *Do any of us on any day ever do "the very best we can"? If we don't, what are the implications in light of God's holiness and demand for perfection? (See Matthew 5:48.) You can contrast this with the Book of Mormon scripture that says, "We know that it is by grace that we are saved, after all we can do" (2 Nephi 25:23).*
- *How wide is the gulf created by your sinful heart that separates you from your Heavenly Father?*
- *Have you ever thought that verses about sinfulness—such as Isaiah 53:6; 64:6; and Romans 3:10-12—apply to you?*
- *What does 2 Corinthians 5:21 mean in this light?*

Discussions with Mormons must be humble and Spirit-led in an atmosphere of discovering truth together. Rather than being critical adversaries, we can become friends and allies in a common quest for truth.

---

*Joel B. Groat (Grand Rapids, Michigan) received his MTS in New Testament from Grand Rapids Theological Seminary in Michigan. He is currently the director of ministries at the Institute for Religious Research (IRR.org) where he has served for the past 30 years. Joel authored the Spanish DVD course* La Fe de Mi Prójimo (My Neighbor's Faith).

22

# Can Something Valuable Really Be Free?
## The Meaning-of-Grace Approach

DR. LOREN PANKRATZ


### Summary

The definition of *grace* in Mormonism is different from what the Bible teaches. Mormons are taught that grace is nothing more than God's "enabling power" to help them keep commandments in order to qualify for exaltation. However, by using the example of Abraham and the teaching of Paul, Christians can explain a clear scriptural understanding of God's grace.


### Introduction

After leading many mission trips into Utah as the college pastor of a church in California, my wife and I concluded that if we really wanted to see the spiritual landscape change in the Beehive state, we needed to plant communities of salt and light in towns and cities where there were no Christian churches.[1] Thus, we moved to Utah in 2010 and launched The Bridge Community in Centerville, Utah, on April 3, 2011.

I recall many conversations in the early days of ministry where I left frustrated because a Mormon seemed to agree with everything I had said about the gospel of grace. I learned that in order to minister to LDS members, I needed to gain a better understanding of different ways we use the same words. I ultimately wrote my doctoral dissertation in 2012 contrasting saving grace as defined by the Bible versus the grace preached by Mormon leadership.

During my study, I discovered important distinctions that have aided my ministry with Mormons. I believe that a Christian's ability to successfully share the good news with Mormons will improve when he or she fully grasps these differences in order to discuss them in evangelistic conversations. Let's compare and contrast the biblical and Mormon views of grace before offering a practical strategy for having conversations with Mormons about grace.

## What Is Everyone's Problem?

To begin, we must start at the fall of humanity. Romans 3:23 says everyone has sinned and comes short of what God expects, which is complete obedience. The result of this is eternal death, as Romans 6:23 adds.

Mormonism offers a much different view by teaching that God procreated spiritual children in a celestial abode called the preexistence. He intends these spirits to gain bodies and come to this earth so they can become "exalted" as gods like him. Adam and Eve transgressed by disobeying something that was formally prohibited, yet in Mormonism this act is not considered a sin because they did not do something inherently wrong.[2]

According to 2 Nephi 2:25 in the Book of Mormon, "Adam fell that men might be; and men are, that they might have joy." Prior to the fall, the following four statements were true of Adam and Eve, according to Mormonism:

1. They had an *intimate* relationship with God.
2. They were *immortal.*
3. They were *innocent* with no capacity for good or evil, joy or sorrow.
4. They were *incapable* of multiplying in their pre-fallen state.

God had instructed Adam and Eve to be fruitful and multiply as well as refrain from eating from the Tree of Life. According to Mormonism, this put Adam and Eve in a catch-22 situation. One church teacher's manual explains it this way:

> Explain that Adam and Eve could not keep both these commandments. If they chose to eat the fruit, they would be cast out of the Garden of Eden. But if they did not eat the fruit and remained in the garden, they would not be able to have children (to "multiply and replenish the earth"). Because the Garden of Eden was a place of innocence, while Adam and Eve lived there they could not change or progress in any way, including having children.[3]

Mormon leaders have taught that Adam and Eve chose to eat the fruit in order to prioritize God's command to be fruitful and multiply. Tenth president Joseph Fielding Smith remarked, "So don't let us, brethren and sisters, complain about Adam and wish he hadn't done something that he did. I want to thank him."[4] Smith also said the "fall of man came as a blessing in disguise, and was the means of furthering the purposes of the Lord in the progress of man, rather than a means of hindering them."[5]

This "fortunate fall" had consequences that are crucial to understanding the meaning of grace in Mormonism. After the fall, each of the four statements above was changed in marked ways. Humans went from being immortal to being *mortal*. Humans who were innocent were blessed with *agency*. Adam and Eve changed from being incapable of multiplying to being *descendent-capable* and from having an intimate relationship with God to being *distant*. The effects of the fall (*Mortal*, *Agency*, *Descendent-capable*, *Distant*) can be recalled by the initials MADD.

In Mormonism, humans are blessed with agency and have the ability to procreate. However, they also inherit a distant relationship with God and a life that will end at the grave, making them unable to progress to their potential to be exalted like God, where, according to

LDS Apostle Stephen L. Richards, they can become "as intelligent and omnipotent as God."[6]

## Grace According to Mormonism

Christians and Mormons both talk about grace as an "enabling power" given by God. For Christians, God's saving grace is the activity undertaken by God to save them from their sins. We received this grace from Him as a gift through faith (Ephesians 2:8-9; Philippians 3:9; Colossians 1:12-14).

Interestingly, LDS theology does not make a distinction between God's enabling grace and the grace that saves. In fact, grace never really escapes the "enabling power" dimension. The onus is on the individual to obey to qualify for exaltation, which is achieving godhood and qualifying to be with one's family forever.

Mormonism teaches that the atoning sacrifice of Jesus Christ heals the two negative effects of the fall for all humans who have ever lived. Jesus "saves" all humans from mortality and allows them to have intimacy with God. We know that people are unable to raise themselves from the dead, no matter how many good works they perform. In Mormonism, this saving work of the atonement is *universal* and *unconditional.* Mormon Apostle Jeffrey R. Holland summarized this thinking when he said,

> Some gifts coming from the Atonement are universal, infinite, and unconditional. These include His ransom for Adam's original transgression so that no member of the human family is held responsible for that sin.[7]

Thus, one of the positive effects of the fall is that humans gained agency, meaning that everyone is able to make the right choices. This creates opportunities for spiritual growth as well as the potential for spiritual death, which occurs as humans use their agency to sin. When people sin, they are kept from reaching their full potential.[8] It's as if sin damages the stairway that humans can use to climb to the peak, making it impossible to achieve the heights that God intends for them.

Mormon leaders teach that Jesus's atonement is key to fixing the staircase. This healing is *individual* and *conditional*.

Joseph Fielding Smith explained the difference between the universal/unconditional and individual/conditional healing power of the atonement:

> Redemption from the original sin is without faith or works; redemption from our own sins is given through faith and works. Both are the gifts of free grace; but while one is a gift forced upon us unconditionally, the other is a gift merely offered to us conditionally. The redemption of the one is compulsory; the reception of the other is voluntary. Man cannot, by any possible act, prevent his redemption from the fall; but he can utterly refuse and prevent his redemption from the penalty of his own sins.[9]

In Mormonism, eternal life (or exaltation) comes with many strings attached. While trusting Jesus for eternal life is necessary, it is insufficient by itself. Seventy Adhemar Damiani explained to a General Conference audience that earning eternal life depends on faithfulness to the commandments:

> Obedience is essential for us to obtain exaltation and eternal life and thus become like our Father—beings of flesh and bone, immortal, exalted, and glorified. Only then will we be heirs of all He possesses. [10]

It should be clear that, in the LDS context, the grace Jesus gives does not elevate the human to a new relationship with God; it merely fixes the staircase allowing humans the chance to climb their way to the top by their obedience. Second Nephi 31:4-20 in the Book of Mormon depicts Jesus as opening a way to eternal life, but that way is traversed by keeping God's commandments.[11]

Recent voices in the LDS Church have emphasized God's love or compassion in explaining this enabling grace. While this is refreshing to some Mormons, I have not yet seen any real shift from traditional

LDS perspectives. BYU professor Brad Wilcox gave a popular address in 2011 titled "His Grace Is Sufficient: How Does God's Grace Really Work?" where he recalls a meeting with a student who knew that she would never measure up to God's standards to merit eternal life.[12]

Wilcox gives a twofold response. First, he affirms the universal and unconditional aspects of the atonement. He says that each person's obedience in this life will determine "what kind of body we plan on being resurrected with and how comfortable we plan to be in God's presence and how long we plan to stay there."

With this response, Wilcox reinforces the traditional LDS perspective that God's grace enables a person to obey, which ultimately qualifies the individual for exaltation. Robert Millet is another Brigham Young University professor who sounds like a biblical Christian to many. But as his book *Grace Works* identifies, the enabling power of grace offered to humans is only as effective as one's obedience to their covenantal commitments.[13] Trusting Jesus's work remains insufficient for eternal life.

## Sharing the Gospel of Grace

Understanding Mormon theology regarding grace can help equip Christians to communicate the gospel effectively. When I speak about grace as a Christian, I am not referring to something that everyone receives universally and unconditionally, nor am I talking about a stairway to heaven where I can become like God through the performance of many works.

To show the Latter-day Saint what the Bible is talking about, I like to organize my conversation several ways to make my points very clear. First, I explain how God gives eternal life as a free gift. Then I explain an important Old Testament text. Finally, I show how Paul saw that text as paradigmatic for our own approach to God.

### *1. Getting the Conversation Started*

A great way to start is to ask, "What is the best part about being a Mormon?" When the Latter-day Saint answers, ask, "May I share with you what I believe to be the best part about being Christian?" I've never had a person say no. This is the perfect opportunity to talk about grace.

### *2. Pointing Out the Abrahamic Prototype*

Once I've announced that eternal life is free because of God's grace, I'll ask, "May I show you why I say that?" Genesis 15:6 explains how Abraham "believed the LORD, and he counted it to him as righteousness." It is absolutely critical that the Mormon does not interpret this text through the lens of Genesis 22 (the sacrifice of Isaac).

I once took an LDS class on the Old Testament at the Institute of Religion near the university where I lived. Following the Old Testament student manual, the teacher claimed that if Abraham had failed the test of Genesis 22, he would have "lost his position."[14] I raised my hand and asked, "Don't you think it is instructive that God gives Abraham his position in an unconditional covenant seven chapters before this 'test' in Genesis 22?"

To help the Mormon experience how radical Genesis 15:6 is, ask him or her to read Genesis 15:12-21. The Old Testament covenant ratification process involves splitting an animal into two parts and having each member of the covenant walk through the animal carcass, which signifies their fate if they did not uphold their covenantal commitments. Jeremiah 34:18 explains the consequences:

> The men who transgressed my covenant and did not keep the terms of the covenant that they made before me, I will make them like the calf that they cut in two and passed between its parts.

I've found that it is important to let the Mormon make the "discovery" that it is God, symbolized by the firepot, who passes through the carcass *alone* and commits Himself to the promises made to Abraham. To help emphasize this, I'll ask, "Who does not pass through the carcass?" Abraham does *not* pass through the carcass, meaning he has no obligations to meet to uphold God's covenant to him. Then I point out that this is a binding business contract signed by only one party: God. God's promises to Abraham were truly a gift. Explaining this, I'll say, "This is what the Bible calls 'grace.' God's favor is not something that Abraham earned." What a radical idea!

### *3. Closing the Deal*

After helping the Mormon see the radical grace involved in God's covenant with Abraham, turn to Romans 4:1-5. Verses 4 and 5 explain:

> Now to the one who works, his wages are not counted as a gift but as his due. And to the one who does not work but believes in him who justifies the ungodly, his faith is counted as righteousness.

A wage is what a person earns such as from working at a job. Ask, "Does Paul see Abraham's standing before God as a wage he earned or a gift he received?" It should be clear that Abraham was considered righteous not because of his labor but based on his faith in God. For emphasis, point out that Abraham was *justified* by grace. Then move a few verses down and read Romans 4:23-25:

> The words "it was counted to him" were not written for his sake alone, but for ours also. It will be counted to us who believe in him who raised from the dead Jesus our Lord, who was delivered up for our trespasses and raised for our justification.

Here Paul argues that Abraham is a prototype of how all humans can come to have a right standing with God. Just as Abraham believed and so inherited God's promises as a gift, so the Christian trusts the life and death of Jesus as sufficient for eternal life. Once the Mormon sees this connection, ask, "If God gave you your wage—what you've earned from your labors—do you think you'd earn God's best rewards?" Then turn to the first part of Romans 6:23 and ask, "What does the apostle Paul think our sins have earned us?" Wait for the answer ("death") and point out the second part of the verse. Ask, "What is the free gift God gives?"

When the Mormon sees how the Bible teaches that trusting Jesus is sufficient for eternal life, say, "This is incredibly good news, isn't it? Trusting Jesus is enough to receive God's graceful gift of eternal life. Does your church teach the same gospel of grace?"

As these examples show, there is a clear distinction between what the Bible explains about grace and what Mormon leaders have taught. Mormons need to be shown that trusting in Jesus alone is all that is required for eternal life. Using this method, it is possible to invite the Mormon to trust in Jesus for his or her salvation and flee any false gospel that is contrary to the grace offered through the atoning blood of Jesus (Galatians 1:8).

---

*Dr. Loren Pankratz (Centerville, Utah) graduated with a double major in religion and philosophy from Chapman University in 2001. After graduating from Princeton Theological Seminary with a master's of divinity, Loren accepted a position as college pastor at a church in Fresno, California, and in 2011, Loren planted The Bridge Community where he serves as the lead pastor. In 2012, Loren graduated from Talbot Theological Seminary with his doctor of ministry degree.*

23

# Are You Considered as Good as Jesus? The Imputation Approach

JOHN KAUER


## Summary

The Bible states that any sin will keep a person separated from God forever (John 3:36). While many people strive to attain God's righteousness, it is impossible in our fallen, sinful state. Instead, the price Jesus paid alone cleanses believers from sin, and His works are credited to Christians the moment they believe.


## Introduction

I have lived in Utah since 2008. When I visit my home state of Texas, Christians often ask, "What do you say to Mormon people when you go witnessing?" I let them know that we have not found *the* way, a silver bullet, but *a* way to get into a gospel conversation quickly and *to the point*. By "to the point," I am referring to the idea that Christianity parts ways with Mormonism, even though Latter-day Saints may claim that faith in Jesus is necessary for forgiveness of sins. However, they probably have never thought it is necessary to be perfectly righteous in the sight of God this side of the judgment seat. Getting Mormons to see beyond their superficial and works-oriented view of salvation is my goal.

I like this approach because it allows me to talk to someone about Jesus without getting into a quarrel about competing versions of Jesus. In Mormonism, Jesus does not have the power to justify sinners; He is only capable of showing the way to live as an example, as a person's own merits are ultimately needed to achieve forgiveness.[1]

Justification by faith alone and through Christ alone was the rallying cry of those who participated in the Reformation. What does it mean to be justified? And what part does Jesus play in it? Christian Reformer John Calvin wrote, "We explain justification simply as the acceptance with which God receives us into his favor as righteous men. And we say that it consists in the remission of sins and the imputation of Christ's righteousness."[2]

Justification is a legal term that means to declare a person righteous before God according to His standard, which is God's own righteousness. It is the opposite of condemnation, which is a declaration of unrighteousness and a guilty sentence. Jesus came to fulfill the law; He obeyed His Father in all things to merit righteousness for all His people. So, a person who is "born again" is *imputed*, or credited, with Christ's righteousness, and the punishment for sin is removed. All of Jesus's works are needed for a person to be considered righteous before God's sight. It is not just a state of never having sinned, which is morally neutral ground, but it is a positive record of having done everything right.

## A Dialogue with Jim

One day during the Provo City Center Temple open house[3] in January 2016, I was positioned on a public sidewalk near the busiest entry. Because the weather was so cold, I was dressed as if I were ice fishing for men. I asked the passersby, "Are you considered as good as Jesus?" No matter the answer, I offered a tract—I call them "gospel cards"—to each one. Few took me up on my offer. However, at just the right time—isn't that the way it works with a sovereign God?—a man named Jim who appeared to be in his sixties approached me and gave the common platitude that "Mormons are Christian too." What this really means is, "Why are you handing out your information at our event?" I ignored his comment and began to engage him with the gospel message.

"Are you considered as good as Jesus?" I asked with a smile. Jim was puzzled and stopped to consider my question.

"Well, no one is perfect," he replied.

"Except for Jesus, you are correct," I responded. Then I added this important phrase: "But we all have *broken His commandments*." I used the phrase "broken His commandments" instead of "sin" when referring to personal guilt. I asked, "What if God could consider you as good as Jesus today? Would that be good news?"

Jim immediately replied, "Of course it would, but it is not possible. I am not through doing all I can do. You don't think we just believe and then do nothing, do you?"

When sharing the faith, it is important to have a Bible readily available to reference appropriate verses that support the Christian position. Thus, I pulled out my copy and turned to 2 Corinthians 5:21. Holding the pages so he could follow along, I read, "For our sake he made him to be sin who knew no sin, so that in him we might become the righteousness of God." Our conversation went like this:

> **Jim:** Yes, this is what the atonement is for. We need Jesus to sacrifice Himself and pay for the sins of the world so we can return to Him.
>
> **Me:** I agree. Jesus had to die to pay for the sins of His people so that they may be forgiven, which is the same as if no commandments were broken. But is this all we need to "become the righteousness of God"? It says here that Jesus never sinned, so that would mean He always kept the law. He did everything Heavenly Father asked Him to do. Would you agree?
>
> **Jim:** Yes, Jesus never sinned.
>
> **Me:** Do you know why Jesus lived 33 years before dying on a cross? It was so He could fulfill the law on our behalf as the second Adam. He could have been put to death as an infant and still paid the penalty of sin; however, He needed to not only *die* for us, but also *live*.

Jim mumbled with a puzzled expression. At this point, I paused in the conversation to give him an opportunity to think. At the same time, I prayed, *Please, Father, let me continue. Holy Spirit, open this man's heart, ears, and eyes, so he may see Jesus high and lifted up for sinners.* There is no sense in rushing things. If God was at work, I knew Jim would remain with me until the providential end. I got out a pencil during this transition and turned to a new page in my notebook. "I will draw it out for you," I said, adding, "I am a visual person, so this may help."

At this point, I drew a cross bar and explained how the top part was an infinite righteousness while the bottom part represented infinite sin. Because a dose of humor at this point in the conversation was needed, I drew tic marks down the vertical axis as I humorously told him how everyone is a sinner, though some are better at it than others. I explained how everyone is doing some type of good works, drawing tic marks up the vertical axis (see below).

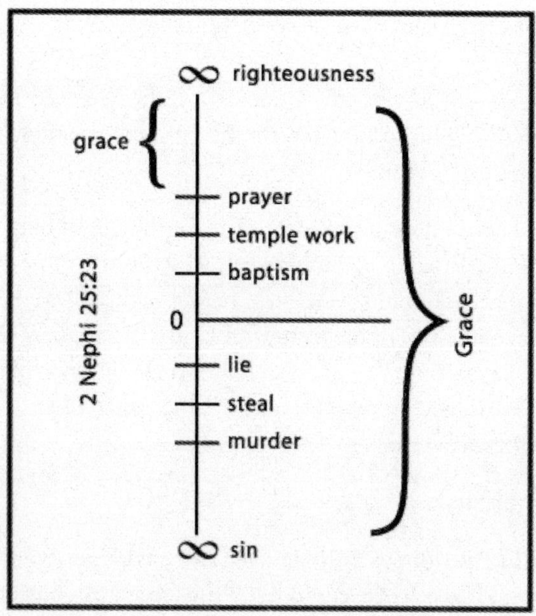


I asked, "Can you tell me some good works you have accomplished?" As Jim listed several of his honorable deeds, I wrote them on the piece of paper. I even included some additional points so he could have plenty of good works from which to choose. However, I left a significant gap at the top. Then I cited 2 Nephi 25:23 from the Book of Mormon, which says, "We know that it is by grace that we are saved, after all we can do." The conversation continued:

> **Me:** Are you *trusting* Jesus to pay for your sins [pointing to the bottom part] *if* you do all you can do [pointing to his list of works]?[4]
>
> **Jim:** Yes.
>
> **Me:** And would you agree that Jesus's grace to you is that portion you lack in perfection [pointing to the portion of the vertical line between Jim's works and infinite righteousness]?
>
> **Jim:** Exactly, you've got it!
>
> **Me:** As a review, what has Jesus done? He has suffered for the penalty of sin we all deserve, and that puts us at a morally neutral point [as I motioned to the intersection, which is 0]. However, this is not the righteousness of God, is it? We also need *His* righteous works added to our account so we would be considered as good as He is.
>
> **Jim:** Oh, now I understand your question, "Are you considered as good as Jesus?" But didn't you say that could happen right now, or something like that?
>
> **Me:** Yes, I did. And the reason we can be considered as good as Jesus right now is because I am trusting in all *His* works already done for me instead of *my* works done for me. If I may, let's think for a minute about some of the things Jesus did as He obeyed the Father. He woke up early before the sun came up and went on a hike into the woods just to pray. It would be a miracle to get me up before the sun to go on a hike to pray; but this is only the beginning. He prayed for the right things, with the right motives, for

as long as He was supposed to, and without falling asleep. Have you always prayed like that?

**Jim:** No, I have not.

**Me:** So, does the quality of Jesus's work exceed yours?

**Jim:** [reluctantly] Yes.

**Me:** Have you raised anyone from the dead, healed the blind, made the lame walk, or even preached an awesome sermon to a crowd of people who were ready to throw stones at you?

**Jim:** [chuckling] No.

**Me:** Well, then, you can see that our works are not as many or as good as Jesus's works. He has better works than we do, both quality and quantity.

Looking back to the chart, I drew an arrow from the bottom all the way to the top and asked, "Do you see how much I am trusting in Jesus?" While Jim thought about that question, I put away the notebook and reached for my Bible, turning to Romans 4:1-5. I asked, "Do you remember the big question, 'Are you considered as good as Jesus?' This is what it means to be justified before God." I then read the good news given to us by Paul:

> What then shall we say was gained by Abraham, our forefather according to the flesh? For if Abraham was justified by works, he has something to boast about, but not before God. For what does the Scripture say? "Abraham believed God, and it was counted to him as righteousness."

I looked at Jim and said, "Here it is again. 'Abraham believed God, and it was counted to him as righteousness.' God gave him a right standing the moment Abraham believed." I read verses 4 and 5:

> Now to the one who works, his wages are not counted as a gift but as his due. And to the one who does not work

> but believes in him who justifies the ungodly, his faith is counted as righteousness.

I said, "The way I see it, Jim, you are working to get paid with the little bit of Jesus's righteousness you need to top off your account. However, you could simply trust in *all* His works and receive them without working for them. Isn't this good news?" I received no answer from Jim and sensed that the discussion was ending. With nothing more to add, I turned to Philippians 3:2-9 as I made a call to repentance:

> Look out for the dogs, look out for the evildoers, look out for those who mutilate the flesh. For we are the circumcision, who worship by the Spirit of God and glory in Christ Jesus and put no confidence in the flesh—though I myself have reason for confidence in the flesh also. If anyone else thinks he has reason for confidence in the flesh, I have more: circumcised on the eighth day, of the people of Israel, of the tribe of Benjamin, a Hebrew of Hebrews; as to the law, a Pharisee; as to zeal, a persecutor of the church; as to righteousness under the law, blameless. But whatever gain I had, I counted as loss for the sake of Christ. Indeed, I count everything as loss because of the surpassing worth of knowing Christ Jesus my Lord. For his sake I have suffered the loss of all things and count them as rubbish [or, my interpretation, "poop"], in order that I may gain Christ and be found in him, not having a righteousness of my own that comes from the law, but that which comes through faith in Christ, the righteousness from God that depends on faith.

I prefer to substitute the word for *rubbish* (Greek: *skubalon*, which means "any refuse, as the excrement of animals") as *poop*. Doing so can add a little bit of levity to a tense moment. At this point, I put away the Bible and brought my notebook back out.

> **Me:** If this was Paul's chart of good works, then he would have placed them here (as I pointed to Jim's list of virtuous

> works). He considers them as poop to gain Christ's works. You see, to put on Christ's works like a robe, it is necessary to come to Him without anything on. You cannot be wearing any of your own works. You must consider them as filthy stained rags, as Isaiah 64:6 says. Can you do that?
>
> **Jim:** [not amused] What do you mean?
>
> **Me:** [pointing to his list of good works on the chart] Do you consider your temple marriage as only for this life and not for eternity? Are you willing to get baptized again because your baptism did not count? Do you consider your missionary work a waste of time? Is your priesthood authority void? Is your tithing record just a way to buy forgiveness? Will you consider it all as "poop," trading it all for Christ's perfect works?

I then let a few seconds go by before I calmly asked, "Do you see how much I am trusting in Christ? I do good works, but I am not *trusting* in them. I trust in Jesus's baptism, *His* preaching and teaching, *His* prayers and not my own. He did it better than me. I want *His* record, not mine."

Jim was either red from exposure to the cold or hot under the collar. He firmly replied, "I see your point, but works *must* have something to do with it. You cannot just say you believe and that's it. You must be baptized to be saved. You need to do your temple work. God called me on my mission." He turned to me, squaring his body with mine, and asked, "Have you ever been a Mormon?" When I told him that I hadn't, he handed back my gospel card and, just before he turned to walk away, said, "Then you just don't understand me."

That was the last time I saw Jim. He did not come back after his temple tour. He did not have any way of contacting me because he had returned the card. I will probably never know if Jim ever searched the Bible to see if these things were true. His reaction to the gospel is commonly seen here in Utah.

Perhaps you think my call to repentance in the manner that I delivered it to Jim might have been too harsh. Maybe the way I did it would not be your method. If that is true, I encourage you to use your own way of calling people to turn from trusting in their works. To me, the illustration on the paper, along with the Bible references, laid out the line I was asking Jim to cross. If God the Father were drawing him to God the Son by the power of God the Spirit, then Jim would be ready to repent of all his works and trust in Christ's works.

In whatever way it is accomplished, sharing the gospel is a worthwhile endeavor. I worshipped Jesus that day, and it was sweet. I opened my heart to let a man named Jim enter my world for a few minutes. I keep a journal where I write the names of those I've witnessed to and record a bit of information to remind me of the conversations. I often go back over the list to think about my encounters and pray for each person. My trust is in a big God who does what He wants, when He wants, and however He wants. I am privileged to be used by Him and be allowed to participate in the sharing of the gospel.

---

*John Kauer (Santaquin, Utah) is the treasurer and lead Utah evangelist for the ministry Think About Eternity (www.ThinkAboutEternity.org). John has been witnessing to Mormons since the 2002 Winter Olympic Games held in Salt Lake City. He received his BA from the University of Texas in Arlington in finance and his master's in biblical studies from Dallas Theological Seminary.*

24

# I'm Trying My Best
## The Impossible-Gospel Approach

KEITH WALKER


### Summary

Many Mormons believe that as long as they are trying and doing their best to keep their church's commandments, God will overlook their sins and allow them to enter the celestial kingdom to be with their family. Explaining that it is impossible to live God's law is a strategy to help Mormons understand how the only chance to succeed is through God's grace.


### Introduction

Showing Mormons how their church's gospel is impossible to live provides many advantages to Christians who take the time to master this approach. Instead of utilizing Bible verses, the approach focuses on references from Mormonism's unique scriptures (known as the Standard Works) to clarify what must be accomplished for a person to receive forgiveness of sins. Instead of confronting the Mormon directly, the impossible-gospel approach assumes that Mormonism's version of the gospel is correct.

However, when followed to its logical conclusion, the doctrine is shown to be absurd. This is what is called a *reductio ad absurdum*, an argument "in which a proposition is disproven by following its implications logically to an absurd conclusion."[1] Those who follow the argument closely will come to this conclusion naturally. Christians who use this approach will leave a much more powerful impression than if they simply tell Mormons that their views on salvation are wrong.

## History of the Approach

My wife Becky and I have been sharing our faith with Mormons at the Mormon Miracle Pageant in Manti, Utah, since June 2000. During our mission trip to Manti in 2001, we met a Christian man who pointed out some interesting quotes from twelfth president Spencer W. Kimball's book *The Miracle of Forgiveness*. These citations describe what God expects from Mormons before they can be forgiven of their sins. For instance, this quote left a big impression:

> It depends upon you whether or not you are forgiven, and when. It could be weeks, it could be years, it could be centuries before that happy day when you have the positive assurance that the Lord has forgiven you. That depends on your humility your sincerity, your works, your attitudes.[2]

As I continued my investigation, I utilized approaches from other Christian apologists while researching Mormon resources to put together an outline that made sense to me. As I continued to encounter troublesome quotes, it occurred to me how impossible it was to do what Mormonism says *must be done* for forgiveness of sins. The next year, I was invited to speak in a training session for Christians. I titled my presentation "The Impossible Gospel of Mormonism." The name stuck, so even though I was not the originator of the approach, this popular strategy is often known by this name.

## The Approach

One key to this approach is to learn how to use questions effectively. Instead of telling Mormons what their religion teaches, it is important to ask probing questions about the meaning of specific verses. When citing any of the unique Standard Works, the goal is not to just tell the Mormons what their scriptures say but let them give their own answers. This provides power to the entire approach. With that as a background, there are several important verses that show why nobody can be forgiven, at least according to Mormon scripture.

### *1. Moroni 10:32 (Book of Mormon)*

To begin this approach, I like to start with Moroni 10:32. The first half of the verse reads:

> Yea, come unto Christ, and be perfected in him, and deny yourselves of all ungodliness; and if ye shall deny yourselves of all ungodliness, and love God with all your might, mind and strength, then is his grace sufficient for you, that by his grace ye may be perfect in Christ.[3]

Point out the "if-then" statement in the passage and then ask the Mormon some questions (and feel free to add others):

- *What are the requirements for grace?* (Deny oneself all ungodliness and love God with all your might, mind, and strength.)
- *When does grace apply?* (Only after a person has met the above requirements.)
- *What would be the result of a person who denied all ungodliness?* (The person would be perfect.)
- *Who is the focus on?* (Instead of Jesus saving a person, the focus is on the person who qualifies to be saved.)

The Mormon may object by asking, "Are you saying that this verse teaches that I have to be *perfect* before I am saved?" If you have asked questions and refrained from using the word *perfect*, you can point out that they have come to this conclusion themselves. At the same time, the conclusion is proper. After all, how *could* it be possible for people to deny themselves all ungodliness and *not* be perfect?

### *2. Second Nephi 25:23 (Book of Mormon)*

This verse reads:

> For we labor diligently to write, to persuade our children, and also our brethren, to believe in Christ, and to be reconciled to God; for we know that it is by grace that we are saved, after all we can do.

Of course, the phrase that contradicts the Bible is "after all we can do." Ephesians 2:8-9 says that salvation comes by grace through faith and *not* by works. To show how this verse stresses the importance of works *in addition to* grace, ask the Mormon if this means that a person can be saved *before* anything that can be done. The answer is obvious.

Because many Christians have challenged the use of the verse in 2 Nephi, there is a movement within Mormonism to deny that the word *after* in this passage refers to a preposition of time but instead denotes a preposition of separation. However, LDS leaders have never interpreted this verse in such a way. Even the *Bible Dictionary*, which is found in Bible versions printed by the LDS Church, defines grace as

> an enabling power that allows men and women to lay hold on eternal life and exaltation *after they have expended their own best efforts*...grace cannot suffice without total effort on the part of the recipient. Hence the explanation, "It is by grace that we are saved, after all we can do" (2 Ne. 25:23). (Italics added)

According to this definition, grace does not mean "unmerited favor." Rather, it is an "enabling power" that helps Mormons gain eternal life after exerting "their own best efforts." According to Mormonism, grace is only sufficient *after* the individual accomplishes the work. With this, ask:

- *Exactly how much is expected of us before we are saved by grace?* (Total effort to do all you can do.)
- *What is all you can do?* (Accomplish all things.)
- *How often?* (All the time.)

- *When does the grace apply?* (Only after you have done all you can do.)
- *Have you ever done all that you can do?* (If they are honest, they will admit nobody but Jesus has done this.)

Mormons who argue about the meaning of this verse should be reminded of the definition of grace as provided by their church.

### *3. Alma 11:37 (Book of Mormon)*

This verse reads in part that God

> cannot save them in their sins; for I cannot deny his word, and he hath said that no unclean thing can inherit the kingdom of heaven...Therefore, ye cannot be saved in your sins.

There are several good questions to ask:

- *According to this verse, what* can't *God do?* (Save people in their sins.)
- *If you cannot be saved in your sins, what condition do you need to be in before you can be saved?* (You need to be out of your sins.)
- *Is it possible to be out of your sins yet still not be perfect?* (No, if you are out of your sins, you are perfect.)
- *Is it possible to be clean yet still sin?* (Sin is what makes us unclean, so it would be impossible to be clean and still sin.)

Using this verse, I once asked a Mormon if he was out of his sins. His response was perfect: "If I can do that, why do I need Jesus?" I told him he asked a great question. If my church taught that I had to stop sinning before I could be forgiven, as the LDS Church does, I would be asking more questions too. At this point in the conversation, most Mormons begin to see the problem. They do not like the idea that they cannot be forgiven until they are perfect.

### *4. Doctrine and Covenants 58:43*

A Mormon may bring up the issue of repentance, which is usually defined in five steps: sorrow for sin, forsaking and abandonment of sin, confession, restitution, and keeping the commandments. The point we will focus on here is the abandonment of sin. One LDS Church teaching manual designed to help teenage boys learn the gospel of Mormonism explains what it means to abandon sins: "Help the young men understand that a truly repentant person will not repeat his sin."[4] This point is emphasized in Doctrine and Covenants 58:43, which says, "By this ye may know if a man repenteth of his sins—behold, he will confess them and forsake them."

Sometimes it is best to communicate by saying nothing and letting the words sink in. Let the Latter-day Saint struggle with the weight of what it means to truly repent according to Mormonism. The individual may have a creative explanation regarding why the text doesn't mean what it says, but Mormonism has consistently taught that true repentance does not permit repeating sin.

Christians may hear many objections to this part of the argument and find themselves circling back to the same points again, as it is very difficult for Mormons to accept what their church expects of them. They may insist that if they sin again, they can repent again. The problem with this thinking is that if a person must forsake a particular sin "again," the sin was never really forsaken in the first place. Remember, "A truly repentant person will not repeat his sin."

One common objection is that repentance is a process. A question may be asked, "How is it possible to stop all sin at once?" Such an objection misses the point. This approach is the end goal of the repentance process. What will the lives of truly repentant people look like? If it is impossible to be truly repentant while sinning, those who are truly repentant have successfully and permanently forsaken all their sins.

Ask:

- *According to D&C 58:43, what demonstrates repentance?* (The forsaking of sin.)

- *Is it possible to be truly repentant if you continue to sin?* (No, true repentance requires abandonment of sin.)
- *According to the priesthood manual, what does it mean to abandon sin?* (Not repeating sin.)

### *5. First Nephi 3:7 (Book of Mormon)*

When Mormons truly understand that the only way to genuinely repent is the complete forsaking of sin, they may claim that perfect obedience is impossible in this life and that they are only expected to do the best they can. This, they will say, does not include perfection. This is the time to address the linchpin of the argument. First Nephi 3:7 states in part,

> I will go and do the things which the Lord hath commanded, for I know that the Lord giveth no commandments unto the children of men, save he shall prepare a way for them that they may accomplish the thing which he commandeth them.

Ask the Mormon to interpret the meaning, which should be similar to how LDS leaders have explained the verse. For example, one church manual states:

> Each of us can repent. Sometimes repentance may seem too difficult for us. We may feel we will never be able to overcome our weaknesses. Satan wants us to believe this so we will keep doing wrong things. We must remember that we can repent. We cannot do it by ourselves. We need help. Each of us is a child of our Father in Heaven, and He has sent Jesus to help us. With Jesus's help we can do all the things our Father in Heaven has commanded us to do…1 Nephi 3:7. (Our Father in Heaven never asks us to do things that are impossible for us to do.) [5]

According to 1 Nephi 3:7, God only gives commandments that people can keep. The manual quoted above applies this verse specifically to the commandment to repent. The Mormon's predicament is that it is impossible to be forgiven without true repentance. Here is the argument in a nutshell:

1. One cannot be forgiven without true repentance.
2. True repentance does not allow for repeating sin.
3. God never gives commandments that cannot be kept.

With that in mind, ask:

- *According to this verse, will God give a commandment that can't be kept?* (No, He only gives commandments that *can* be kept.)
- *What is the best you can do?* (Keep the commandments.)
- *Have you ever kept a commandment?* (If so, then *that* was your best. Now you must keep all the other commandments.)
- *Who wants you to believe that you cannot repent?* (Satan wants you to think you cannot repent so you can keep sinning.)

### *6. Alma 34:32-35 (Book of Mormon)*

Mormons who understand that perfection is required for forgiveness may claim that repentance can be completed in the next life. Alma 34:32-35 disagrees with this notion, saying in part that "this life is the time for men to prepare to meet God" and "if ye have procrastinated the day of your repentance even until death…ye have become subjected to the spirit of the devil." The passage includes warnings that no labor can be performed after death and that a person who procrastinates repentance is subjected to the Devil forever.

Any honest reading of this passage indicates that it is impossible to repent in the afterlife. The words "this life" appear five times! Alma 42:13 adds that "the plan of redemption could not be brought about, only on conditions of repentance of men in this probationary state." The *probationary state* means *this* mortal life. Not only are Mormons unforgiven until they repent and cease the sin, but this work must be accomplished entirely in this life.

Ask:

- *According to this passage, when must you complete your repentance?* (Before you die.)
- *Where must you perform your labor?* (On the earth.)
- *When do we prepare for eternity?* (In this life.)
- *What happens if you procrastinate your repentance until death?* (You have become subjected to the Devil and he seals you as his.)
- *Can this fate be changed?* (No, this is the final state of the wicked.)

This is clearly a problem because the goal always remains unfulfilled. The only other response to this passage is to reinterpret it, which some Mormon sources will do, but the burden of proof should be placed back on the Latter-day Saint to reconcile these contradictory views with Alma 34 in the Book of Mormon.

Even if it is believed that repentance is possible after death, all Mormons agree that repentance in the next life is even harder than in this life. This is a dire situation. If complete repentance is impossible in *this* life, how can Latter-day Saints take comfort in the idea that they can repent in the *next* life if it is even harder? What do you even call something that is harder than impossible?

## Conclusion

This approach will need to be practiced many times before the evangelist becomes proficient in its use. A common mistake some Christians make is to treat this approach as just a list of verses that need to be covered instead of a conversation that should flow. Not every verse has to be cited, and they don't even need to be addressed in the order given in this chapter. Until the Mormon understands the point, do not rush to the next verse. This is a conversation, not a conquest!

It may take repeating an idea numerous times to get a point across; with patience, perseverance, and creative questions, however, it is possible to help the Mormon see exactly what the LDS scriptures say to show how forgiveness is contingent on successfully keeping the commandments. Getting the Mormon lost before presenting the good news of the biblical gospel has many benefits in dealing with the heart of the issue, which is that sinful humans cannot keep all God's commandments. It is, I believe, the most loving way possible to introduce the biblical gospel of grace. Try it out and see if this could work for you.

---

*Keith Walker (San Antonio, Texas) is president of Evidence Ministries (www.evidenceministries.org) that reaches out to Jehovah's Witnesses and Mormons while warning the Christian community about the dangers of these groups. Keith enjoys showing Christians how to lovingly engage those who come to their doors.*

# Spotlight

## JAMES WALKER

*James Walker is the president of Watchman Fellowship (www.watchman.org), a Christian apologetics organization based in Arlington, Texas, that researches a variety of religious movements, including Mormonism, and presents information in churches throughout the United States as well as on the Internet. Besides speaking in churches, James produces videos for the Internet and works with those who have recently left Mormonism or are thinking about it.*

**Eric and Sean: Can you tell us a little bit about your own personal testimony and how you left Mormonism?**

James: I was a fourth-generation Latter-day Saint and fully believed in Joseph Smith. As early as the seventh grade, I had a Christian friend, Tom, who challenged my belief in multiple gods by showing me Isaiah 43:10 in the Bible. Ultimately, it was the Mormon gospel of works righteousness and always feeling "unworthy" contrasted with the biblical gospel of salvation by grace through faith alone (Ephesians 2:8-9) that brought me to Christ at age 21.

**Eric and Sean: Why do you visit churches around the country to teach Christians about Mormon beliefs?**

James: God used Christian friends in my life to draw me to His gospel of grace, so I want to be that kind of friend to other Mormons. I also want to encourage and train Christians to share Christ with their Mormon friends "with gentleness and respect" (1 Peter 3:15).

**Eric and Sean: Suppose someone said that, by even talking about Mormonism with committed Christians in a church setting, there**

**is a risk of someone possibly joining the LDS Church. How would you respond?**

James: Spiritual maturity is the only effective way to avoid spiritual deception (Ephesians 4:14-15). Attempts to ignore the problem or hope that Christians never come into contact with people of other religions are not the best strategies to protect those who are young or weak in their faith. Maturity is greatly accelerated when believers are exposed to the error contrasted with biblical truth while being equipped and trained for gospel ministry.

**Eric and Sean: Watchman Fellowship produces short videos and posts them on the Internet. What are some of the things discussed?**

James: We produce these videos to train Christians to better understand and reach out to their Mormon friends. Here are a few examples:

- Explaining Grace to a Mormon (4 minutes): www.watchman.org/WitnessTip.htm
- Street Interview with a Mormon (10 minutes): www.watchman.org/LDS_Interview.htm
- Mormons in Transition Interviews (10 minutes): www.watchman.org/MIT_Video.htm

And here is a 21-minute video produced by truelife.org where I talk about the question, "Is Mormonism True?" www.truelife.org/answers/is-mormonism-true

**Eric and Sean: Tell us about your program called Mormons in Transition.**

James: Mormon leaders have acknowledged that an unprecedented number of Latter-day Saints are having serious doubts about their faith or are leaving Mormonism entirely. Unfortunately, most who lose their faith tend to become atheists or agnostics. We want to build relationships with current Mormons who have questions as well as with former

Mormons. We use MeetUps.com to advertise three monthly gatherings hosted in different areas of the city. We have no agenda or lesson. We share a meal, have open conversations, and try to facilitate new friendships. All views are respected wherever people may be in their journey of transition. We try to model biblical Christianity as a viable option for Mormons who question their faith.

**Eric and Sean: As someone who used to be a Mormon, what is the best advice you could give to a Christian who wants to have a productive conversation with a Latter-day Saint?**

James: Well, reading this book is a great start. It is important to take advantage of good Christian books and other resources. These tools help us to have the basic understanding of Mormon doctrines and terminology needed to have truly productive discussions.

I would also encourage you to pray for your Mormon friends and entrust the results of your discussions to God. Try not to judge the effectiveness of your conversations by the initial responses you get. When I was Mormon, I never let my Christian friends know that their questions were hitting home. I assured them that I knew "beyond a shadow of a doubt" that Mormonism was true. I would tell them that their questions actually increased my faith in Joseph Smith. In the end, however, God did use their questions, testimonies, and relationships to enable my journey from Mormonism to Christianity.

# EPILOGUE:

## Go for It!

DR. SEAN MCDOWELL

A few years ago, I wanted to utilize social media more effectively. A friend gave me a copy of the book *Platform: Get Noticed in a Noisy World* by Michael Hyatt, and I devoured it.[1] Hyatt offers some remarkable steps to help people build websites and blogs and use other social media platforms like Twitter with greater effectiveness. There is good reason his book is a bestseller.

I started the book enthusiastically, but I was completely overwhelmed by the time it was over. As a result, I put it down and moved on. Why? The answer is simple: *Hyatt gave so many steps that I simply didn't know where to start.* I didn't have the time or resources to perform all the steps he suggested; the amount of work to be done simply overwhelmed me and kept me from taking any steps at all.

But later I had a game-changing thought: Rather than feeling the need to do *everything*, I would simply start by doing *something*. Doing something, I figured, is better than doing nothing. So I started with a few basic steps and learned to develop my social media presence over time. Rather than trying to hit a grand slam, so to speak, I focused on base hits. And while some people are much savvier than I was on social media, I have had some success and influence.

If you have made it this far in this book, you might be having similar thoughts as I did when first reading *Platform*: *There are so many ideas; where do I even start?* Here's my suggestion: *Just pick one strategy that seems most appealing to you, and go for it*. That's it!

Don't feel the need to do everything. In fact, please don't try every approach in this book. You will simply overwhelm yourself. But trying one strategy is much better than trying no strategy. Can you imagine the difference we could make if a significant number of Christians simply adopted *one* strategy in this book and put it to use? I am confident we would see droves of Mormons seriously considering the historic Christian faith.

But rather than imagining what *could be*, focus on what *you can do*. So, here's the question: Which of the strategies seems most appealing and interesting to you? Is it the strategy by J. Warner Wallace, analyzing Mormonism through the lens of a detective? Is it the LISTEN approach by Dr. David Geisler and Brian Henson? Is it the "Impossible Gospel" by Keith Walker? Is it the Internet strategy by Fred Anson? Or is it one of the others? The key is not so much *which* strategy you adopt, but that you adopt a strategy and go for it.

If things seem to go well, keep at it, and give God the credit. And please let us know about it.[2] Lord willing, you will see fruit from your efforts. If things don't go as you hope and plan, learn from it, and move on to another strategy.

The good news is that God is pleased with our efforts if we are genuinely aiming to bring glory to Him (1 Corinthians 10:31). We are not responsible for the results. But we are responsible to use the gifts and opportunities God has given us to build His kingdom. What better way than lovingly reaching out to Mormons?

There's no time to waste. Go for it.

Appendix 1

# The Gospel (Good News) According to the Bible[1]

There has only ever been, and ever will be one eternal God (Isaiah 43:10). He is perfect, unchangeable, and without limitation (Malachi 3:6). He has revealed Himself to us through His Word, the Bible. He created everything that exists (Genesis 1:1): every universe, every cell (Psalm 147:4); every star, to every blade of grass, every atom that has ever existed…and every person…including you and me (John 1:3). And he gave us a code to live by and placed it in our hearts as a conscience to know right from wrong (Romans 2:15).

But you and I, on many occasions, have chosen wrong (Isaiah 53:6). The Bible tells us, "All have sinned and fall short of the glory of God" (Romans 3:23). That "no one is righteous, no, not one" (Romans 3:10).

Because of this rebellion against our Creator, we have caused a separation between us and God (Isaiah 59:2). And it is a gap so wide that we can never cross it by our efforts (Ephesians 2:12). But many have tried. In realizing their sin, some people have tried to do good things to outweigh the bad. But God has declared that even all of our righteous deeds are like filthy rags to Him (Isaiah 64:6).

Others have thought that if they could just stop doing bad things, they would be good enough. But the Bible says that if we've done even one thing wrong, we are lawbreakers, and subject to the full penalty of the law (James 2:10).

This penalty is death (Romans 6:23). Eternal separation from God.

Because God is perfect and we are not...He is just in His judgment, and you and I stand guilty before a Righteous Judge (Romans 2:2).

But God loved us so much that He sent His one and only Son, Jesus, to come to earth (John 3:16), to enter into our mess, and live the perfect life we should have lived (Hebrews 4:15), and in regard to our standing before God, He traded places with us (2 Corinthians 5:21). He was blameless but He took our punishment of death. We stand guilty, but we can have His reward of eternal life (Romans 3:24-25).

"God demonstrated His love for us in this, that while we were still sinners Christ died for us" (Romans 5:8).

Jesus died the death that we should have died, but He didn't stay in the grave (Acts 2:24). He rose from the dead defeating sin and death, and sharing His victory with all who will believe in Him (1 Corinthians 15:57). Now we can be seen as innocent in the eyes of God (Isaiah 43:25)!

A man once asked Jesus, "What must we do to be doing the works of God?" Jesus answered him, "This is the work of God, that you believe in him whom he has sent" (John 6:28-29).

And that is the gospel: that anyone who will repent of sin and turn not to good works, religious systems, or traditions of men, but to belief in the one and only Son of God, Jesus Christ, will be saved (Acts 3:19; 16:31).

The Bible says that it is by grace that we have been saved through faith and not by our works (Ephesians 2:8). That it is not possible for us to earn God's forgiveness through any deeds that we can do (Romans 11:6). God says that anyone who relies on his own works is under a curse (Galatians 3:10), because no one can be justified by his accomplishments (Romans 3:20).

This gospel is so important to God that He warns us if anyone tries to add anything to, or take anything from this message, even if that messenger is an angel from heaven, he will be eternally condemned (Galatians 1:8). God has guarded His true gospel throughout the ages (Matthew 16:18), and through His servants, He shares it freely to all who will hear it (Romans 10:14-17).

Today God has freely offered you His gift of grace and salvation. And that is good news!

Appendix 2

# 101 Mormon Terms Defined (from Aaronic Priesthood to Zion)

It's impossible to communicate with your Latter-day Saint friend unless you have an understanding of the definition of vocabulary terms. Some words used in Mormonism are also used in Christianity, although these typically have different meanings. Meanwhile, many LDS terms are unique to Mormonism. This is the purpose of Appendix 2; we will define the words as typically understood by the Mormon community. Feel free to use this resource throughout your reading of the book.

We will use italics with words used in a particular definition that are defined in this section. Words in parentheses that follow a particular term are synonymous with the term being defined.[1]

**Aaronic Priesthood:** The authority to perform certain ecclesiastical tasks, allegedly bestowed by John the Baptist onto *Joseph Smith* and his friend Oliver Cowdery on May 15, 1829. Baptized Mormon males 12 years and older are eligible to receive this *priesthood.*

**Agency:** The ability to choose right from wrong, referring to both people on the earth today as well as all spirits in the *preexistence.*

**Anti-Mormon:** Usually a pejorative term used to refer to those (typically Christians) who are critical of Mormonism and therefore are considered hateful by many Mormons. It can also refer to any information from any source that places the LDS Church in a bad light.

**Apostasy, Great:** The belief that true Christianity lost its authority after the death of Christ's apostles, which made it necessary for God to restore the true church through *Joseph Smith* and the founding of the LDS Church in 1830.

**Apostle:** One of 12 members in the second-highest governing body of the LDS Church and considered to be a *General Authority*. The most senior member is the President of the Quorum of the Twelve Apostles, who is next in line to become the church's *president*.

**Atonement:** A work accomplished through the suffering of *Jesus* at *Gethsemane* and His death on the cross that allows all humans to rise in the resurrection to one of three *kingdoms of glory*. The Mormon atonement also paves the way for potential *exaltation* in the *celestial kingdom*.

**Baptism:** Required for the remission of sins and membership in the LDS Church. Baptismal candidates must be eight years or older. A Mormon male who holds *Melchizedek priesthood* authority immerses the candidate in water, usually at a local LDS *chapel*. A *covenant* with God is made at this time, with the candidate promising to keep all the *commandments*.

**Baptism for the Dead:** Also known as "baptism by proxy" or "vicarious baptism," this *ordinance* is performed in Mormon temples by living church members on behalf of someone who is deceased. The soul for whom the work is done is given a chance to receive the gospel in *spirit prison*.

**Bible:** One of the four *Standard Works*. The official translation used is the King James Version of the Bible. According to the Eighth Article of Faith, the Bible is true only "as far as it is translated correctly."

**Bishop:** An unpaid leader of a local Mormon *ward* whose duties are similar to the responsibilities of a Christian pastor.

**Book of Mormon:** One of the four *Standard Works.* Contains the alleged story of an ancient Jewish civilization that existed on the American continent. It was originally compiled on *gold plates* that were buried in a hill in New York and translated by LDS Church founder *Joseph Smith. Missionaries* often use Moroni 10:4, found at the end of the scripture, to challenge prospective converts to receive the confirmation of this book's truthfulness.

**Branch:** A Mormon congregation that is not large enough to form a *ward.*

**Brethren:** See *General Authority.*

**BYU:** Brigham Young University. A university and graduate school located in Provo, Utah, owned by the LDS Church. Extension campuses are located in Hawaii, Idaho, and Israel.

**Calling:** Invitation that a member receives for a particular assignment in the local church congregation.

**Celestial Kingdom:** The highest *kingdom of glory* reserved for those Mormons who demonstrate complete obedience to LDS laws and ordinances. This is where one may enjoy the presence of *God the Father* and *Jesus Christ* as well as abide with one's family forever. See Exaltation.

**Chapel:** A building used for church services and events.

**Child(ren) of God:** All humans, both righteous and wicked. *God the Father* and *Heavenly Mother* procreated each spirit in the *preexistence.*

**Commandments:** Laws and rules as taught by the LDS Church. Keeping these is necessary to receive *exaltation.*

**Confirmation:** A *Melchizedek priesthood* member lays his hands upon the head of a recently baptized convert, thus bestowing membership into the LDS Church as well as the *gift of the Holy Ghost.*

**Council in Heaven:** A council of the gods called by *God the Father* in the *preexistence* to determine how the spirit *children of God* could come to earth as physical beings. *Jesus* and Lucifer offered two competing plans, with two thirds of the spirits siding with *Jesus.*

**Covenants (Oaths):** Two-way promises made by members with God in *baptism/confirmation*, the weekly *sacrament*, temple *endowment*, and temple marriage (*sealing*), all of which must be kept to gain *exaltation*.

**Creeds:** Generally associated with historical Christian statements of faith, which are rejected by LDS leaders as part of the *Great Apostasy*.

**Damnation:** Being prevented from reaching one's full potential as a *child of God* due to a person's lack of faithfulness to the whole law of the LDS *gospel.* It does not refer to an eternal *hell.*

**Deacon:** Office in the *Aaronic priesthood* given to males beginning at the age of 12. Among other duties, deacons serve the *sacrament* on Sunday mornings.

**Doctrine and Covenants (D&C):** One of the four *Standard Works.* Primarily a collection of divine revelations mostly revealed to *Joseph Smith.* Most contemporary LDS doctrine is recorded in this scripture.

**Elder:** A male 18 or older who holds the *Melchizedek priesthood.*

**Endowment:** A ceremony within a Mormon *temple* that prepares the participants for *exaltation* in the afterlife.

***Ensign*:** An official monthly church magazine. The May and November issues contain transcripts of all the talks given at the semiannual *General Conference* gatherings in April and October.

**Eternal Increase:** The ability of qualified Mormons who have become gods to procreate throughout eternity in the *celestial kingdom*.

**Exaltation (Eternal Life):** Becoming glorified as gods in the highest level of the *celestial kingdom* and living forever in the family unit.

**Fall of Adam and Eve:** Adam's transgression (not "sin") that took place in the Garden of Eden, causing them to become mortal and making them subject to physical death. It has been called "a blessing in disguise" because, without it, spirits would never have been allowed to enter mortality.

**Family Home Evening:** A recommended gathering for families on Monday nights, with the primary activity of studying the Mormon *gospel*. Church activities do not happen during this time, as church buildings are closed. Families often use this time to strengthen relationships and have fun together.

**Fast and Testimony Meeting:** Practice of members sharing their personal testimonies at church services on the first Sunday of each month.

**Fast Offering:** An offering designated for the poor, contributed during a *Fast and Testimony meeting*. Mormons are encouraged to refrain from two consecutive meals, donating the savings to the church.

**First Presidency:** The three top leaders of the church consisting of the church's *president* and his two counselors.

**First Vision:** An event that Mormons are taught took place in 1820, according to the official account, when *God the Father* and *Jesus Christ* appeared to 14-year-old *Joseph Smith* in the Sacred Grove near Palmyra, New York. In this vision, Smith was told that all the Christian churches were wrong.

**Garments, Temple:** Also known as the "garments of the holy priesthood," a sacred undergarment worn by faithful Mormons who are qualified to attend the *temple*. The garments are believed to be a spiritual (and possibly physical) "shield and protection."

**General Authority:** The highest leaders of the church, including the *First Presidency*, Quorum of the Twelve *Apostles*, and the first two quorums of the *Seventy*.

**General Conference:** An assembly of LDS membership held in Salt Lake City, Utah, on the first weekend of each April and October. These meetings are for official instruction, announcements, and teaching given by *General Authorities* and other LDS leaders.

**Gethsemane:** The primary location where the *atonement* took place when *Jesus* sweated drops of blood.

**Gift of the Holy Ghost:** Fullness of blessings available to LDS members after *baptism*. The *Holy Ghost* remains with those who stay worthy, though he will withdraw when the *commandments* are not kept.

**God the Father (Elohim, Heavenly Father):** First member of the *Godhead* who once lived as a righteous human in another realm before he became exalted. He has a resurrected, tangible body of flesh and bones (D&C 130:22) and is the literal father of every premortal human being in the *spirit world*.

**Godhead:** In rejecting the Christian doctrine of the Trinity (i.e., one God in three persons), Mormonism's Godhead consists of three distinct gods (*Heavenly Father*, *Jesus Christ*, and the *Holy Ghost*) who are united in purpose.

**Godhood:** Humans can reach this status through obedience and then becoming exalted like *God the Father* in the *celestial kingdom*.

**Gold Plates:** According to the angel *Moroni*, the *Book of Mormon* was written upon plates of gold. *Joseph Smith* claimed to translate these plates into English from "Reformed Egyptian" characters.

**Gospel:** All doctrines, principles, laws, *ordinances*, and *covenants* necessary for a Mormon to achieve *exaltation*.

**Grace:** God's enabling power that is provided to all humans through the work of *Jesus* and His *atonement*. Because of this, everyone receives an inheritance to a *kingdom of glory*.

**Heavenly Mother:** The wife of *God the Father*, or "Heavenly Father." Early Mormon leaders openly taught that Heavenly Father was a practicing polygamist, making Heavenly Mother merely one wife among many.

**Hell:** Depending on the context, there are several possible meanings. Generally, this is a reference to *spirit prison*, a temporary holding place for those who did not accept Mormonism during their lifetimes.

**High Priest:** An office usually given to more experienced members within the *Melchizedek priesthood* who oversee the spiritual welfare of church members.

**Holy Ghost:** The third member of the *Godhead* who is sometimes described as the Holy Spirit and other times described as distinct from the Holy Spirit. He is a *child of God* but does not have a body of flesh and bones like *Jesus* and *God the Father*. The influence of the Holy Ghost is said to help *investigators* know whether the *Book of Mormon* (and Mormonism) is true.

**Institute of Religion:** An LDS school offering college-level classes on various subjects of Mormonism, usually located near major university campuses.

**Investigator:** Someone who is considering joining the LDS Church and is being visited by *missionaries*.

**Jack Mormon:** Generally, a term that describes Mormons who are not fully practicing their faith.

**Jesus:** Second member of the *Godhead*. He was the literal firstborn son of *God the Father* in the *preexistence* where he was known as Jehovah and worked his way to perfection.

**Joseph Smith (1805–1844):** The founder of The Church of Jesus Christ of Latter-day Saints.

**Kingdoms of Glory (Three Degrees of Glory):** The *celestial*, *terrestrial*, and *telestial kingdoms* where all humans but the *sons of perdition* will reside after the final judgment.

**Laying on of Hands:** The act of priesthood leaders putting their hands on the head of a person to bestow a blessing or *ordination*.

**LDS:** Abbreviation for "Latter-day Saints." The Church of Jesus Christ of Latter-day Saints is the official title.

**Melchizedek Priesthood:** Known as the higher or greater *priesthood*, a special authority given to baptized Mormon men 18 years and older through the *laying on of hands*. This *priesthood* authority is believed to have been originally given to *Joseph Smith* and his friend Oliver Cowdery sometime between May 15, 1829, and April 6, 1830, through the biblical apostles Peter, James, and John.

**Missionary:** A volunteer sent to national and foreign locations around the world in service to the LDS Church. The most familiar are those tasked with spreading the LDS *gospel*: young men ages 18 to 25 (who serve for two years), young women 19 to 25 (who serve for 18 months), and retired couples (who serve for six months to three years).

**Mormon:** Two possible meanings: (1) An ancient Nephite prophet who abridged and compiled the records of his people known today as the *Book of Mormon*. (2) A nickname commonly used to refer to a member of the LDS Church, also known as a Latter-day Saint.

**Moroni:** The son of *Mormon* in the *Book of Mormon* who supposedly buried the *gold plates* containing the record of the Nephite people. In 1823, the angel Moroni is said to have appeared to *Joseph Smith* and revealed to him the location of the buried plates. A golden statue of Moroni holding a trumpet is put on a spire at most LDS temples.

**Mortal Probation (Second Estate):** Mortal life on this earth wherein physical bodies are given to those who were faithful in the *preexistence*.

**New Name:** A name received by *patrons* during a *temple* ceremony that will be used in the next life. Only the husband is allowed to know his wife's new name, which usually has its origins in the *Bible* or the *Book of Mormon*. The wife is not supposed to know her husband's new name.

**Ordain:** To bestow *priesthood* authority on a worthy male member through the *laying on of hands*.

**Ordinance:** Ceremonies in which a Mormon makes a *covenant* with God. Included are *baptisms*, *sacraments*, and works performed in an LDS *temple*.

**Outer Darkness:** Severe punishment for eternity, primarily reserved for Satan, his demons, and the *sons of perdition*.

**Paradise:** Temporary place in the postmortal *spirit world* for Mormons who have been properly baptized and who remained faithful until death.

**Patriarchal Blessing:** A conditional, personal prophetic utterance given to a Mormon, either by a relative or by an ordained patriarch appointed by the LDS Church.

**Patron, Temple:** A person who performs works and makes *covenants* with God in an LDS *temple*.

**Pearl of Great Price:** One of the four *Standard Works*. Contains books such as the Book of Abraham, Moses, Joseph Smith's History, and Smith's retranslation of a portion of the Gospel of Matthew.

**Plan of Salvation:** A plan allowing the *children of God* to become like *God the Father* (see *Godhood*). As a spirit child in the *preexistence*, a person who rightly chose *Jesus* as Savior is given the chance to be born onto the earth with a physical body and the opportunity to progress to a *kingdom of glory*.

**Preexistence (Premortality, First Estate):** A *spirit world* existence preceding the second estate. All spirits born of *God the Father* had to choose between the salvation plans offered by *Jesus* and Lucifer. Those who chose Lucifer were cast out of heaven and were prohibited from obtaining physical bodies. Those who sided with *Jesus* are allowed to be born on the earth with physical bodies, necessary to achieve *exaltation*.

**President (Prophet, Seer, Revelator):** A *General Authority* who holds the highest office in the LDS Church. Others in Mormonism also hold the title "president," including the President of the Quorum of the Twelve Apostles, mission presidents, and the president of the Presiding Bishopric.

**Priesthood:** Understood to be the power and authority to act in God's name. May also refer to Mormon males who hold this authority. Also see *Aaronic priesthood* and *Melchizedek priesthood*.

**Relief Society:** Organization for female members who are 18 or older.

**Repentance:** The process by which a Mormon receives forgiveness. True repentance involves six steps, including confession and a successful abandonment of all sin.

**Restoration:** Reestablishment of true gospel principles when *Joseph Smith* founded the LDS Church in 1830. *Priesthood* authority was returned after it had been taken from the earth during the *Great Apostasy*.

**Resurrection:** All human beings will be physically raised to a *kingdom of glory* through the *atonement* provided by *Jesus*.

**Sabbath:** Sunday. This is a day Mormons are told to "keep holy" by attending church services while refraining from shopping, doing chores, and participating in recreational activities.

**Sacrament:** Similar to the Protestant version of communion, or the Lord's Supper. Observed weekly in LDS services, with bread and water serving as elements, to renew the *covenants* made at *baptism*.

**Salvation:** Two possible meanings, depending on the context: (1) General Salvation (see *resurrection*); (2) Individual Salvation (see *exaltation*).

**Scripture:** The four written works (the *Bible*, the *Book of Mormon*, the *Doctrine and Covenants*, and the *Pearl of Great Price*) are called the *Standard Works*. In addition, this could also include the inspired words of the living *prophet*, official church writings, and *General Conference* addresses.

**Sealing:** A *temple* ceremony binding a husband and wife together for eternity, or binding children to their parents if the children were born outside of Mormonism.

**Seminary:** Elective religious classes offered at LDS buildings, often located near public high schools or in members' homes. In Utah, high school students are given the chance to leave the school's campus so a paid Mormon teacher can instruct them about the *Standard Works* and church history. In other states, students typically gather in the mornings before school begins and may be taught by a volunteer.

**Seventy:** A man who holds a leadership position following the positions of the *First Presidency* and the *apostles*. These men known as the Seventies fit into eight quorums. The men belonging to the first two quorums are known as *General Authorities* while the others are referred to as area authorities.

**Sons of Perdition:** Those who rebelled with Lucifer in the *preexistence*. The term can also apply to Mormons who willfully and deliberately deny the *Holy Ghost* and the truth of Mormonism while knowing it is true.

**Spirit Prison:** Temporary place for deceased non-Mormons who are waiting for vicarious *temple* work to be done on their behalf by living Mormons.

**Spirit World:** See *Paradise* and *Spirit Prison*.

**Stake:** A regional administrative grouping of five to ten *wards*. In the US a minimum of 3,000 members comprise a stake, while outside the US 1,900 members are required.

**Standard Works:** See *Scripture*.

**Telestial Kingdom:** The lowest *kingdom of glory* to which "liars, sorcerers, adulterers and whoremongers" are assigned for eternity after death. The residents of this kingdom will be visited by the *Holy Ghost*, but not by *God the Father* or *Jesus*.

**Temple:** Special buildings located throughout the world where members who are deemed worthy get married and participate in *ordinances*, including work on behalf of the dead.

**Temple Recommend:** A barcoded card that allows a member of good standing in the LDS Church access to a *temple* for two years at a time. This is given only after an interview with the Mormon's *bishop* if the applicant is deemed *worthy*.

**Terrestrial Kingdom:** The middle *kingdom of glory* to which honorable non-Mormons and less-than-faithful Mormons are assigned after death. The residents of this kingdom will be visited by *Jesus Christ* but will be separated from *God the Father* throughout eternity.

**Tithing Settlement:** If less than a tenth of a Mormon's income was given to the church (tithe) during the previous year, the deficit is encouraged to be made up during a private meeting the member has with the *bishop*, especially if the member wants to qualify for or keep a *temple recommend.*

**War in Heaven:** Conflict in the *preexistence* that was started by Lucifer when his bid to become the savior of the world was rejected. A third of the spirit *children of God* were prevented from getting physical bodies when they were cast out of the *preexistence*.

**Ward:** A local Mormon congregation presided over by a *bishop* made up of members from a particular geographic location, usually consisting of between 150-500 members. When a ward becomes too large, it is split up. Smaller congregations are called *branches*.

**Washing and Anointing:** Initiatory *temple* ceremony that purifies the *patron*.

**Word of Wisdom:** A health law found in Doctrine & Covenants 89 commanding Mormons to abstain from hot drinks (interpreted as coffee and tea), tobacco, excessive amounts of meat, and alcoholic beverages.

**Worthy (Temple Worthiness):** Mormons who fully live their religion, demonstrating their adherence to the requirement of Mormonism to be considered righteous so they can participate in *temple* ceremonies. Mormons who hold an active *temple recommend* are often referred to as "worthy" members.

**Zion:** Several possible meanings in Mormonism, but for contemporary Mormonism it generally means the "pure in heart"; as a community of people, it refers to those who belong to the LDS Church.

# Subject Index

# Scripture Index

BOOK OF MORMON

## DOCTRINE AND COVENANTS



## PEARL OF GREAT PRICE

*Moses*



*Joseph Smith—History*



*Articles of Faith*

# Notes

### Introduction: Should Christians Share the Good News with Mormons?—*Eric Johnson*

1. In this book, we will refer to Christians in several ways by using adjectives such as *biblical*, *Bible-believing*, *evangelical*, and *born again*. Those who have contributed to this book align themselves with Protestant (evangelical) Christianity.

2. *Mormons Believe... What?! Fact and Fiction about a Rising Religion* (Orange, CA: The Parameter Foundation, 2011), 7.

3. For a fuller treatment of this question, see chapter 1 of Bill McKeever and Eric Johnson, *Answering Mormons' Questions* (Grand Rapids, MI: Kregel, 2013).

4. According to Appendix 2, the Great Apostasy is the belief that true Christianity lost its authority after the death of Christ's apostles, which made it necessary for God to restore the true church through Joseph Smith and the founding of the LDS Church in 1830. See original quotes by a variety of LDS leaders at Mormonism Research Ministry, "Is This Bigotry? A Response to Latter-day Saints Who Say, 'We Never Criticize Christian Churches,'" http://www.mrm.org/we-never-criticize.

5. To a Mormon, "scripture" can include one of the four written works called the Standard Works; this is comprised of the Bible (King James Version), the Book of Mormon, the Doctrine and Covenants, and the Pearl of Great Price. In addition, words spoken by the leadership can also be accepted as "modern" scripture.

6. Visit our website SharingWithMormons.com for LDS Church citations on these issues.

7. Unless otherwise noted, we will use the English Standard Version (ESV) in biblical citations.

8. Saint Francis was known for preaching the gospel as much as living in a righteous fashion. For information to show how the quoted statement was never cited by Saint Francis, see an article by *Christianity Today*'s Mark Galli titled "Speak the Gospel," May 21, 2009, www.christianitytoday.com/ct/2009/mayweb-only/120-42.0.html.

### 1. Helping Our Friends Evaluate Truth Claims: The Straight-Thinking Approach—*Mark Mittelberg*

1. I present these in detail in my book *Confident Faith: Building a Firm Foundation for Your Beliefs* (Carol Stream, IL: Tyndale, 2013).

2. *History of the Church*, ed. B.H. Roberts (Salt Lake City, UT: Deseret Book, 1950), 6:319-320. The *History of the Church* is a seven-volume set produced by the LDS Church providing details about the earliest years of the religion.

3. For more information, see chapter 2 of this book, "Sharing the Reasons for God: The Evidence Approach," by Sean McDowell.
4. To see the citation, visit www.youtube.com/watch?v=TVsNEIOXTQc.
5. See, for example, my section on the 20 "Arrows of Truth" in *Confident Faith*. Also recommended are Lee Strobel's *The Case for Christ* (Grand Rapids, MI: Zondervan, 1998) and *The Case for Faith* (Grand Rapids, MI: Zondervan, 2000).

### 2. Sharing the Reasons for God: The Evidence Approach—*Dr. Sean McDowell*

1. For instance, see exmormon.org and exmormonstories.org. Both sites are atheistic in nature.
2. The LDS Church is trying to address historical findings that contradict earlier Mormon teachings to prevent the exodus of Mormons from the faith. See "Gospel Topics Essays—Introduction and Links," Mormonism Research Ministry, www.mrm.org/gospel-topics.
3. Victor Reppert, "The Argument from Reason," in *The Blackwell Companion to Natural Theology*, eds. William Lane Craig and J.P. Moreland (West Sussex, UK: Blackwell, 2009), 344-390.
4. J.P. Moreland, *Consciousness and the Existence of God: A Theistic Argument* (New York: Routledge, 2008).
5. Stephen Meyer, *Darwin's Doubt* (New York: HarperCollins, 2013).
6. Guillermo Gonzalez and Jay W. Richards, *The Privileged Planet* (Washington, DC: Regnery Publishing, 2004).
7. Josh McDowell and Sean McDowell, *Evidence that Demands a Verdict* (Nashville, TN: Thomas Nelson, 2017).
8. Ibid.
9. For a helpful articulation of the ontological argument, see Douglas R. Groothuis, *Christian Apologetics* (Downers Grove, IL: InterVarsity Press, 2011), 185-206.
10. Sean McDowell and Jonathan Morrow, *Is God Just a Human Invention?* (Grand Rapids, MI: Kregel, 2010), 71-82.
11. Francis J. Beckwith, Carl Mosser, and Paul Owen, eds., *The New Mormon Challenge* (Grand Rapids, MI: Zondervan, 2002).
12. Michael R. Licona, *The Resurrection of Jesus: A New Historiographical Approach* (Downers Grove, IL: InterVarsity Press, 2010).
13. Josh McDowell and Sean McDowell, "The Historical Existence of Jesus," in *Evidence that Demands a Verdict* (Nashville, TN: Thomas Nelson, 2017).
14. Sean McDowell, "Was Joseph Smith a Martyr?" SeanMcDowell.org, November 17, 2015, http://seanmcdowell.org/blog/was-joseph-smith-a-martyr.

### 3. Did God Really Say So? The Reliability-of-the-Bible Approach—*Matt Slick*

1. To see these changes, see *3913 Changes in the Book of Mormon* (Salt Lake City, UT: Utah Lighthouse, 1996).

2. "After the books of the New Testament were written, they were carried all over the Roman Empire. The Christians everywhere took care of them, and copied and multiplied them in the century immediately following their production" (Ira Maurice Price, *The Ancestry of Our English Bible*, 3rd rev. ed by William A. Irwin and Allen P. Wikgren (New York: Harper and Row, 1956), 154. And "many of the first copies of the Gospels were made, not by professional scribes, but by literate lay copyists. As the early church rapidly expanded throughout the Roman world in the first centuries A.D., there was a pressing need for multiple copies of authoritative Christian documents, including Matthew, Mark, Luke, and John. Nonprofessional copyists must have stepped in to meet this need" (Mark D. Roberts, *Can We Trust the Gospels? Investigating the Reliability of Matthew, Mark, Luke, and John* (Wheaton, IL: Crossway Books, 2007), 28.

3. "Care for the precise wording of the biblical text is attested, therefore, at the start of the Christian era" (A.R. Millard, "In praise of ancient scribes," *Biblical Archaeologist* 45, no. 3): 143.

4. Lloyd Anderson, "Manuscript Discoveries of the New Testament in Perspective," Papers of the Fourteenth Annual Symposium on the Archaeology of the Scriptures, presented April 13, 1963, 57-58. Brigham Young University, Provo, Utah. BYU is an official university of the LDS Church.

5. In 2013, I personally visited each of these historical sites in Israel as well as walked into Cave 1 in Qumran. For more, see my article "Archaeological evidence verifying biblical cities," on the Christian Apologetics & Research Ministry website, www.carm.org/archaeological-evidence-verifying-biblical-cities.

6. Two books that deal with contradictions are Gleason Archer's *New International Encyclopedia of Bible Difficulties* (Grand Rapids, MI: Zondervan, 2001) and Norman L. Geisler and Thomas Howe's *The Big Book of Bible Difficulties* (Grand Rapids, MI: Baker, 2008).

### 4. Who Is the Real Jesus? The Christ-Centered Approach—*Dr. Robert M. Bowman Jr.*

1. See Robert M. Bowman Jr., *Jesus and the Inerrancy of Scripture: A Simple Argument for Those Who Believe in Jesus* (Cedar Springs, MI: Institute for Religious Research, 2015), http://bib.irr.org/jesus-and-inerrancy-of-scripture.

2. The groundbreaking study was Richard A. Burridge, *What Are the Gospels? A Comparison with Graeco-Roman Biography*, 2nd ed. (Grand Rapids, MI: Eerdmans, 2004).

3. See, for example, the entries on the four Gospels in *The Oxford Encyclopedia of the Books of the Bible*, Michael D. Coogan, editor-in-chief (Oxford: Oxford University Press, 2011), a secular/liberal reference work. Even the agnostic scholar Bart Ehrman dates the Gospels between AD 70 and 100, in *The New Testament: A Historical Introduction to the Early Christian Writings*, 6th ed. (New York: Oxford University Press, 2016), 100.

4. In *The Complete Works of Tacitus*, translated by Alfred John Church and William Jackson Brodribb, edited by Moses Hadas, Modern Library College Edition (New York: Modern Library, 1942), 380.

### 5. Investigating Mormonism: The Case-Making Approach—*J. Warner Wallace*

1. For verification from the official LDS Church website, see "Plural Marriage in Kirtland and Nauvoo," https://www.lds.org/topics/plural-marriage-in-kirtland-and-nauvoo?lang=eng.

2. Although Joseph did convince Emma to support polygamy for a short time, she quickly retracted her support and despised the practice for the rest of her life. See Linda King Newell and Valeen Tippetts Avery, *Mormon Enigma: Emma Hale Smith,* 2nd ed. (Urbana, IL: University of Illinois Press, 1994), 143-145, 151-156.

3. Richard Lyman Bushman, *Joseph Smith: Rough Stone Rolling* (New York: Alfred A. Knopf, 2005), 328-332. Read more about the Kirtland bank failure in "Joseph Smith's Kirtland Bank Failure," Utah Lighthouse Ministry, http://www.utlm.org/onlineresources/josephsmithsbank.htm.

4. Bushman, *Joseph Smith: Rough Stone Rolling,* 413, 423-424, 514-517.

5. Ibid., 48-52.

6. See the trial document at Fawn M. Brodie, *No Man Knows My History: The Life of Joseph Smith the Mormon Prophet* (New York: Alfred A. Knopf, 1983), 427-428.

7. For instance, compare Matthew 6:13 to 3 Nephi 13:13. For more information on Smith's plagiarism from the KJV, see Jerald and Sandra Tanner, *Joseph Smith's Plagiarism of the Bible in the Book of Mormon* (Salt Lake City, UT: Utah Lighthouse Ministry, 1998).

8. For example, compare John 10:9, 14, 16, spoken by Jesus in AD 32 to 1 Nephi 22:25, allegedly spoken by Nephi in 588 BC.

9. Compare 1 Nephi 22:20 with Deuteronomy 18:15, 19 as quoted in Acts 3:22-23. Smith quoted the New Testament paraphrase, but 1 Nephi was allegedly written more than 600 years prior to this paraphrase.

10. For more on this issue, watch a one-hour documentary titled *The Lost Book of Abraham,* from the Institute for Religious Research and Grooters Productions, which can be found online on YouTube, published by Aaron Shafovaloff, June 26, 2007, https://www.youtube.com/watch?v=hcyzkd_m6KE.

### 6. Undermining Confidence in a Mormon's Personal "Testimony": The Police-Lineup Approach—*Dr. Corey Miller*

1. To see my full approach on the testimony and addressing the notion of salvation using the Book of Mormon prior to the biblical presentation, see Corey Miller and Lynn K. Wilder, *Leaving Mormonism: Why Four Scholars Changed their Minds* (Grand Rapids, MI: Kregel, 2017). Also see Corey Miller, "The Use and Misuse of Testimony: A Stealth Strategy for Effective Dialogue with Mormons," *Christian Research Journal* (December 2017).

2. Boyd K. Packer, *That All May Be Edified* (Salt Lake City, UT: Bookcraft, 1982), 340; italics in original.

3. Boyd K. Packer, "The Candle of the Lord," *Ensign* (January 1983): 55.

4. Dallin Oaks, "Teaching and Learning by the Spirit," *Ensign* (March 1997): 13.

5. Gene R. Cook, "Are You a Member Missionary?" *Ensign* (May 1976): 103. D&C 9:8-9 says, "But, behold, I say unto you, that you must study it out in your mind; then you must ask me if it be right, and if it is right I will cause that your bosom shall burn within you; therefore, you shall feel that it is right. But if it be not right you shall have no such feelings, but you shall have a stupor of

thought that shall cause you to forget the thing which is wrong; therefore, you cannot write that which is sacred save it be given you from me."

6. *Preach My Gospel: A Guide to Missionary Service* (Salt Lake City, UT: Intellectual Reserve, 2004), 38.

7. Here is just one of Spencer W. Kimball's comments: "Monthly there are testimony meetings held where each one has the opportunity to bear witness. To by-pass such opportunities is to fail to that extent to pile up credits against the accumulated errors and transgressions." See *The Miracle of Forgiveness* (Salt Lake City, UT: Bookcraft, 1969), 206.

8. See definitions of LDS terms in Appendix 2.

9. There are dozens of splinter Mormon groups, many of which are found in or near Utah. For instance, the polygamist Fundamentalist Church of Jesus Christ of Latter-day Saints (FLDS), formerly led by Warren Jeffs, teaches that the LDS Church based in Utah went apostate for changes over the years, including the elimination of polygamy and allowing those with African heritage to hold the priesthood. Based in Independence, Missouri, the Community of Christ (formerly Reorganized Church of Jesus Christ of Latter-Day Saints) denies that Brigham Young was a legitimate prophet and claims that Smith's son, Joseph Smith III, was the legitimate successor to his father.

10. Examples may include the Community of Christ, based in Independence, Missouri; Church of Christ (Temple Lot), based in Independence, Missouri; and the Fundamentalist Church of Jesus Christ of Latter-day Saints (FLDS), a polygamist group based in Hildale, Utah, and Colorado City, Arizona. Dozens of other splinter groups can be named.

11. To see my approach on presenting the gospel using the Book of Mormon (and *The Miracle of Forgiveness* mentioned above) as well as problems with the Mormon concept of God and a treatment on the nature and value of testimonial evidence, see chapter 2 of *Leaving Mormonism.*

12. The phrase "eternal life" in Mormonism denotes celestial glory (Doctrine and Covenants 14:7).

13. The word *has* is present tense in the verse's original Greek.

### 7. Joseph Smith's First Vision and the Book of Mormon: The Historical Approach—*Bill McKeever*

1. *Teachings of Gordon B. Hinckley* (Salt Lake City, UT: Deseret Book Company, 2016), 226-227.

2. Joseph Smith—History 1:17.

3. Joseph Smith—History 1:19.

4. Joseph Smith—History 1:22.

5. See Joseph Smith's Handwritten 1832 First Vision at http://www.utlm.org/onlineresources/firstvisionjosephsmith1832.htm.

6. Richard Abanes, *One Nation Under Gods* (New York: Four Walls, Eight Windows, 2002), 16. Also see *Joseph Smith's 1832-34 Diary* (Salt Lake City, UT: Modern Microfilm, 1979), 5.

7. Ibid., 11-12.

8. Ibid., 11-22.

9. *Preach My Gospel* (Salt Lake City, UT: The Church of Jesus Christ of Latter-day Saints, 2004), 36.

10. Wesley Walters, *The Palmyra Revival and Mormon Origins* (Salt Lake City, UT: Mormonism Research Ministry, 2012). For more, visit Mormonism Research Ministry, www.mrm.org/first-vision.

11. For more information on the different First Vision stories, visit Mormonism Research Ministry, www.mrm.org/first-vision-stories.

12. Jeffrey R. Holland, *Christ and the New Covenant: The Messianic Message of the Book of Mormon* (Salt Lake City, UT: Deseret Book, 1997), 345-46.

13. Tad R. Callister, "God's Compelling Witness: The Book of Mormon," *Ensign* (November 2017): 107.

14. See Richard L. Bushman, *Rough Stone Rolling* (New York: Alfred A. Knopf, 2005), 60. See also *Church History in the Fullness of Times: Religion 341 through 343* (Salt Lake City, UT: The Church of Jesus Christ of Latter-day Saints, 2003), 44-45.

15. Lucy Mack Smith, *History of Joseph Smith by His Mother* (Salt Lake City, UT: Stevens and Wallis, 1945), 108.

16. *History of the Church*, ed. B.H. Roberts, vol. 4 (Salt Lake City, UT: Deseret Book Company, 1973), 537.

17. John A. Widtsoe and Franklin S. Harris Jr., *Seven Claims of the Book of Mormon* (Salt Lake City, UT: Deseret News Press, 1937), 37.

18. Ibid.

19. John L. Sorenson, *An Ancient American Setting for the Book of Mormon* (Provo, UT: Foundation for Ancient Research and Mormon Studies, 1996), 283.

20. H. Putnam, "Were the Golden Plates Made of Tumbaga?" *The Improvement Era* (September 1966), 789.

21. Ibid.

22. From 2013 to 2015, a series of essays written by LDS scholars were published on the official LDS website, lds.org. Topics included the First Vision and the Book of Mormon. The church has dealt with some of the obvious problems in these essays. You can find links to these essays and also see MRM's reviews of each one by visiting the Mormonism Research Ministry, www.mrm.org/gospel-topics.

### 8. Using Surveys to Reveal Truth to Mormons: The Polling Approach—*Chip Thompson*

1. *Gospel Principles* (Salt Lake City, UT: The Church of Jesus Christ of Latter-day Saints, 2009), 9. An earlier edition of this manual added, "The first spirit born to our heavenly parents was Jesus Christ. He is thus our elder brother."

2. F. Burton Howard, "Eternal Marriage," *Ensign* (May 2003): 92.

3. *History of the Church*, ed. B.H. Roberts, vol. 4, (Salt Lake City, UT: Deseret Book, 1950), 461. See also *Teachings of the Prophet Joseph Smith* (Salt Lake City, UT: Deseret Book, 1977), 194.
4. *Gospel Principles*, 67.
5. For more on this topic, see chapter 3 of this book, "Did God Really Say So? The Reliability-of-the-Bible Approach," by Matt Slick.

### 9. Sharing with a Mormon Family Member: The Keeping-Good-Relations Approach—*Carl Wimmer*

1. The article by Paul Rolly, a columnist for *The Salt Lake Tribune*, was published on October 11, 2013. The headline read, "Carl Wimmer goes from Mormon to Evangelical: Former Lawmakers, ex-Latter-day Saint wants to be a Christian preacher" http://archive.sltrib.com/article.php?id=56982850&itype=CMSID. The article started out this way: "Carl Wimmer was the bull-in-a-china-shop, take-no-prisoners legislator whose uncompromising conservatism and in-your-face approach toward adversaries earned him a fair share of antagonism from some colleagues, while becoming a hero to the far right." After listing some nefarious traits of my political career, he then wrote using a sarcastic tone, "That was the old Carl Wimmer, the world-class weight lifter, gun-loving cop and super-ambitious politician who showed disdain for liberals and RINOS (Republicans in Name Only). The new Wimmer is about peace and love and is working toward being a Christian minister."
2. David Earley and David Wheeler, *Evangelism Is...How to Share Jesus with Passion and Confidence* (Nashville, TN: B&H Academics, 2010), 80.

### 10. When the Elders Come Calling: The Missionaries-At-Your-Door Approach—*Sandra Tanner*

1. See at www.lds.org/ensign/2017/05/saturday-afternoon-session/statistical-report-2016?lang=eng.
2. L.L. (Don) Veinot, Lynn K. Wilder, and Cory B. Willson, "Should Christians Confront Mormon Missionaries When They Knock on the Front Door?" *Christianity Today*, May 2015, www.christianitytoday.com/ct/2015/may/should-christians-confront-mormon-missionaries.html.
3. See at www.lds.org/manual/preach-my-gospel-a-guide-to-missionary-service?lang=eng.
4. For more definitions, see Appendix 2 in this book. Also visit www.utlm.org/onlineresources/terminologymain.htm.
5. Joseph Fielding Smith, ed., *Teachings of the Prophet Joseph Smith* (Salt Lake City, UT: Deseret Book, 1977), 312, 342-354, 370-373. One of Smith's sermons is published at www.lds.org/ensign/1971/04/the-king-follett-sermon?lang=eng.
6. See Doctrine & Covenants 7:1-3.
7. For example, see Steven L. Shields, *Divergent Paths of the Restoration* (Independence, MO: Herald Publishing House, 2001).
8. See Galatians 1:7-12 and 1 John 4:1.

9. For more on this topic, visit www.utlm.org/onlinebooks/mclaims7.htm.

10. For more information on the reliability of the Bible, see chapter 3, "Did God Really Say So? The Reliability-of-the-Bible Approach," by Matt Slick.

11. See F.F. Bruce, *The New Testament Documents: Are They Reliable?* (Grand Rapids, MI: Eerdmans, 1981).

12. *Gospel Principles* (Salt Lake City, UT: The Church of Jesus Christ of Latter-day Saints, 2009), 62-65.

13. See 2 Timothy 2:23-26 and Titus 3:2-9.

14. For more information on this topic, I recommend *Missionary 911: A Guide to Productive Conversations with Mormon Missionaries* (Brigham City, UT: Main Street Church of Brigham City, 2016). For more questions to ask the missionaries, go to www.utlm.org/onlineresources/sharingyourfaithwithlds.htm.

### 11. Sharing the Truth with LDS Women: The Compassion Approach—*Becky Walker*

1. *Zion* in Mormonism means the LDS Church on earth.

2. For definitions of LDS terms, see Appendix 2.

3. For more, see chapter 21 of this book, "When Being Good Is Not Good Enough: The Awareness-of-Sin Approach," by Joel Groat.

4. This is according to one study done in 2002. See Julie Cart, "Study Finds Utah Leads Nation in Antidepressant Use," *LA Times,* February 20, 2002, www.articles.latimes.com/2002/feb/20/news/mn-28924. The primary cause for the depression in Utah could be high altitude; or perhaps the strict guidelines in the state's majority religion is responsible. Whichever it might be, this topic has been widely debated.

5. Polygamous groups hold to the teachings of Joseph Smith, Brigham Young, and John Taylor—the first three presidents of the LDS Church—but are not aligned with The Church of Jesus Christ of Latter-day Saints based in Salt Lake City, Utah.

6. To see a short video about this outreach, see "10,000 Tissues, The Outreach in Utah," posted on YouTube by "MormonDoctrinedotnet," October 1, 2012, https://www.youtube.com/watch?v=HvtJvBvbyZE.

7. For more on this topic, visit JosephsWives.com.

8. For another perspective by a woman on how to share the truth with Latter-day Saint females, go to www.SharingWithMormons.com.

### 12. Preaching from an Asbestos Suit: The Reasoning-with-Mormons-on-the-Internet Approach—*Fred W. Anson*

1. Since Trinitarianism versus Mormonism's doctrine of tri-theism is such a common point of discussion, gaining a proficient grasp of the doctrine of the Trinity is essential. While there are many good resources on this doctrine, I recommend James White's book *The Forgotten Trinity* (Minneapolis, MN: Bethany House, 1999).

2. Aaron Shafovaloff, "The Creed of Practical Mormon Atheism," Mormonism Research Ministry, March 14, 2013, http://blog.mrm.org/2013/03/the-creed-of-practical-mormon-atheism.

3. Richard and Joan Ostling, *Mormon America: The Power and the Promise* (New York: Harper San Francisco, 2007), 249.

4. There are many excellent websites that will help build understanding of authentic church history and doctrine. For example, the sites run by Mormonism Research Ministry (mrm.org), Utah Lighthouse Ministry (utlm.org), Institute for Religious Research (irr.org), and Mormon Think (mormonthink.com) are my favorites. Besides *Mormon America* as referenced above, I recommend two books by Mormonism Research Ministry's Bill McKeever and Eric Johnson: *Answering Mormons' Questions* (Grand Rapids, MI: Kregel, 2013) and *Mormonism 101* (Grand Rapids, MI: Baker, 2015).

5. Pew Research Center, "A Portrait of Mormons in the U.S.," July 24, 2009, Pew Forum, www.pewforum.org/2009/07/24/a-portrait-of-mormons-in-the-us.

6. John Dehlin, "Top 5 Myths and Truths about Why Mormons Leave the LDS Church," Why MormonsLeave.com, February 1, 2014, www.whymormonsleave.com/top-5-myths-and-truths-about-why-mormons-leave-the-lds-church.

7. Os Guiness, *Fool's Talk: Recovering the Art of Christian Persuasion* (Downer's Grove, IL: InterVarsity Press, 2015), 163. Ellipsis mine.

8. The link I used when I made this argument was Robin Ngo, "Top 10 Biblical Archaeology Discoveries in 2016," *Bible History Daily*, December 30, 2016, www.biblicalarchaeology.org/daily/news/top-10-biblical-archaeology-discoveries-in-2016.

9. See "Revelation Book 1," The Joseph Smith Papers, www.josephsmithpapers.org/paperSummary/revelation-book-1?p=15; or "The Attempt to Sell the Book of Mormon Copyright," Mormonism Research Ministry, www.mrm.org/attempt-to-sell-copyright.

10. The link used in support of this argument was Caroline Winter, "How the Mormons Make Money," *Bloomberg*, July 19, 2012, www.bloomberg.com/news/articles/2012-07-18/how-the-mormons-make-money#p5.

11. According to the LDS Church website, "where Latter-day Saints differ from other Christian religions is in their belief that God and Jesus Christ are glorified, physical beings and that each member of the Godhead is a separate being" (www.lds.org/topics/godhead). This is where an understanding of the basic tenets of the Trinity comes into play.

12. Jim Whitefield, *The Mormon Delusion, Volume 4: The Mormon Missionary Lessons a Conspiracy to Deceive* (Raleigh, NC: Lulu Press, 2011), 429.

### 13. Engaging in Gospel Discussions: The Keep-It-Simple Approach—*Aaron Shafovaloff*

1. For more on these approaches, see chapter 18 of this book, "Extra! Extra! Read All About It: The Newspaper Approach," by Sharon Lindbloom and chapter 17 of this book, "Let Your Voice Be Heard: The Open-Air-Evangelism Approach," by Andrew Rappaport.

2. For a clear presentation of the gospel, see Appendix 1.

3. The diversity of thought within Mormonism is astounding. One phenomenon within Mormonism is that of nonbelieving participants, which are those who associate with Mormonism and who defend its theology and culture yet who do not personally believe the core truth claims of the religion. Be aware that while the person may say she is Mormon, you may be talking to someone who is essentially agnostic.
4. For more on this topic, see chapter 3 of this book, "Did God Really Say So? The Reliability-of-the-Bible Approach," by Matt Slick.
5. A good online resource for this complex (yet biblical!) doctrine is Matt Slick, "What Is the Trinity?" Christian Apologetics and Research Ministry, November 24, 2008, https://carm.org/what-is-the-trinity.

### 14. LISTEN: The Conversational Approach—*Dr. David Geisler and Brian Henson*

1. We are referring to groups that claim to be Christian, yet in some way depart from the essential teachings of traditional Christianity, including Mormons and Jehovah's Witnesses.
2. As contained in the first four Ecumenical Councils of the Church, and as explained in *Conviction Without Compromise* by Norman L. Geisler and Ron Rhodes (Eugene, OR: Harvest House Publishers, 2008).
3. David Geisler and Norman Geisler, *Conversational Evangelism: Connecting with People to Share Jesus* (Eugene, OR: Harvest House Publishers, 2014).
4. The LISTEN acrostic was first introduced into our second edition of our book *Conversational Evangelism* in 2014.
5. In our *Conversational Evangelism* model, we explain that the Christian needs to learn to be like a musician, able to hear the sour notes people are singing to us. Every day in our conversations with nonbelievers, we can train our ears to hear problematic beliefs that others hold, just as we can hear off-key or sour notes in someone's singing.
6. See Mormon definitions of terms in Appendix 2.
7. See 1 Corinthians 1:18. To contradict literally means to say *yes* and *no* at the same time in the same sense. Paul's point here is that Christian beliefs are not contradictory. The further implication is that we cannot believe that Jesus is the only way (John 14:6) to God and, at the same time, believe that He is not the *only* way to God. There may be mysteries in the Bible, but never contradictions. God's truth certainly goes beyond reason but it never goes against reason.
8. For example, Doctrine and Covenants 130:22 says, "The Father has a body of flesh and bones as tangible as man's." Thus, man is made in the image of the body of God (Moses 6:9). This is in contrast with John 4:24, which teaches that "God is spirit."
9. For more on these arguments, see chapter 2 of this book, "Sharing the Reasons for God: The Evidence Approach," by Sean McDowell.

### 15. Authentic, Humble Dialogue with Mormons: The Columbo Approach—*Dr. Lynn K. Wilder*

1. Our family's story is found in the book *Unveiling Grace: The Story of How We Found Our Way Out of the Mormon Church* (Grand Rapids, MI: Zondervan, 2013).

2. Michael Lipka, "Mormons more likely to marry, have more children than other U.S. religious groups," Pew Research Center, May 22, 2015, www.pewresearch.org/fact-tank/2015/05/22/mormons-more-likely-to-marry-have-more-children-than-other-u-s-religious-groups.
3. Aleksandra Sandstrom and Becka A. Alper, "6 facts about U.S. Mormons," Pew Research Center, September 30, 2016, www.pewresearch.org/fact-tank/2016/09/30/6-facts-about-u-s-mormons/.
4. *Preach My Gospel* (Salt Lake City, UT: The Church of Jesus Christ of Latter-day Saints, 2004), 70.
5. Pastor Jim Caitlin talks about land mines in *Missionary 911: How to Have Meaningful Discussions with Mormon Missionaries* (Brigham City, UT: Main Street Church, 2016).
6. Adam's Road Ministry's "LDS Doctrine Topical Guide" is available online at their website, http://adamsroadministry.com/bible_topic_guide_list/. Also see the doctrinal comparison chart at the back of my book *Unveiling Grace.*
7. Gregory Koukl, *Tactics: A Game Plan for Discussing Your Christian Convictions* (Grand Rapids, MI: Zondervan, 2009), 46.
8. Ibid., 47.
9. See Doctrine and Covenants 20:9; 27:5; 42:12; 135:3.
10. For more information, see chapter 3 of this book, "Did God Really Say So? The Reliability-of-the-Bible Approach," by Matt Slick.
11. See James R. White, *Forgotten Trinity: Recovering the Heart of Christian Belief* (Minneapolis, MN: Bethany House Publishers, 1998).

### 16. The Power of a Simple Invitation: The Come-and-See Approach—*Dr. Bryan Hurlbutt*

1. Jonathan Edwards, *The Works of Jonathan Edwards*, vol. 1 (Carlisle PA: The Banner of Truth Trust 1834), 119-120. Ellipsis mine.
2. For further research see Whitney Cross, *The Burned-over District: The Social and Intellectual History of Enthusiastic Religion in Western New York, 1800–1850* (Ithaca, NY: Cornell University Press, 1950).
3. This couplet that was coined by Snow in 1840 was approved by Joseph Smith. According to Seventy Milton R. Hunter in a book that was used as a church manual, this "today is still a doctrine understood primarily by members of the Church of Jesus Christ of Latter-day Saints" and has been approved by a variety of other church leaders, even those who currently hold office (Milton R. Hunter, *The Gospel through the Ages* (Salt Lake City, UT: Steven and Willis, 1945), 105-106. For more on this, see Bill McKeever, "Does Lorenzo Snow's famous couplet no longer have a functioning place in LDS theology?" Mormonism Research Ministry, www.mrm.org/snow-couplet.
4. *Teachings of the Presidents of the Church: Joseph Smith* (Salt Lake City, UT: The Church of Jesus Christ of Latter-day Saints), 210.

### Spotlight Shane Jones

1. For more on this issue, see "Why are Mormons not allowed to drink coffee?" Mormonism Research Ministry, www.mrm.org/word-of-wisdom-coffee.

**17. Let Your Voice Be Heard: The Open-Air Evangelism Approach**—*Andrew Rappaport*

1. Listen to the December 15, 2016, broadcast here: www.str.org/podcasts/strask-december-15-2016#.WiwhiEqnFaR. More resources from Stand to Reason can be found at www.str.org.
2. More resources from Living Waters can be found at www.LivingWaters.org. For more on the example of how I think open-air evangelism works well, check out the resources there.
3. For an example of using someone's name to disarm the opponent's defenses, see the video "Open Air Preaching with a Demon Possessed Heckler," posted on YouTube by "StrivingforEternity," https://www.youtube.com/watch?v=xbwL4C9wMXE.
4. Greg Koukl, *Tactics: A Game Plan for Discussing Your Christian Convictions* (Grand Rapids, MI: Zondervan, 2009), 42-71.

**18. Extra! Extra! Read All About It: The Newspaper Approach**—*Sharon Lindbloom*

1. Nauvoo, Illinois, was a Mormon settlement from 1839 to 1846. Today, restored buildings serve as tourist attractions staffed by LDS missionary docents.
2. A PDF copy of the four-page "Temple Square Visitors Guide" is available online at Mormonism Research Ministry, www.mrm.org/wp-content/uploads/2015/11/Newspaper-Square-Project-pdf.pdf.
3. These public events are held for several weeks before a new or remodeled Mormon temple is dedicated. A PDF copy of this newspaper is available online from Mormonism Research Ministry at www.mrm.org/temple-newspaper.
4. The Book of Mormon purports to be "a record of God's dealings with the ancient inhabitants of the Americas" (Book of Mormon Introduction). For one example of horses in the Book of Mormon, see 1 Nephi 18:25.
5. For more on this topic, visit JosephsWives.com.
6. As described by Christian missionary Wally Tope.
7. The tract was "Citings of Joseph," 1998, printed and distributed by the Nauvoo Christian Visitors Center.
8. *History of the Church*, vol. 6, ed. B.H. Roberts (Salt Lake City, UT: Deseret Book, 1950), 408-409.
9. The four keys: "(1) You are in trouble (Romans 3:23; 6:23). (2) God has provided a Savior (Romans 5:8). (3) Receiving the Savior repairs your broken relationship with God (John 1:12). (4) You must have faith (Romans 10:9-10)."

**19. *The Miracle of Forgiveness*: The Free-Book Approach**—*Eric Johnson and Randy Sweet*

1. Perry cited Joseph Smith, "We Believe All that God has Revealed," *Ensign* (November 2003): 86.
2. "Lord, I Believe; Help Thou Mine Unbelief," *Ensign* (November 2003): 22.
3. *Lengthen Your Stride: The Presidency of Spencer W. Kimball* (Salt Lake City, UT: Deseret Book, 2005), 79.

4. Sara Long, petition directed at Deseret Book, "Deseret Book: Please stop publishing The Miracle of Forgiveness (1969)," www.change.org/p/deseret-book-please-stop-publishing-the-miracle-of-forgiveness-1969. Ellipsis mine.

5. See Eric Johnson, "*The Miracle of Forgiveness* is now out of print: Why?" Mormonism Research Ministry, www.mrm.org/miracle-out-of-print.

6. Richard G. Scott, "Finding Forgiveness," *Ensign* (May 1995): 76.

7. Richard G. Scott, "Peace of Conscience and Peace of Mind," *Ensign* (November 2004): 16.

8. Bruce C. Hafen, "Beauty for Ashes: The Atonement of Jesus Christ," *Liahona* (April 1997): 41.

9. *Teachings of Presidents of the Church: Spencer W. Kimball* (Salt Lake City, UT: The Church of Jesus Christ of Latter-day Saints, 2006). Two chapters of this manual per month (the book contains 24) were supposed to be read and talked about in church Sunday school meetings in 2007.

10. See the tract by visiting the website TheMiracleofForgiveness.com. The highlighted portions of the book can be found at Mormonism Research Ministry's website, www.mrm.org/highlighted-portions.

11. See the bill at Mormonism Research Ministry's website, www.mrm.org/kimball-bill.

12. This part is cited in the church manual *Teachings of Presidents of the Church: Spencer W. Kimball* (Salt Lake City, UT: The Church of Jesus Christ of Latter-day Saints, 2006), 96.

13. *Gospel Principles* (Salt Lake City, UT: The Church of Jesus Christ of Latter-day Saints, 2009), 231.

14. For more on this topic, see chapter 24 of this book, "I'm Trying My Best: The Impossible-Gospel Approach," by Keith Walker.

15. See a highlighted and scanned copy of what we consider the best quotes online at the Mormonism Research Ministry, www.mrm.org/wp-content/uploads/2014/08/scan0003.pdf.

16. For example, see Doctrine and Covenants 1:31-32; 14:7; 25:15; 58:43; and 82:7, among others.

### 20. Website Advertising: The Sign Approach—*Rob Sivulka*

1. Peter Henderson and Kristina Cooke, "Special Report: Mormonism besieged by the modern age," *Reuters* (January 31, 2012), www.reuters.com/article/us-mormonchurch-idUSTRE80T1CM20120131.

2. Both website domains go to the same page. During the day, I use a cloth sign with PVC pipe on the inside to hold it up; this can be dismantled and is much more attractive and durable than a cardboard sign. During the night, I use a lighted LED sign designed by friend Jeff Baran that simply says "JosephLied.com."

3. There has been some recent effort on the part of the LDS Church to dissemble the fact that they really teach this doctrine. See "Will Exalted Mormons Get Their Own Spirit Children and Worlds?" at Mormonism Research Ministry's website, www.mrm.org/spirit-children-and-planets.

4. For a brilliantly humorous cartoon that extrapolates the point further, see "Mormon Secrets: What the Missionaries Don't Tell," posted on YouTube by "Saved XMormon," October 6, 2014, https://youtu.be/-VKT4hrBTuk.

5. "LDS Are Told Not To Research Their Religion," posted to YouTube by "isthechurchtrue," October 29, 2015, https://youtube/Qv3UdvcI21k .
6. Robert L. Millet, "Milk Before Meat—But Meat," *More Holiness Give Me* (Salt Lake City, UT: Deseret Book, 2001), 143-156.
7. *Discourses of Brigham Young* (Salt Lake City, UT: Deseret Book, 1954), 11.
8. Ibid., 126.
9. Written permission to quote granted by a friend who wishes to remain nameless (December 11, 2017).
10. Written permission to quote granted by Anita Hoak (December 9, 2017).
11. Walter Martin and Jill Martin Rische, *Through the Windows of Heaven* (Nashville, TN: Broadman & Holman, 1999), 16-17.
12. For those who want to pursue this method of evangelism, you have my permission to use any of my sites in your own advertising. Bumper stickers with the site's address are available to order. You may also want to consider creating your own site to advertise.

### 21. When Being Good Is Not Good Enough: The Awareness-of-Sin Approach—*Joel B. Groat*

1. *Exaltation* is synonymous with eternal life. *Gospel Principles* (Salt Lake City, UT: The Church of Jesus Christ of Latter-day Saints, 2009), 141-142, 277-279.
2. See *Gospel Principles,* 109-113. For a treatment on the impossibility of forgiveness and repentance in Mormonism, see chapter 24 of this book by Keith Walker: "I'm Trying My Best: The Impossible-Gospel Approach."

### 22. Can Something Valuable Really Be Free? The Meaning-of-Grace Approach—*Dr. Loren Pankratz*

1. While reports indicate that approximately 60 percent of all Utah residents are affiliated with the LDS Church, most estimates show that fewer than 3 percent of Utahans are evangelical Christian. Out of Utah's 29 counties, several don't have any Christian churches with Sunday services.
2. See Seventy Tad Callister's book *The Infinite Atonement* (Salt Lake City, UT: Deseret Book, 2000).
3. *Preparing for Exaltation Teacher's Manual* (Salt Lake City, UT: The Church of Jesus Christ of Latter-day Saints, 1998), 14.
4. "Adam's Role in Bringing Us Mortality," *Ensign* (January 2006): 53.
5. Joseph Fielding Smith, *Doctrines of Salvation,* vol. 1 (Salt Lake City, UT: Bookcraft, 1954), 114.
6. Stephen L. Richards, *About Mormonism* (Salt Lake City, UT: The Church of Jesus Christ of Latter-day Saints, 1944), 10.
7. Jeffrey R. Holland, "The Atonement of Christ," *Ensign* (March 2008): 35.
8. *Gospel Principles* (Salt Lake City, UT: The Church of Jesus Christ of Latter-day Saints, 2009), 109. See also Robert Millet, *Precept Upon Precept* (Salt Lake City, UT: Deseret Book, 2016), 353.

9. Joseph Fielding Smith, *Doctrines of Salvation*, ed. Bruce R. McConkie (Salt Lake City, UT: Bookcraft, 1955), 2:10.
10. Adhemar Damiani, "The Merciful Plan of the Great Creator," *Ensign* (March 2004): 10.
11. See also D&C 14:7; 25:15; 1; Nephi 22:31; Joseph Smith Translation of Romans 4:16; Mosiah 4:10-12; Ether 2:15; Alma 11:37 and 42:24.
12. This talk was delivered at BYU on July 12, 2011. Text of the talk may be downloaded from BYU's website at: https://speeches.byu.edu/talks/brad-wilcox_his-grace-is-sufficient/ (accessed September 1, 2017). For a Christian response to this talk along with an eight-part Viewpoint on Mormonism podcast, visit the Mormonism Research Ministry, www.mrm.org/wilcox-speech.
13. Robert Millet, *Grace Works* (Salt Lake City, UT: Deseret Book, 2003), 143.
14. *Old Testament Student Manual Genesis-2 Samuel (Rel. 301)* (Salt Lake City, UT: The Church of Jesus Christ of Latter-day Saints, 1981), 79.

### 23. Are You Considered as Good as Jesus? The Imputation Approach—*John Kauer*

1. For more on this topic, see chapter 24 of this book, "I'm Trying My Best: The Impossible-Gospel Approach," by Keith Walker.
2. John Calvin, *Institutes of the Christian Religion*, vol. 1, bk. 3, ch. 11.2 (Louisville, KY: Westminster John Knox Press, 1960).
3. A temple open house is an event open to the public just before a new or remodeled temple is opened for members in good standing only.
4. In his book *The Story of Reality* (Grand Rapids, MI: Zondervan, 2017), Greg Koukl explains that he is "not fond of the English word *faith*...since it is too easy to mentally add the words *blind* or *leap of* to it" (133). According to the early Christians, the word *trust* is a better choice because "true faith was neither belief without knowledge (a 'leap of faith'), nor a simple assent to certain truths. Rather, faith was knowledge in motion" (135).

### 24. I'm Trying My Best: The Impossible-Gospel Approach—*Keith Walker*

1. Bo Bennett, *Logically Fallacious* (Archieboy Holdings LLC, 2015), 186.
2. *The Miracle of Forgiveness* (Salt Lake City, UT: Deseret Book, 1989), 325. For more on how to use Kimball's book in evangelism, see chapter 19 of this book, "*The Miracle of Forgiveness:* The Free-Book Approach," by Eric Johnson and Randy Sweet.
3. Most LDS source references in this chapter can be found on the LDS Library app available for free on both Apple and Android devices.
4. *Aaronic Priesthood Manual 1* (Salt Lake City, UT: The Church of Jesus Christ of Latter-day Saints, 2002), 83.
5. *Gospel Fundamentals* (Salt Lake City, UT: The Church of Jesus Christ of Latter-day Saints, 2002), 69-70. Ellipsis mine.

**Epilogue: Go for It!**—*Dr. Sean McDowell*

1. Michael Hyatt, *Platform: Get Noticed in a Noisy World* (Nashville, TN: Thomas Nelson, 2012).
2. Contact information can be found on this book's website, SharingWithMormons.com.

**Appendix 1: The Gospel (Good News) According to the Bible**

1. Used with permission from God Loves Mormons, www.godlovesmormons.com/gospel.

**Appendix 2: 101 Mormon Terms Defined (from Aaronic Priesthood to Zion)**

1. The first term is generally the more common term. For a more complete list of terms related to Mormonism, visit Mormonism Research Ministry's "A-Z: A Simple Introduction to Terms Used by Latter-day Saints" by Eric Johnson, www.mrm.org/a-z.

Other Good Harvest House Reading

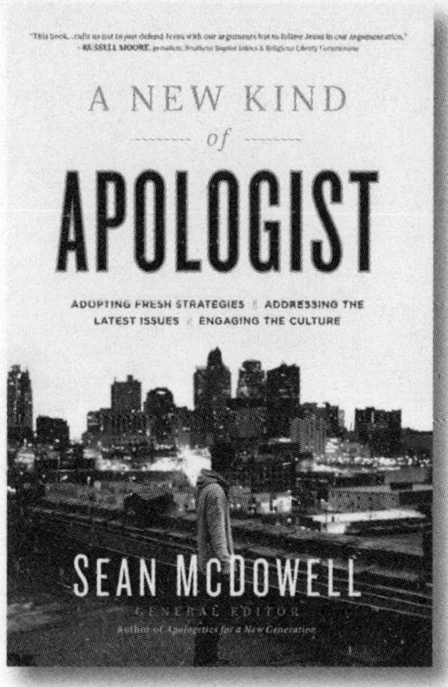


## A NEW KIND OF APOLOGIST

SEAN MCDOWELL, GENERAL EDITOR

Edited by Sean McDowell with contributions from more than 20 leading apologists, *A New Kind of Apologist* is the go-to resource for effectively defending the Christian faith in our changing culture. In it you'll discover:

- important topics often ignored by apologists, such as transgender issues, religious freedom, and the intersection of economics and apologetics
- a new kind of apologetics that is relational, gracious, and holistic
- interviews with both seasoned apologists and skeptics, providing insights into how to do apologetics effectively in today's culture